THIS BOOK BELONGS TO

Dr. Jess Guth

PASSING/OUT

Dedicated to Kelsey and Mr. Jack

Passing/Out
Sexual Identity Veiled and Revealed

Edited by

DENNIS R. COOLEY
North Dakota State University, USA

and

KELBY HARRISON
Union Theological Seminary, USA

ASHGATE

Published by
Ashgate Publishing Limited
Wey Court East
Union Road
Farnham
Surrey, GU9 7PT
England

Ashgate Publishing Company
Suite 420
101 Cherry Street
Burlington
VT 05401-4405
USA

www.ashgate.com

British Library Cataloguing in Publication Data
Passing/out : sexual identity veiled and revealed.
   1. Sexual orientation. 2. Passing (Identity) 3. Outing
   (Sexual orientation) 4. Queer theory.
   I. Cooley, Dennis R. II. Harrison, Kelby.
   306.7'6-dc23

Library of Congress Cataloging-in-Publication Data
Cooley, Dennis R., 1965-
   Passing/out : sexual identity veiled and revealed / by Dennis R. Cooley
and Kelby Harrison.
      p. cm.
   Includes bibliographical references and index.
   ISBN 978-1-4094-3582-2 (hardback) -- ISBN 978-1-4094-3583-9 (ebook)
   1. Outing (Sexual orientation) 2. Passing (Identity) 3.
Gays--Family relations. 4. Transsexuals--Family relations. I. Harrison,
Kelby. II. Title.
   HQ76.25.C666 2012
   306.76'8--dc23

2012002396

ISBN 9781409435822 (hbk)
ISBN 9781409435839 (ebk)

Printed and bound in Great Britain by the
MPG Books Group, UK

Contents

List of Contributors

Maren Behrensen is Ph.D. candidate in Philosophy at Boston University, U.S.A. Her areas of interest include contemporary issues in ethics, Kant, philosophy of law, metaphysics of personhood and free will.

Samantha Brennan is Professor of Philosophy at the University of Western Ontario, Canada. Her areas of interest include contemporary normative ethics, particularly at the intersection of deontological and consequentialist moral theories. She also has active research interests in feminist ethics.

Mark Chekola is Emeritus Professor of Philosophy at Minnesota State University Moorhead, U.S.A. His areas of interest include ethics and the philosophy of social sciences. His current research focuses on the concept of happiness.

Dennis R. Cooley is Associate Professor of Philosophy and Ethics at North Dakota State University, U.S.A. His areas of interest include theoretical and applied ethics, such as bioethics and death.

Rob Cover is Senior Lecturer of Media at The University of Western Australia, Australia. His areas of interest include minority identities, community and media cultures, as well as digital, participatory/interactive media and communication theory.

Kelby Harrison is Post-Doctoral Fellow in Social Ethics at Union Theological Seminary, U.S.A. Her areas of interest include constructive ethics for LGBTQ persons as well as the critical evaluation of cultural, theological, and secular sexual ethics. She has a strong interest in the past, present, and future of queer liberation theology.

Daniel Hurewitz is Professor of History at Hunter College, U.S.A. His areas of interest include the cultural roots of identity politics, the emergence of a gay rights movement, the politics of homophobia, and the history of Los Angeles and New York.

Janna Jackson Kellinger is Assistant Professor in the College of Education and Human Development at University of Massachusetts Boston, U.S.A. Her areas of interest include English education, secondary education, queer pedagogy, the intersection of education and queer identity.

Alice MacLachlan is Assistant Professor of Philosophy at York University, Canada. Her areas of interest include ethics, focusing especially on feminist ethics and virtue ethics, social and political philosophy, and the politics of sexuality. Her research topics include forgiveness, reconciliation, reparation and apology, as well as the philosophy of Hannah Arendt.

Nancy Arden McHugh is Associate Professor of Philosophy at Wittenberg University, U.S.A. Her areas of interest include the philosophy of women's lives, knowledge and social change, and knowing bodies, with a special focus on the connection between theory and practice, philosophy and lived experience, and epistemology and politics.

Christine Overall is Research Chair and Professor of Philosophy at Queen's University, Canada. Her areas of interest include feminist theory, applied ethics including bioethics, and philosophy of religion.

Karin Sellberg is Post-Doctoral Research Fellow at Edinburgh University, Scotland. Her areas of interest include contemporary literature, transgender and queer theory and discourses of embodiment.

C. Riley Snorton is Assistant Professor of Communication at Northwestern University, U.S.A. His areas of interest include transgender and queer theory, media anthropology, Africana studies, cultural studies, performance studies, and popular culture.

Susanne Sreedhar is Assistant Professor of Philosophy at Boston University, U.S.A. Her areas of interest include political philosophy, especially the history of political philosophy, early modern philosophy, and feminist philosophy.

Willie Tolliver is Director of Africana Studies, and Director of Film Studies and Associate Professor of English at Agnes Scott College, U.S.A. His areas of interest include African-American literature, nineteenth-century American literature, Henry James, and film.

Introduction

Dennis R. Cooley and Kelby Harrison

Richard Mohr argues that questions of passing and outing are not *a* set of ethical questions, but *the* set of ethical questions in the life of gay, lesbian, bisexual, and queer persons. In order to ask the ethical life organizing questions about how one should veil or reveal a sexual identity, one must also ask difficult questions about the nature of identity, the history of sexual identity, and how identity, sexual or otherwise, functions within our personal and social relationships.

Passing as heterosexual often seems better to closeted LGBTQ people than revealing one's actual sexual identity. Veiled people avoid being singled out as deviant and receive benefits from being "normal." However, do they have an ethical duty to be out?

Many people and all moral philosophers working in this area recognize that there is a moral dilemma. We want people to be authentic and live according to who they truly are. At the same time, obviously, there can be grave moral costs to passing, deeply problematic social implications to passing, and moral sympathies for some who choose to pass. In times of trouble, those who belong to persecuted classes can often be tempted to pass as a member of the oppressor group. Unfortunately, no matter when or where someone lives, it can be a time of trouble because there always seems a societal need to make one or more group the focus of social dislike if not hatred; so there is always an incentive to pass. How to resolve the dilemma is difficult. After all, we are rather reluctant about forcing people, to endanger themselves just to live as they should in an ideal world.

Outing oneself and outing others is a moral minefield at the best of times. Being unveiled or unveiling oneself comes with utilitarian considerations such as political advancement and community health, questions of autonomy, privacy, self-respect, and respect for others, and a plethora of other moral factors that have to be given their proper weight in any final decision we make. Passing/outing is inextricably bound with moral questions whose answers require complex, nuanced answers that take into account general moral principles and ideals as well as each individual situation's particular set of circumstances, including the metaphysical issue of who each person is as a person in general and who each person is as a person in particular. The former set of characteristics all persons share in common, while the latter is what makes each person the individual she is. Each has its own impact on each case of passing or being out.

Within the LGBTQ community/ies the understanding of sexual identity has been impacted radically by a group of researchers known as queer theorists: a set of literary, cultural, and philosophical thinkers who sought to expose the socially constructed aspects of sexual identity. These thinkers and writers have been prolific since the early 1990s and have significantly altered the way intellectuals and even activists conceive of sexual identity. Without a doubt, queer theory has made the rhetorical and critical inquiry into sexuality a more sophisticated and nuanced endeavor. It has shirked off layers of assumptions and burdens about the truths of sexual identity. But, queer theory has also come with a moral cost. Taken at its most extreme, the deconstructive endeavors of queer theory have left the markers of sexual identity as nothing more than political and social markers of the privileged and the marginalized. That is, sexual identity markers signify only differences in power. Because queer theory denies any essential value to sexual identity, queer theory makes passing/outing ethical impossibilities; passing/outing are only instruments of social and political mobility empty of normative meaning.

The Methodology of this Book

In *On Liberty*, John Stuart Mill argued that a marketplace of ideas is necessary in the continuous search for truth. Because people cannot know whether their opinions are in error, they must constantly examine them, especially those that are fundamental to each person's decision making.

> In the case of any person whose judgment is really deserving of confidence, how has it become so? Because he has kept his mind open to the criticism of his opinions and conduct. Because it has been his practice to listen to all that could be said against him; to profit by as much of it as was just, and expound to himself, and upon occasion to others, the fallacy of what was fallacious. Because he has felt, that the only way in which a human being can make some approach to knowing the whole of a subject, is by hearing what can be said about it by persons of every variety of opinion, and studying all modes in which it can be looked at by every character of mind. No wise man ever acquired his wisdom in any mode but this; nor is it in the nature of human intellect to become wise in any other manner. (Mill 1988: 88)

For any individual to assume, with absolute certainty, that his view is the right one is to fail in his duty as a person no matter how difficult it is to do (Mill 1988: 87). We know that it is the devil's own business to have to examine, and then to decide whether to discard or keep beliefs that receive some of their evidentiary justification from a false belief. How much do they rely upon the false data? Are the data really that unreliable? And other questions have to be answered before we begin the process of trimming our belief sets. The task becomes even more difficult if the belief is central to the core of who the person is. Those alterations would require significant changes in the person's identity, which are harder as the person ages and becomes more settled in who she is as an individual, or the belief is one of the more fundamental ones bordering on ideological. The latter types of beliefs are so interwoven into each person's set of beliefs that it might be impossible to separate one of them, clean out all beliefs that were sufficiently dependent upon it, and then go on with the person's life as if nothing significant has happened. In fact, these alterations to our mental states are like large earthquakes in our reality. They disrupt, disjoint, and tear at who we are as individual people. But to be better people as people in general, and in most cases, in particular, we must do it.

Bettering ourselves is not the end of the story for why we have a duty always to be engaged in examining the veracity of the things we believe. We are obligated to recognize that many of our actions involve other people: some as contributors to the action; some as people affected by the consequences of what we do. How we affect others can be determined, in part, by a variety of moral factors. Perhaps most importantly, every person is a member of a concrete, interdependent, and interconnected web of relationships. Whenever one person in the relationship acts, then others connected to that person can be affected in good or evil ways mitigated or enhanced by the relationship they have with the actor. We thus have greater impact on certain others, which requires us to take greater care of them than we would of ourselves. Since those in relationships with us are more vulnerable to our actions than we are because the former cannot control those actions nor do they have a chance, at the very least, to acquiesce in what we are doing or what will happen to them, then we must ensure that our actions are based on legitimate evidence.

By improving ourselves by way of having opinions that are closer to the truth than not, we can make better decisions and act in ways more fitting for the impact we have on those in our webs of relationships or in society around us in general. We can limit unwarranted damage to others, while, hopefully, improving their lot in life so that they can flourish more efficiently than would be the case if we were acting out of false beliefs. Hence, our duty to be actively engaged in a marketplace of ideas is a duty to oneself and a duty to others. To do otherwise, would be to fail to take due care in our interactions.

Mill's approach is the centerpiece of how this anthology examines the question of out versus veiled people. We have brought together scholars with a variety of opinions to create dialogues on the subject that add to the diversity of the book's marketplace of ideas in three ways. First, in each of the seven chapters there are representatives from different disciplines within the social sciences and humanities. The discipline specific forms of thinking present fascinating new ways of understanding a central position, conflicting positions, or in some cases, clear differences on a particular issue. The interdisciplinary nature of the work provides more nuance to the complicated questions addressed in the text much the way that obtaining more and more oral and other histories of a significant event moves us away from what might be an idiosyncratic tale to a rich, depth narrative that captures the event as a whole through collective memory.

Second, contributors were encouraged to identify and develop what they individually thought most important in regard to the issues of revealing or veiling sexual identity. We took this approach so that our contributors could freely identify areas of importance rather than having to fit their work with what we as editors believed to be of paramount concern. By acting in this manner, we did not allow what might be mistaken about our views to stifle the marketplace of ideas.

Moreover, the dialogue form employed in this work allowed for a natural, organic discussion to take place between the paired authors. Each produced a stand-alone essay, which allowed each contributor to state what he or she thought should be addressed. This essay was then addressed by the other author as he or she thought fit. At times, the other author strove to develop the ideas of the other author. In some instances, there were clarifications of positions in the scholar's own work that might be brought into question by the other author's original contribution. Authors sometimes chose to point out errors, and this was the start of a conversation. Regardless of the approach taken, the commenter did whatever he or she found most important to do in his or her second contribution. The last components of the dialogues—the responses—were also left open to the contributors to develop whatever they thought most useful to the discussion. The flowing nature of the exchange of ideas promotes a wider, deeper understanding of the subject matter.

Third, and most importantly, this anthology collects a series of chapters from two intellectual generations: scholars who began their writing and intellectual careers before queer theory hit the academy and those who began after it was likely to be wide-spread. Each contributor was asked to address questions of passing and outing in light of the theories of identity and thinking they thought most relevant to the issues at hand.

We chose 1995 as our dividing line because in 1990 Teresa de Lauretis coined the term "queer theory." We expected to find that the generation whose graduate work came before the widespread dissemination of the new paradigm would tend toward pre-queer theory's characteristic traits, such as essentialism. We thought that five years would be enough time for Lauretis' ideas to spread in a significant way throughout relevant disciplines. After all, the mere fact that the term is coined in one year does not entail uniform penetration in that same year. Since five years is about the time a person would begin and end her doctoral student career, a lustrum for adequate dispersal seemed about right. Those scholars who graduated after 1995, our second intellectual generation, were hypothesized to be more closely aligned with post-queer theory.

Each pre-queer theory generation scholar was paired with a post-queer theory generation scholar and asked to comment and reply to the theoretical content of the other's work. By doing this, the anthology became a site for dialogue between two generations standing on either side of a pivotal shift in our trajectory towards justice and equality. The dialogue illustrates significant differences and similarities in some approaches to this vital issue. We do not claim that these dialogues capture every plausible approach to the subject, but they do provide valuable insights that advance the discussion in beneficial ways.

For those who are generally influenced by the pre-queer theory state of their discipline, one might expect to see a heavy reliance on the Enlightenment ideas exemplified by John Locke and others from that era. First, essentialism in regard to identity maintains that there is a certain set of characteristics a person has that are necessary to who the person is. Unlike accidental traits that can change over time without affecting the person's identity, an essential property can on its own alter the person's identity to make the person a different person. For example, what a person wears on a particular day is an accidental property of his. If he had worn something else, then he would still be the same person. Hair color, scent, and other secondary qualities are morally irrelevant to who the person is as an individual. Changing an essential characteristic, on the other hand, will not be as innocuous to the existence of the person. Sexual orientation is often thought to be an essential trait of who a person is. If that were altered to a different orientation, then that person would cease to exist the moment the change occurred to become a different entity with the new characteristic. In addition, for essentialism, the set of characteristics that make an entity a person qua a person in general was thought to be complete, absolute, and universal. All people have to have each of the essential traits within the set in order to be a person or a particular type of thing. If he failed to have any of them, then he should be classified as a different thing that fell under a different type or category.

Second, pre-queer theorists might tend to place a great deal of emphasis on rationality and minds as an essential and central fixture to identity. For example, who a person is will be determined by the mental states and other characteristics that she has. That is, the body can change radically, while the person remains the same entity because the mind retains its necessary properties. However, if the mind changes sufficiently, then the person essentially alters regardless of whether the body remains in the same state it was at the start of the mental alteration period.

In addition, since minds are somehow different from bodies, then features thought inherent to minds are often considered to be superior to characteristics of bodies extended in space and time. For example, acting primarily because of desire or emotion is essentially defective in comparison to acting out of pure reason alone, if Kant is right.[1] The idea is that when we act without sufficient rationality, then we basically degrade ourselves by using characteristics of the body that we share with lower life forms, such as dogs and cats. Therefore, when it came to identity, rationality took precedence over mere emotions in who a person really is at her central core, which she holds in common with all persons, as well as the particular essential core she has as an individual being. Rationality is also the central component of moral conduct and thinking because of this privilege it has been given for so long.

The role that identity politics played prior to 1995 should not be ignored when discussing the possible generational differences that can be found among scholars. Because there was such a stigma to being LGBTQ, it was often far safer for people

---

1 Of course, Hume would beg to differ.

to remain closeted than to unveil that they were not in the heterosexual norm. Employment, social acceptance, safety, and many other social benefits that people accept without question could be denied to those who were different in this way. The result was that by not being in the social mainstream that would allow those with irrational beliefs about non-heterosexuality to see that they were mistaken, and then change their beliefs accordingly, non-heterosexual remained hidden, which encouraged the view within the LGBTQ and heterosexual communities that there was something morally wrong with being non-heterosexual.

Identity politics has many facets, but the one most relevant to this work is the approach it advocated for coming out of the closet. In order to challenge the social conventions in regard to sexual orientation and being queer, it was vital to be out. The more heterosexuals saw those who were out acting according to their identity, then the less deviant and different non-heterosexuality would be to them, and therefore, the more acceptable it would become. In this case, familiarity did not breed contempt. It was intended to create— if not a welcoming society—at least one in which people could live authentically. With greater acceptance would come greater power in political and social circles in order to make LGBTQ livesas good as was offered to those who were heterosexual. In order to advance the interests of the group as a whole, then it is often argued that those who can be out have a duty to be out.

The tension that arises in identity politics is clear if we consider sexual orientation to be a morally irrelevant characteristic, as race should be. If sexual orientation is irrelevant, then being out would be a very odd duty for an individual to have. Heterosexuals had no obligation to state that they are heterosexual— because of heterosexism—but LGBTQs would be obligated in many cases to come out to those who made or might make assumptions about their sexual orientation. Therefore, an additional burden was placed on non-heterosexuals, whose position was already weaker than heterosexuals, to reveal what is supposed to be of no moral concern. This additional obligation reveals what appears to be two different moralities: one for heterosexuals and one for LGBTQ which gives this group a greater burden to bear even though they are already more vulnerable.

In post-queer theory there was a significant change in thinking about these issues. In the United States the activist watershed moment for sexual identity disclosure came with the 1969 Stonewall riots. As activists worked throughout the 1970s and 1980s towards visibility, the younger generations of LGBTQ folks became used to the narratives and expectations of "coming-out." The political assumptions were clear—our collective future and freedom depended on visibility, and the dangers of outing oneself were lessened with each passing year and each new individual commitment to LGBTQ visibility. LGBT scholarship in these years mirrored these same political assumptions. But, the intellectual watershed moment in thinking about sexuality and visible sexual identity came in the early 1990s with the introduction of academic "queer theory." Particularly notable is Judith Butler's 1990 publication of *Gender Trouble* which began to unravel the supposed essentialism of gender identity, and by association sexual identity through exposing the mechanism of reproduction of gender as normatively enforced repetitions of behavior, embodiment, and stylization such that something which is very much performed is experienced as natural. This process of denaturalization opened the intellectual door for sexuality to be explored as socially constructed and regulated through processes of power that are both productive and destructive of the docile bodies under its control.

Queer theory thinkers have a tendency to share at least three basic assumptions in the study of sexuality: it is socially constructed, it is all about power, and ethics are to be held as suspect.

There are multiple aspects to the first basic assumption, that sexual identity is socially constructed. First there is an historical sensitivity about how sexuality has been interpreted. The historical work of academics such as David Halperin (see e.g. 1989, 2004) and Jonathon Katz (2007) convincingly demonstrate that sexual practices throughout history have been understood in different ways. The notion of sexual practices as constitutive of an identity is a fairly recent phenomenon tracing back to the early 1860s. This background knowledge allows for greater flexibility in deconstructing our contemporary understandings of sexual practice as identity.

Secondly, through deconstructive exposure of moments in the history of non-normative sexuality it becomes evident that the processes of construction of aspects of LGBTQ identity are not always recognizable: The structures are quickly hidden by the process of history. This is evidenced by the work of both Michel Foucault (see e.g. *History of Sexuality V.1* (1990)) and George Chauncey (1995). The ubiquitous presence of the closet, for example, within LGBT identities was a construction of the early 20th century, as Chauncey demonstrates in his book *Gay New York*. The recognition that the elements of sexual identity that we take the most for granted in contemporary culture are a product of socio-historical forces allows for greater rethinking of possibility in sexual ideology.

Thirdly, the work of theorists such as Eve Sedgwick demonstrates that things are not always as they seem. In her work, *The Epistemology of the Closet*, Sedgwick argues that the closet is universalizing—that it impacts everyone's sexuality, not that it is minoritizing—as we often suppose it only impacts LGBT sexual minorities (2008). Rereading the impact of sexual identity on culture and human subjectivity becomes a central impetus of queer theory.

In regards to the second basic assumption— it is all about power—queer theorists are avid thinkers in regards to how power functions and influences behavior, ideologies, and even the most natural seeming elements of embodiment. Power is seen as a more nuanced and productive force than simply top down oppressive regimes (although this form of power is also recognized). Post-modern inquiries into the production and employment of power also figure centrally in understandings of sexuality in social and political contexts. Foucault's work (1990, 1995) has been formative in this assumption.

The third shared basic assumption is a general suspicion of the workings of ethics on sexual—namely queer—bodies. Epistemology takes front seat in most of queer theory while ethics does not come along for the ride. Questions tend to focus on the production of sexual knowledge, and ways of knowing and understanding subjectivity. Recently, there has been a shift in this trend and the critical role of ethics is returning to the scholarly scene. This anthology is a part of that recent trend.

At the same time as these considerations are all firmly in place, post-queer theory scholars are also often the most likely to have had the opportunity to be out as lesbian, gay, bisexual, transgendered, or queer for a significant percentage of their careers and to take on LGBTQ or queer topics of research or even specializations. Queer theory may have influenced these scholars in breaking from the traditional methodologies of their academic disciplines and exploring new avenues in the quest for knowledge. It may have resulted in career trajectories that might not otherwise have been taken. Queer theory is certainly likely to have influenced the ways the scholar understands her/him/hir-self.

A final note of context for this anthology: There are pre- and post-queer tensions within LGBTQ communities, with various adherents not feeling seen, understood, or respected in their experiences and understandings of what it means to be a sexual minority. Although this text does not specifically explore those tensions, it does manage to recreate them—exposing them on the level of intellectual commitments, and moral assumptions about identity and social obligation. In this regard it is a microcosm of a broader social-ethical issue for LGBTQ people. Creating a platform for dialogue and exchange is the best way forward through these tensions. We must find spaces in which to face each other and explain our viewpoints and listen to one another, even make interventions into the worldview of one another. In this regard, we believe that this anthology is a step in the right moral direction of building communication in locations where communication is fraught. The book itself is a moral experiment.

The Chapters

As can be seen in the following chapters, the anthology shows that there is no hard and true line of demarcation between pre and post-queer theories, their respective theorists, and the two generations. Clearly, neither pre nor post-queer theory generations has monolithic positions that must be adopted. At times, concepts and arguments are shared between the pairings, and some contributors' approaches do not fit neatly with that of their generational cohort. But the diversity of approaches and thinking is useful in promoting a deeper understanding of passing's ethical issues and how the selected contributors think about them.

In Chapter 1, Mark Chekola and Nancy Arden McHugh conduct a pre- and post-queer theory discussion of what it is to be a person and the role that sexuality plays in that concept. Using the Billy Tipton case as a focal point, Chekola's contribution lays the classical foundations for why passing is inherently deceptive. He also provides an essentialist account of identity that would apply to all human persons and examines identity from an individualistic standpoint. McHugh provides a different narrative about identity which influences her work on the morality of passing. As she writes, "My purpose is to make clear that the kind of management forced upon people so that they pass (as black, white, male, female) is done so under the misguided and dangerous belief that bodily stability, reflective of an inner self, can be achieved and is necessarily desirable." McHugh's approach reflects post-queer theory's notion that identity is more cultural and fluid than in the essentialist accounts. Finally, the case studies of Tipton, Max Beck, and Adrian Piper show similarities and differences of the different types of passing, including intersexuality and race.

In Chapter 2, post-queer theory co-authors Alice MacLachlan and Susanne Sreedhar engage with pre-queer theory author Dennis R. Cooley on questions of the ethical duty to be out, and the moral complications of being out that are raised in the case of queer femmes. Cooley argues the limits of the duty to be out, establishing the parameters. On the negative end: one must not be in a position to lose something of comparable worth, and it cannot pose significant danger to the person's flourishing. And on the positive end: one must consider the possible increases in flourishing, self-respect, and it must entail the reasonable chance of success in influence people in the right direction. For MacLachlan and Sreedhar, queer femmes face a dilemma in being visible in that it may cost them a sense of authenticity in terms of gender expression. This is both a burden and a privilege, and it is clear that the privilege comes along with power and responsibility to undo stereotypes. Throughout the dialogue, interesting questions arise about the role of utilitarianism, moral luck, flourishing, and duties in relationship to passing and outing oneself.

Chapter 3 pairs Daniel Hurewitz with Kelby Harrison in a discussion of different types of power and how it affects identity. Hurewitz talks about the difficulty of discovering what has been carefully hidden by those who are in the closet. By finding out the secrets, those who have them are given an enormous amount of power over those who are trying to keep their passing secret for whatever reasons they believe to be legitimate. Even the veiled person's death does not destroy the power the possessor of the secret has over those who cared for the closeted individual. By revealing the secret, the possessor can alter the survivors' perception of the deceased and those experiences the survivors had with the departed when he or she was alive. Harrison argues that aspects of power should be considered as it has been understood by feminists, followers of Foucault, and critical race theorists. Once again, the fluidity of identity and subjectivity are the central themes to understanding power and passing. Finally, in their dialog each author considers power in circumstances of oppression.

In Chapter 4, post-queer theory author Rob Cover and pre-queer theory author Janna Jackson Kellinger discusses the employment of the term "queer" and its affiliate methodologies vs. the identity markers of "gay and lesbian" in two different contexts. Kellinger revisits a book she published on gay and lesbian teachers, reifying her decision to use the identity markers of "gay" and "lesbian" which were the preferred identities of her participants. Rob Cover critiques the literature on gay and lesbian youth suicide for not including a queer theory tool, despite the presence of queer methodologies and thinking about identity and its prevalence in academia for the last 20 years. In the discussion Kellinger and Cover discuss the inherent problems with the binary of coming out vs. passing, with Kellinger supporting and advocating for coming out, and Cover advocating an ethical responsibility to undo the dichotomy and pluralize the options of identity disclosure and performance.

In Chapter 5, Willie Tolliver and C. Riley Snorton examine the intersection of sexual and racial passing, with a special focus on African American celebrity. Tolliver weaves together a study of being out versus being veiled based on literature and history, including the Harlem Renaissance. By orienting his essay on characters from Monique Truong's *The Book of Salt*, Tolliver explores sexual and racial passing in a setting of "colonialism, displacement, [and] nostalgia," which puts into perspective cultural conditions and rules about passing and exploitation that have bearing on the subject in the 21st century. C. Riley Snorton's work focuses on the "down low" of black culture and how it is exploited by celebrities such as Oprah Winfrey. Snorton's "glass closet" serves as a metaphor for understanding "public black sexualities as already figured as deviant, while simultaneously read as mysterious and untenable in mediated space." The intersection of race and sexuality provides a broader and deeper development of the subject of passing that queer theory alone cannot provide. In the dialogue that follows the two essays, the authors consider the impact that sexual orientation, race, and celebrity have on the rules and conditions of passing.

Chapter 6 explores marginal identities by focusing on the communities of sexual minorities: bisexuals and intersexuals. Pre-queer theory author Samantha Brennan explores bi-invisibility, using political philosophy, critiquing the notion of sexual citizenship, and advocating an understanding of the communicative process of fashion, performance, and visibility. Post-queer theory author Maren Behrensen asks whether intersexual is a queer identity—which she answers with a qualified yes; and asks whether intersex passing is similar to other kinds of LGBTQ passing—which she answers with a qualified no. In the discussion, ascribing of the term "queer" to those whom do not self-employ it is debated. The key features of sexual citizenship and its relationship to political recognition are teased out, and the importance of the role of medical trauma in intersex community building and queer activism is established.

Chapter 7 contains a dialogue between Christine Overall and Karin Sellberg. Overall focuses on transgender passing and deception. Unlike much of the argument on sexual orientation passing, when transgender people are veiled they are not being deceptive. Overall argues that "gender is an aspirational identity, a fundamental personal characteristic such that, if its possessor values it, s/he must maintain and reinforce it through ongoing action." By being successful in their attempts to pass as a different gender, then transgender people are merely maintaining a fundamental personal characteristic. To be revealed would make it impossible to be authentic. Sellberg adopts a position based upon the work of Judith

Butler and other notables from the post-queer theorists. As does Overall, Sellberg argues that gender is aspirational and something that needs constant renewal. Moreover, identity is formed through language as a form of self-formation through performance which is required at all moments in order to maintain the constant renewal. In this manner, Sellberg rejects the pre-queer theorists' essentialism and fundamental continuity to be replaced with deconstructionism.

References

Butler, J. 1990. *Gender Trouble.* New York: Routledge.

Chauncey, G. 1995. *Gay New York: Gender, Urban Culture, and the Making of the Gay Male World, 1890-1940.* New York: Basic Books.

Foucault, M. 1990. *The History of Sexuality, Vol. 1: An Introduction*, translated by Robert Hurley. New York: Vintage.

Foucault, M. 1995. *Discipline and Punish: The Birth of the Prison.* New York: Vintage.

Halperin, D. 1989. *One Hundred Years of Homosexuality: And Other Essays on Greek Love.* London: Routledge.

Halperin, D. 2004. *How to Do the History of Homosexuality.* Chicago, IL: University of Chicago Press.

Katz, J. 2007. *The Invention of Heterosexuality.* Chicago, IL: University of Chicago Press.

Sedgwick, E. 2008. *Epistemology of the Closet.* Berkeley, CA: University of California Press.

Mill, J.S. 1988. *Utilitarianism, On Liberty, and Considerations on Representative Government*, edited by H.B. Acton. London: J.M. Dent & Sons Ltd.

Chapter 1

The Ontological Foundations of Passing

Mark Chekola and Nancy Arden McHugh

Introduction

Mark Chekola and Nancy Arden McHugh develop pre- and post-queer theories on identity and passing. Chekola considers certain traits to be essential to the identity of each person, which in turn can lead to a moral impact on whether passing is deception. McHugh rejects the essentialist account whilst she develops the concept of the imposed pass.

The Moral Dimensions of Passing

Mark Chekola

In a story, the prince pretends he is a low-ranking, ordinary person, in order to find out whether the woman he loves, loves him for his own sake, and not because he is a prince. When jazz musician Billy Tipton died in 1989, it was discovered that he was, unbeknownst to most (including his adopted sons) really a woman ('A Secret Song' 1989: 41, 'Musician's Death' 1989: A18). A black person, light in color, pretends to be white to gain privileges. A Polish Jew passes as a Christian during World War II. At work, a homosexual, when conversing with colleagues about the past weekend, changes the sex of the person she is dating. All of these are cases of "passing," pretending to be something one is not. Sometimes passing is regarded as amusing and even touching, as when it turns out the prince is really loved himself and not for his position. Sometimes passing is regarded with wonder and questioning, as in the Tipton case: how could she get away with it? Why were the adopted children deceived? Sometimes it is regarded as a plausible protective strategy, such as the homosexual concealing her sexual orientation from co-workers.

My contribution will examine passing, distinguishing different varieties or categories of passing and raising moral considerations, social and individual. I will argue that it raises some serious moral questions, making it a much less casual phenomenon than sometimes assumed. Whether it is wrong and what about it is wrong will vary, depending on the situation and reasons.

Passing is, basically, pretending or being taken to be what one is not. The *Oxford English Dictionary*'s definition of "to pass for, as" is "To be accepted as equivalent to; to be taken for; to be accepted, received, or held in repute as.

Often with the implication of being something else." Its first citation is from 1596 (*Oxford English Dictionary* 1989: 294). Erving Goffman in his classic work *Stigma* refers to it as "the management of undisclosed discrediting information about self" and notes "Because of the great rewards in being considered normal, almost all persons who are in a position to pass will do so on some occasion by intent" (1963: 42, 74). Sometimes it is done for other reasons, such as testing (the prince disguising his status, or the minority person from a human rights office pretending to want to rent an apartment).

Passing, then, as we shall be focusing on it, is a method of managing information about oneself which, if known, would, the passer believes, lead to being discredited. At this point, we need to consider the passer's role with regard to the information being hidden, as well as the reasons. Some passing is done unintentionally, by virtue of others presuming the person is, in Goffman's terms, "normal." For example, a light-skinned African American might be presumed to be white. Much homosexual passing occurs passively: "Unless given evidence to the contrary, most people in most social situations assume others are heterosexual" (Berger 1992: 85). In this discussion of passing, I will use the term "passing" to refer to cases where some degree of intentionality or deliberateness is involved. At a minimum, passing individuals accept the fact that they are passing, approve of its occurring, and avoid doing anything to give out the information that the assumption (such as of one's being white or heterosexual) is incorrect. The standard case will be one where the person is actively passing: avoiding others' finding out the information, actively doing things to lead people to believe that this person lacks the stigmatized trait, etc. However, if others presume I am heterosexual when I am not, and I avoid discussing my relationship or change the sex when talking about a date I am, by these actions, beginning to change the unintentional passing into a form of intentional passing.

Turning to reasons, we find that they vary. In some cases passing may be done for sheer survival. For example, a Jew in Poland under Nazi rule might pass as a Christian to survive. It might be resorted to in order to avoid forms of discrimination lesser than being killed, but still fairly serious. For example, a black person of light skin color might pass as white in order to get a desired job, a better education or the opportunity to live in a better area, a practice reported to have been common in the United States as well as in South Africa under apartheid.[1] In reports about Billy Tipton, the reason given for her passing as a man was to be able to be a jazz musician: "There were certain rules and regulations in those days if you were going to be a musician" ('A Secret Song' 1989: 41).[2] One might pass to avoid being thought ill of by others, particularly

---

1   Graham Wilson, in *Passing for White: A Study of Racial Assimilation in a South African School* writes about how common such passing was in South Africa during apartheid.

2   This statement was made by the woman, to whom Tipton claimed to be married for 19 years.

where one might be *reduced* to that category. This is a reason often avowed by gay and lesbian people, and sometimes by people who are Jewish. As a defense of passing, I call it the "master/multiple identity argument," which I will discuss later. Yet another sort of reason is to avoid unwanted attention, a desire to be left alone. Celebrities pretending to be ordinary tourists would be one example. We could also her include cases of someone's not disclosing information where it would likely lead difficult or complicated discussion, such as with a person on a plane flight. Finally, there is passing where it is used to test someone: the prince mentioned earlier, or the human rights worker.

Initial Moral Considerations

Passing involves a secret and, typically, deception, lying. Like keeping secrets and lying, it will sometimes be morally justified and sometimes not; and sometimes our moral evaluation of it will be complicated. At the outset I would like to stress that it will not work to treat passing in a casual way, suggesting, for example, that as long as there are some understandable reasons for it (wanting to control information believed to be discrediting) an individual's decision to do it is then justified, and that is that. Even in the most obvious cases, I will argue, it is done at some moral cost.

There are some situations which do seem to be clear cases of justified passing, such as a Polish Jew passing as Christian during the Nazi era. Here the risks are clear and very serious. Our strongest moral judgments would be against the society and the government: no one should be treated in that way. Though the heaviest responsibility rests on the society in cases such as these, in what ways might we see passing individuals as having some moral responsibility?

Morality and the Passing Individual

Let us now focus more directly on passing from the individual's perspective. For the Polish Jew under Nazi rule it is hard for us to feel anything but moral support. What about situations that are less extreme, such as that of Billy Tipton, a passing black person, or a gay man or lesbian passing as straight? My aim is to show that even though typically some degree of moral responsibility rests on the society there are issues of individual morality that arise. Passing is a kind of moral compromise, and as such, people passing often become tools of their own oppression. Our moral judgments will be complicated, and sometimes we may want to be critical of someone's passing, as will be shown later, even though the society has created the context in which passing is chosen. I am not seeking to "blame the victim," but to note the moral complexity of the phenomenon, a complexity which includes in some cases moral culpability on the part of the passing person.

Passing as Lying

As mentioned earlier, some passing is done unintentionally. Homosexual persons are often presumed to be heterosexual. A light-skinned black person lacking significant features typically associated with being black will probably be taken to be white.

Insofar as others make the assumptions, there is no lie. But when one does something to foster assumptions, it is a form of deception. Immanuel Kant in an essay on truthfulness writes of a Mississippi speculator who carried on as usual so people would not guess his intention to abscond. It cannot be said that the person in this situation has *lied* by those actions, but there is deception (Kant 1963: 226-7). In situations of passing, unless contact is very limited and casual, it will be hard to avoid some lying. When I change the sex while telling a coworker about a date last weekend, I am intentionally deceiving—in other words, lying. And if lying is *prima facie* wrong, then this act is, too.[3] Sometimes there is fairly overt lying involved in passing. Billy Tipton, a woman living as a man, deceived members of the band, people in the audience, and even her adopted sons.[4] Sometimes the lying may be covert. While changing one's last name and undergoing surgery to alter facial characteristics that may be regarded as Jewish do not seem to be direct lies, the underlying aim appears to be to claim "I am not Jewish."

For homosexuals, the closet, as a form of passing, will typically involve some lying. Often lovers are referred to as roommates, and living quarters are arranged so that it can be claimed (falsely) to some visitors (such as parents, colleagues) that each person has a separate bedroom.

As lies, all of these cases will be *prima facie* morally wrong. It may be that in certain situations they will turn out to be justified morally, overall, in terms of being the most satisfactory alternative in a difficult situation. However, they are not without moral consequence.

In addition, a common phenomenon with regard to lies is that it becomes more and more complicated to keep them up: the "tangled web" phenomenon. Goffman calls this "in-deeperism," the "pressure to elaborate a lie further and further to prevent a given disclosure" (1963: 83). There is also, of course, the risk that the lie will be found out, and in some cases (such as Tipton's) the virtual certainty. So lies tend to breed more lies, and as a strategy lying brings problems from a pragmatic point of view.

---

3   Sissela Bok argues that while lying and secrets intertwine and overlap, one important difference is "Whereas I take lying to be *prima facie* wrong, with a negative presumption against it from the outset, secrecy need not be" (1989: xv).

4   In 'Musician's Death', son Jon Clark says "I'm just lost. He'll always be Dad. But I think he should have left something behind for us, something that would have explained the truth" (1989: A 18).

Passing and Self-Hatred

Self-hatred seems difficult to avoid in situations of stigmatization where people may pass. Kurt Lewin in an essay entitled "Jewish Self-Hatred" gives an analysis of self-hatred that will work well for other cases. Lewin says:

> It is recognized in sociology that the members of the lower social strata tend to accept the fashions, values and ideals of the higher strata. In the case of the underprivileged group it means that their opinions about themselves are greatly influenced by the low esteem the majority has for them. This ... heightens the tendency of the Jew with a negative balance [of forces leading him to wish to remain in the group] to cut himself loose from things Jewish ... Being unable to cut himself entirely loose from his Jewish connections and his Jewish past, the hatred turns upon himself. (1948: 194)

From a moral point of view, supporting shame based on unfounded stereotypes amounts to supporting and entrenching unwarranted patterns of harm. Taking the societal norms seriously enough to have this shame is a form of servility to the society, accepting the views of oppressors and doing exactly what they want. A serious problem with servility pointed out by Thomas Hill, Jr. is that a servile person fails to respect morality: "A person who fully respected a system of moral rights would be disposed to learn his proper place in it, to affirm it proudly, and not to tolerate abuses of it lightly" (Hill 1977: 178). Not fully respecting himself, such a person is at risk of not respecting others. Insofar as self-respect is a necessary element of morality, the lack of it implicit in passing undermines the individual's morality. To whatever degree this is due to social coercion, it is a socially fostered servility.

Passing and Group Membership

A strategy sometimes used by people who are members of stigmatized groups is to point out a lack of clarity with regard to what counts as being a member of the group. A Jewish person might note that there is a lack of clarity with regard to what it is to be Jewish (is it racial, religious, cultural?) and also might claim to be different from other Jews (not observant, etc.) A gay or lesbian person might note similar issues: Does being gay mean being sexually active, in a relationship, participating in gay events, etc.? Such a person might claim difference from stereotypical gay people and be annoyed at being grouped with them.

Kurt Lewin, focusing on what it is to be Jewish, has a helpful response. He sees this as a self-deceptive error in understanding the nature of groups, and in particular an underprivileged, oppressed group. He claims "it is not similarity or dissimilarity of individuals that constitutes a group, but interdependence of fate." Members of groups are often very different (even members of a family may be more like other, unrelated people than each other). "[T]wo individuals will belong to the same group if their fates are interdependent," even if their character, interests, religion and political ideas differ (Lewin 1948: 165-6). And it is the majority which, by its marginalization of the group, makes for the interdependence of fate of its members. So, try as one wishes, the Jewish person cannot choose to not be a Jew.

Lewin's analysis is apt with regard to other oppressed groups. Gay and lesbian people often claim they have little in common with other gay people, or that they are not like "those effeminate men, drag queens or diesel dykes." In addition, one often hears criticism of terms like "the gay and lesbian community," noting ways in which the word "community" seems inappropriate. Following Lewin, we could note that they are a group, a community, because of their "interdependence of fate," which has to do with how the society, the majority, reacts to them.

The Master/Multiple Identities Argument

One argument sometimes used to justify passing with regard to some stigmatized category such as being black, gay or lesbian, Jewish, etc., is that one might, by virtue of revealing such information, end up being fully identified with that category, or reduced to it. James Stramel, in writing about the outing issue and the caution some have about coming out as gay or lesbian, notes that for some gay people:

> their gayness is at the forefront of everything they do, and being gay becomes a "master identity." But, for others, being gay is only one relatively minor component of who they are. For many gay people, sexual identity is not the central feature of their lives. (1996: 81)

So, this argument would see passing as a strategy for avoiding a "master identity" that one does not want, or does not see as true of oneself, but which would be forced upon one by others.

This is the fear that writer and critic Anatole Broyard had, who passed for white until his death, even hiding it from his children, which caused anguish for his wife, who knew. He "passed for white because he wanted to be a writer, and he did not want to be a Negro writer" (Gates 1996: 68). Writing about someone who happened upon Broyard's copy of a magazine with an article by him in which the contributor's note was cut out later finding out the note included the claim the author "knows at first hand" the life of the American Negro, Henry Louis Gates, Jr. claims about Broyard:

> He knew that the world was filled with such snippets and scraps of argument, all conspiring to reduce him to an identity that other people had invented and he had no say in. Broyard responded with X-Acto knives and evasions, with distance and denials and half denials and cunning half-truths. Over the years, he became a virtuoso of ambiguity and equivocation. (ibid.: 66)

This argument is also put forward by Peter Davies. He warns open gay men that because their sexual identities are predominant aspects of their identities, they are easily tempted to falsely see their experience as universal, believing one's being gay should always be a "master identity." Davies points out:

> For it remains the case that, for many men, sexual identity is not the central feature of their lives; and there are yet others for whom it is simply not feasible to construct a fully gay lifestyle. We should not be tempted to see these individuals somehow as "failed gays," men who have not managed to attain the final stage of a process that we have followed. Rather, we need a postmodern account of identity, which recognizes multiple identities and life as a process of achieving a more or less satisfactory *modus vivendi* with them. Rather than the idea of a gay identity as a superordinate organizing principle, we might pursue the idea of the sexual identity as one element of a man's life vying for space and energy with other aspects. (1992: 77)

Passing then might be justified on the grounds that it protects one's identity from being usurped by being gay, black, Jewish, etc. A common way that gay and lesbian people put this argument is by saying "my being gay is a small part of me," suggesting that being gay is insignificant enough that a failure to disclose it is not a case of lying or deception.

I believe there are a number of confusions in this argument, which I call the "master/multiple identities argument." The real issue is, I think, the question whether, under the circumstances, the failure to disclose is justified. If it is a situation of real danger, we could say that while unfortunate in terms of being deceptive, it is justified. There may be good reasons for passing. But, it is passing. It is not as if it just "didn't happen to come up." Broyard, fearful of his identity as a writer being taken over by his race, continued to pass long after it ceased to make sense, even hiding it from his children. The disclosures avoided by gay and lesbian people who are in the closet have to do with the sorts of things that are regarded as fairly routine information to share among others, such as with whom one lives, the sex of the person one dated last weekend, etc. As such, the avoidance would appear to be intentional.

Ironically, the same thing that the passer fears (being taken over by that identity) is what makes the claim that it is "only a small part of me" in a sense false. As Lewin argued, in an oppressive society this is something one cannot avoid: one is a member of the category, the group, by virtue of a shared fate. It is not a small part of you. Society, by its reactions, does not let it be just a small part of you.

The argument then amounts to a ruse: the avowed reason (it is a small part of me) is not the real reason for the failure to disclose and appealing to it as an argument is self-contradictory. The real reason is danger, shame, fear, timidity or some such thing. And the reason may be a good one or a weak one. It is a moral compromise. Perhaps early in Broyard's career his passing may have been a plausible choice. He might have been put into the category of "Negro writer," and may have found it difficult to pursue the writing career he wished to pursue. As time went on this concern becomes less convincing, particularly in the light of the extensive "web" of lies it required.

Integrity, Relationships, Complicity

I have argued that passing has moral implications. While our strongest moral judgments might be made against the society and its institutions for allowing and supporting the conditions that make passing a tempting strategy, there are moral costs. Sometimes, particularly when done to avoid serious consequences, it may be overall morally justified. The concept of integrity is useful here. Integrity can be understood as involving honesty and forthrightness and a disposition to stand up for what is right and not being tempted by the easy path. Passing as a way of dealing with stigma often involves some loss of integrity.

One aspect of this I have not yet noted that since passing involves hiding information about oneself from others, it impairs relationships, both casual and close, and fosters isolation. Even casual relationships, such as those among coworkers, involve some sharing of information about one's life. The level of intimacy of a relationship is determined by how much of his self a person reveals. Passing severely restricts relationships one develops.

In an article about passing in the film *Europa, Europa*, Julie Inness writes about how the main character, Solly, who is Jewish, initially passes as German in a threatening situation. However, afterward it becomes clear that a deeper reason he uses passing as a strategy is to seek human connection in the face of loneliness (1995: 220). Instead of connection the strategy leads to isolation. Inness writes:

> Passing has revealed its hidden logic of escalating estrangement. People who pass neither make a complete transition into the world in which they pass, nor do they effortlessly step back into the world they left behind. Attempting to develop friendships with people who occupy the passing world, they find themselves trapped. (ibid.: 231)

Finally, it is a strategy that ends up supporting the oppression that makes it an inviting strategy. The passer reinforces the oppressive structure for his own personal gain or ease. The poet Adrienne Rich writes forcefully about these effects: "The retreat into sameness—assimilation for those who can manage it—is the most passive and debilitating of responses to political repression, economic insecurity, and a renewed open season on indifference" (1993: 204).

Passing at the Margins of Race and Sex

Nancy Arden McHugh

I explore the inner experience of passing, making connections between personal narratives of race passing and sex/gender passing. I focus on a common element in the different inner experiences of being judged as trying to pass and being forced to pass, calling these "imposed passes" for reasons that are spelled out later. I explore how the imposed pass is formative of a sense of self that becomes diminished through others' and one's own interpretation of an individual as false, fraudulent, and inauthentic. I begin by reviewing some key literature on passing. I then move on to address identity and essentialism and their relation to passing. Next I focus on the imposed pass through two first person narratives of imposed passing. I argue that these narratives make clear the danger of essentialist notions of identity and their manifestation in the imposed pass. My purpose is to make clear that the kind of management forced upon people so that they pass (as black, white, male, female) is done so under the misguided and dangerous belief that bodily stability, reflective of an inner self, can be achieved and is necessarily desirable.

The Anxiety of Passing

In *Making the Body Beautiful,* Sander Gilman points out that the term "passing" originated in the nineteen century as a "pejorative term for the act of disguising one's 'real' (racial) self" (2001: 20). This racial self was not only a black self, but also included Irish, Jewish, and Eastern European selves. Passing, whether through cosmetic surgery or through the "convenience" of possessing Western European (and non-Irish) features, was a threat to European class and race boundaries and "showed how tenuous the boundaries in the social order were" (ibid.). The fear that someone could pass for something they "were not" became a source of social fear and anxiety. The anxiety produced by passing provided a critique of European cultural and racial identity because it subversively illustrated the instability of the European self. This critique went unnoticed because of the "naturalness" of European identity. Yet, the fear of passing became a normative force because minimizing the threat from passing required that "real" Europeans had to assert their European nature by acting and trying to appear to be more European through engaging the very same body modification practices that those passing engaged. To be European one had fit into the racial category designated as European as well as look as if one fit. The body, at the same time, could and could not be an indicator of an essential identity. In the nineteenth century, European identity was continually re-inscribed by the threat from passing.

Elaine Ginsberg, in *Passing and the Fictions of Identity*, argues that:

passing is about identities: their creation or imposition, their adoption or
rejection, their accompanying rewards or imposition. Passing is also about the
boundaries established between identity categories and about the individual
and cultural anxieties induced in boundary crossing. Finally, passing is about
specularity: the visible and the invisible, the seen and the unseen. (1996: 2)

Passing is about the identity one creates of oneself or the identity that is created
for oneself by others, an imposed identity. Passing also requires reciprocity. To
pass as something, whether or not it is my intention to try to pass, there must be an
experiencer of my passing. Furthermore, for one to pass there must be perceived
boundaries of what one is and what one is not. There must be some assumed natural
or essential identity that one deliberately or accidentally disguises from others that
negates the category that others take the passer to belong. In other words, a passer
appears to belong to one group, but "really" is part of another. As Gilman argues,
passing "presupposes decisive categories of inclusion and exclusion" (2001: 21).
To pass is to become part of a group, either intentionally or unintentionally, and to
become invisible within that group (ibid.: 22). The success of my pass is measured
by how unnoticed, how unremarkable, I am within a particular group.

Passing and Essentialism

The practice of passing requires that people take there to be stable, fixed, essential
categories of identity that "a self" can fill. Most members of the academy are
familiar with the critique of essences and essential categories that have been part of
the postmodern project and the problems this critique creates for identity. Briefly,
the reasoning goes like this: the modern subject is a self that has certain essential
features that make that self what it is. The inner self is, in a sense, a timeless whole.
One might not know oneself well, but the process of self-discovery, the modern
project of personal progress, will reveal a self that one comes to recognize as
authentically real. Ladelle McWhorter argues, "for most essentialists, the process
of developing self-awareness is the process of learning about something already
present, a self who already is homosexual, lesbian, or gay" (1999: 82). This self
is taken to be unchanging. Perceived changes are the result of coming to know
oneself better and revealing more of the stable self.

Outward appearances are thought to be sure indications of the inner, essential,
timeless self. A person's blackness or a person's whiteness reveals something about
that person's essential inner nature, as would a person's maleness or femaleness.
We look at the outside to understand what is essentially inside. In *Essentially
Speaking*, Diana Fuss notes, "[e]ssentialism is most commonly understood as a
belief in the real, true essence of things, the invariable and fixed properties which
define the "whatness" of a given entity" (1989: xi). Part of the postmodern project
has been a dispelling of the idea of essences. The "[a]nti-essentialists are engaged
in interrogating the intricate and interlacing processes which work together to
produce all seemingly 'natural' or given objects" (ibid: 2).

In the process of working through the essentialist constructivist debate in sexual identity, McWhorter makes a useful distinction between essential natures and identities:

> What an object is in itself is a matter of its essence. That the object is able to remain "the same" over time is *an effect* of its essence. Thus identity in the sense of maintenance of oneself in the selfsame is an effect of essence. (1999: 82)

She argues that an essence by its definition is not something that can appear to our senses because an essence is unchanging and our senses only experience those things that do change (ibid: 83). So even if there are essences, the outside perceiver could not discover another's essence. As McWhorter says "[w]e're never going to stumble across a homosexual essence at a party or a homosexual essence in a laboratory" (ibid.: 83).

The question must be asked then, what do we think we find when we have "found" another's essence or when a person talks about an essential nature or an essential identity? McWhorter responds what we may have found is a product of socialization. She provides a rather convincing example:

> Having spent a great deal of my life in a region of the U.S. where one of the most salient aspects of anybody's identity is his or her religion, I insist that the answer is yes: Sometimes socialization alone is enough to create very deep kinds of self-awareness and a fundamental sense of one's identity and place in the world. No one is born a Christian; no one inherits Christianity through the genes. Yet in Alabama to identify or not to identify as a Christian in not something a person can deliberate about; it pervades our lives from the day we are born. (ibid.: 84)

McWhorter points out that the purpose of the Christian church is to make Christians. The act of baptizing makes this quite obvious. When one is baptized as a child her parents are making a commitment to raise her as a Christian, i.e., to form a Christian identity in the child. When one is baptized as an adult or when in Christian religions, such as Catholicism, where one goes through the process of confirmation, an individual is choosing to be a Christian and to live a Christian life. By definition Christianity is a constructed and chosen identity, not a found or an essential identity.

Essentialism is a Folk Philosophy

Most people outside of the academy (therefore most people) are essentialists, as are many people inside the academy, even though we treat the discussion of essentialism as passé. Most people view individuals and groups as having some fixed, immutable nature. Those making policy decisions, medical decisions, and going about the normal mundane tasks of life are essentialists. It is folk philosophy. The common claim that one can create oneself as one wants oneself to be is really made under the guise of self-discovery or a revealing of the self. Gilman points out, the pass created by cosmetic surgery is contingent upon the idea of remaking oneself into what one really is (2001: 25). The whole new you with the different nose and the tummy tuck is not really a whole new you; it is really you and others will recognize and "accept the external appearance as a true indication of the internal reality" (ibid.).

Candace West and Don Zimmerman's writings support my claim of essentialism as a folk philosophy. Referring to sociologist Erving Goffman's empirical work on gender, they write, "Goffman contends that when human beings interact with others in their environment, they assume that each possesses an 'essential nature'—a nature that can be discerned through the 'natural signs given off or expressed by them'" (1987: 129). Gilman concurs. He argues "our categories seem to be real in our world. They are rooted, we think, in the natural categories of our world and our society. The screaming man on the corner looks dangerous, acts dangerous, must be dangerous—and we respond with fear, a fear generated by the category through which we have organized our impressions of him" (Gilman 2001: 330).

What does this mean for passing? In the academy what many think of as a non-issue, essentialism, is in fact a very material issue that has substantial impact on the daily lives of some individuals and groups. Because passing requires that there are stable, fixed, essential categories of identity, it needs a belief in essences to even exist. Because there is the expectation that individuals have readily visually identifiable essences, we seek to find those in individuals. Amy Robinson argues that "the "problem" of identity, a problem to which passing owes the very possibility of its practice, is predicated on the false promise of the visible as an epistemological guarantee" (1994: 716). Gilman's screaming man who looks dangerous, act dangerous and therefore must be dangerous illustrates Robinson's claim quite well. The outer reveals to us what we take to be an inner essential dangerous nature.

There is a sense of cognitive safety when a person's appearance meets our expectations, but there is also a sense of safety in just being able to clearly identify what a person "is." When the visible does not identify an individual's self, most people seek to impose an identity upon them—we force them to pass as something. "'Passing' is the other side of the coin of our persistent and constant need to generate stereotypes in order to organize the world" (Gilman 2001: 330).

To have a pass imposed upon one requires that others have some expectations of who they think an individual is and what they appear to be, i.e., there is a discontinuity between appearance and assumed essence. One seeks to impose an essence upon another to resolve the discontinuity. Furthermore, with the imposed pass and the imposed essence, the assumed right to self-authority is frequently negated. One is viewed to lack self-authority, to be mistaken about their true self. This lack of authority requires that someone with authority impose an essence. Fuss argues that when essentialism is deployed one should ask "*what motivates its deployment?*" (1989: xi).[5] In the case of the imposed pass, essentialism is deployed in an attempt to make individuals fit into categories that are safe and do not challenge others' sense of self, normalcy, and stability. As the quote by Gilman points to above, the pass, imposed or chosen is generated by the need for neat, unchallenging stereotypes. The two narratives of imposed passing presented below illustrate these points in a startling fashion.[6]

Narrating Passing

Adrian Piper is a light-skinned African American philosopher and artist who is usually mistaken for white. In her autobiographical essay, "Passing for White, Passing for Black" she recounts her experience of others' reactions to the discontinuity of what they take to be her natural or real essence and her perceived essence (Piper 1996). Piper states that upon entering Harvard as a graduate student in philosophy at the first department social the "most famous and highly respected member of the faculty observed me for a while from a distance and then came forward. Without introduction or preamble he said to me with a triumphant smirk, 'Miss Piper, you're about as black as I am'" (ibid.: 234). On Piper's application to Harvard she checked African American as her racial category because she did not want to be perceived to be passing as white, yet in this case the professor clearly thought she was trying to pass for black, that essentially she was white.

Marilyn Frye argues that whiteness as a concept is "wielded" and that whites guard the defining of who is white and who is not white. When a person like Piper "has been clearly and definitively decided to be white *by* whites, her claim that she is *not* white must be challenged.... To such a person, a white person is saying: I have decided you are white, so you are white, because what I say about who is white and who is not is definitive" (Frye 1983: 115). The deployment of white essentialism is the prerogative of whiteness. The authority is with the white person, not with Piper.

In her essay, Piper also recounts one of her colleagues "who glared at [her] and hissed, 'Oh, so you want to be black, do you? Good! Then we'll treat you like one!'" (1996: 257). This reflects the more common experience that Piper had of others' perceptions that she was trying to pass for white because she did not announce her "blackness" in "appropriate" ways that indicated blackness. In other words, because she did not have what they took to be essential black features and because her behavior did not fall into their categories of black behavior, she was responsible for actively announcing her blackness in a way that those that more clearly fit the "essential" qualities were not responsible for. Frye argues that

---

5   Fuss's emphasis.

6   For example, most people are familiar with narratives of light-skinned African Americans passing as white during Jim Crow not only to avoid Jim Crow laws, but also merely to live. Gilman's *Making the Body Beautiful* chronicles the history of passing by use of cosmetic surgery.

blackness is expected to be announced in a way that whiteness is not because whiteness is taken to be an "in-group, a kin group, which is self-defining" (Frye 1983: 115). Whiteness does not need announcing, but blackness does. Piper states,

> [f]or most of my life I did not understand that I needed to identify my racial identity publicly and that if I did not I would be inevitably mistaken for white. I simply didn't think about it. But since I made no special effort to hide my racial identity, I often experienced the shocked and/or hostile reaction of whites who discovered after the fact. I always knew when it happened, even when the person declined to confront me directly: the startled look, the searching stare that would fix itself on my features, one by one, looking for the telltale "Negroid" feature, the sudden, sometimes permanent withdrawal of good feeling or regular contact—all alerted me to what had transpired. Uh-oh, I would think to myself, and watch another blossoming friendship wilt. (Piper 1996: 257)

Piper explains how she experienced others' "shocked and/or hostile reaction" to her racial identity. Piper's own inner experience of this common event is one of shame, of feeling like an imposter. She experienced:

> the groundless shame of the inadvertent imposter, exposed to public ridicule or accusation. For this kind of shame, you don't really need to have done anything wrong. All you need to do is care about others' image of you, and fail in your actions to reinforce *their positive image of themselves*. (ibid.: 235)[7]

Piper experiences having done something wrong, when of course she did not. What is important here is not only her experience of shame and feeling like an imposter, but how her body, her blackness where previously others saw whiteness, affects others' "positive images of themselves." Piper's blackness contests others' bodily integrity, others' sense of a fixed self, their essential nature, their sense of safety. If Piper is black, when she was assumed to be white and displayed what others took to be essential behaviors and features of whiteness, then others' sense of self as white becomes contested also. If blackness cannot be determined by one's appearance and behavior, then there are no criteria upon which to judge whiteness. Whiteness become de-essentialized at the same time blackness does. There becomes no authentic way to be white or black because these categories become destabilized. Whiteness cannot provide the epistemological privilege and social safety it is thought to provide if it cannot be readily and certainly identified.

Not surprisingly other marginalized individuals experience similar, though not identical, reactions to their bodies that others perceive to be incompatible with their selves. This is especially the case with intersexed individuals. Max Beck was born with mosaic cells in his body, some XY and others XO. He also had a "rudimentary phallus" and "fused labio-scrotal folds" (Beck 2001: 1.1). Beck's

---

7   My emphasis.

parents were told to raise him as a girl, so they took him home and attempted to raise him as Judy. Beck was able to "pass" as a tomboy as a child, though not well. He says "I grew into a rough-and-tumble tomboy, a precocious, insecure, tree-climbing, dress-hating show-off with a Prince Valiant haircut and razor-sharp wit who was constantly being called 'little boy' and 'young man'" (ibid.).

As Beck proceeded into adolescence passing as a tomboy, the androgyny that frequently is accepted in children became increasingly unacceptable to others, including his parents and doctors. West and Zimmerman explain how the folk philosophy of essentialism functions with sex by quoting anthropologist Harold Garfinkel. They state:

> Garfinkel (1967) notes that in everyday life, we live in a world of two—and only two—sexes. This arrangement has moral status, in that we include ourselves and others in it as "essential, originally, in the first place, always have, always will be, once and for all, in the final analysis, either 'male' or 'female'". (West and Zimmerman 1987: 133)

Beck's life and that of many other members of the intersexed community supports this claim.

> I quickly came to understand that tomboy—the gender identity with which I had escaped childhood—was less acceptable in adolescence. Yearly visits to endocrinologists and pediatric urologists, lots of genital poking and prodding, and my mother's unspoken guilt and shame served to distance me considerably from my body: I was a walking head. (Beck 2001: 1.2)

Beck began to realize that the instability of his body did not fit with the essentialized expectations of the categories of male and female. The medical management of his body, the "genital poking and prodding" by endocrinologists and urologists made this quite clear, as did his mother's guilt. Kessler (1998) argues that "physicians 'psychologize' the issue [of intersexed infants] by talking about the parent's anxiety and humiliation in being confronted with an anomalous infant. They talk as though they have no choice but to respond to the parents' pressure for a resolution of psychological discomfort and as though they have no choice but to use medical technology in the service of a two-gender culture" (ibid.: 32).

The medical community and the parents are complicitous in reinforcing not just behavioral gender norms, but the expectations of genital difference so that the essential congruity between sex and gender and the expectations of sexual dimorphism are replicated. Beck could not be genderless or a third gender, there is no room for these options in a two-gender system. He had to be something, so they made him a "girl" and worked to make everything else from genitalia, to hair, dress and toy choice fit "girl/female." Essentialism is deployed in an attempt to fix something—Beck's body—that challenges the two-gender system.

   Subsequent surgeries to construct female genitalia and hormone injections left Beck physically scarred and unfeeling and emotionally scarred. Beck describes himself as "wander[ing] through [this] labyrinth for another ten years, with a gender identity and desires born of those medical procedures. I began to experience myself as a sort of sexual Frankenstein's monster" (Beck 2001: 1.2). This analogy to Frankenstein's monster seems apt. Like Frankenstein's monster Beck's bodily and emotional sense of self was constructed by medical professionals with expectations of what it is like to be a real man or a real woman. Their attempts to give him a stable body, a body that would reflect a conventionally sexed body reflecting conventional gender norms, resulted in a fragmented body, one that Beck did not even know, one that others continued not to know how to categorize.

   Max Beck as Judy eventually begins to identify as a lesbian. But even this label is contested by her perceived lack of bodily stability. He asks, "how could I be a butch if I was "really" a man? How could I call myself "lesbian" when I wasn't even a woman? I felt like an imposter, a fraud, and now more than ever, a freak" (Beck 2001: 2.2). Like Piper, Beck felt like an imposter. One discovered to not fit the one category with which he wished to identify—lesbian. As an individual not fitting the male/female dichotomy or the masculine/feminine, Beck had no community in which he essentially, naturally fit.

   Beck begins to recognize his self as queer, as contesting the essential fixity of rigid gender, sex and sexuality categories. He finds himself a:

> [t]omboy, unfinished girl, walking head, Frankenstein, butch—these were all so many wonderful/terrible, sharp/ill-fitting suits; the body wearing them was and is transgendered, hermaphroditic, queer. And an important, even essential element of that queerness was the trauma that accompanied it, the medicalization, the scars, the secrecy, the shame. I was born a tiny, helpless almost-boy, but the way my world responded to me is what made and makes me intersexed. (Beck 2001: 2.2)

Beck's constructed sense of self is that of an intersexual, a different kind of identity category, a category more like McWhorter's constructed Christian and less like what our expectations are of essential fixed sexed identities. His self is so overtly constructed that it allows most others to feel comfortable in their own seemingly unconstructed, essential selves. Beck, unlike most others, was and is reminded on a daily basis of the instability of self.

   Beck decides to transition to living as a man, thus becoming Max. He begins to replace his estrogen with testosterone and eventually has a mastectomy. He begins to actively contest sex, gender, and sexuality categories by living androgynously as intersexual. But this body felt "naked" to Beck. He finds himself "scaring little old ladies out of public restrooms, making seemingly simple tasks, such as shopping, surprisingly difficult" (Beck 2001: 2.3). Again, just like an "unfinished girl" or a half-made boy, Beck as intersexual and androgynous cannot live easily in a culture that places its comfort and security in a two-gender system. Beck has to come to live as something, male or female, because in a two-gendered system to be intersexed is to be nothing or perhaps worse than nothing—it is a threat to the system itself.

Though he now lives as a man, is married, and is a father, Beck finds himself, in his words:

> [l]ooking in the mirror every morning, I am reminded of just how outward outward appearances are. Moving through the world, I'm just a guy: a husband, a father, a computer geek, a manager.... . Does the Y chromosome in (only) some of my cells and the facial hair I'm growing make me any less a girl, a tomboy, a lesbian, a butch, a woman? I have worn all of these identities, so surely they are mine, even if they no longer fit, even if they were never my birthright, never mine to wear. I cannot undo my history, and I am sick to death of regretting it, so those hard-won horrifics will have to stand. When I look in the mirror, I see all of them. (Beck 2001: 2.3)

The End and Maybe Not a Satisfying One

Beck now passes as man, a guy, a pass he feels more at home with than his other forced alternative. Just like Piper has only a choice of black or white and is put into those categories at others' convenience, Beck has options of male or female, straight or lesbian. Both of them experience the sense of being perceived as what they are not. Both inhabit contested bodies because our categories are too narrow, unimaginative and entrenched to allow for more or different categories. Piper's narrative reflects more of her struggle with others' perceptions of herself. Beck's reflects his struggle with his bodily instability, the management and reaction to his body by others and the frustration of binary sex and gender categories. As Ginsberg makes clear in her description of passing, Piper and Beck contest "the boundaries established between identity categories" and create "cultural anxieties [by their] boundary crossing" (Ginsberg 1996: 2). Beck's and Piper's narratives also show how passing undermines assumptions of privilege. To contest bodily stability and stability of the self is to trouble the essential privileging of whiteness and the privileging of maleness, for these categories become meaningful in a different way when they are in flux.

Beck's and Piper's experiences and selves are incredibly significant because their sense of diminished self, the betrayal of identity and a body that does not fit is at least in part the result of a culture that produces categories that it takes to be essential, fixed and meaningful. Beck and Piper show how these essential categories are productive of practices that are physically and psychologically harmful. Our reliance upon essentialism as a folk philosophy led to the mutilation of Beck's body and Beck's and Piper's senses of themselves as fraudulent and without a social location. The metaphysic of essentialism is much more ethically worrisome and dangerous than it might appear in philosophers' lexicon. The Intersexed Society of North America makes frighteningly clear just how harmful essentialism can be: Five children in the United States are mutilated every day in attempts to normalize sex and gender. Some medical professionals are becoming more willing to rethink treatment protocols for intersexed infants, but most argue that surgery is a necessary first step, because parents cannot accept a child whose gender they cannot see (Kessler 1998: 126).

There is a moral imperative to shift the way we engage people who trouble our essential categories. Max Beck and Adrian Piper bravely recount their experiences with essentialism and the imposed pass, but the responsibility for unseating these privileged categories should not just lie with people in Beck's and Piper's situation. It lies with all of us who recognize this harm. We should speak out about the privileging of certain kinds of bodies and the mutilation of bodies conducted under the guise of social fit and social categories. As Marilyn Frye suggests we should unseat the privileging of whiteness and its prerogative of labeling and identification. She argues that whites should be publicly explicit about a disloyalty to whiteness and the privileges of whiteness, that whites should disassociate with those activities that further this privilege (Frye 1983: 116). Recognizing the relation between cases like those of Beck and Piper can help show how morally problematic essentialism can be. Many people would be willing to consider what happens to Piper to be ethically worrisome, yet consider Beck's case to be a medical emergency. The damage caused to Max Beck makes clear that the emergency was not Beck's infant body, but the socially mandated mutilation of infants done under the guise of social fit and parental comfort. These smaller, more pointed interventions that trouble essentialized categories seem to me to provide a means at getting at and chipping away essentialism as a folk philosophy. They may also disrupt the misguided and dangerous belief that bodily stability, reflective of an inner self, can be achieved, is necessarily desirable and can be done without costs.

Comments on McHugh's "Passing at the Margins of Race and Sex"

Mark Chekola

Rigid, narrow categories, ways of seeing the world, particularly when there are negative views applied to some of the categories, can cause great harm when the categories have to do with people and the people do not quite fit. McHugh shows this with her vividly described cases of Adrian Piper and Max Beck. Adrian Piper is a black person who do not look black and affirms her being black and does not want to hide it. She has to deal with people who do not like not being able to readily identify someone as black, particularly if they mistakenly take someone to be white on the basis of appearance. Max Beck is an intersexed person born with mosaic genetics, with a mixture of XY and XO cells, and atypical genitalia (a "rudimentary phallus" and "fused labio-scrotal folds" (Beck 2001: 1.1). His parents, at the suggestion of physicians, attempt to raise Max as a girl. Beck does not fit, and goes through a number of changes, including surgery to construct female genitalia and hormone treatments, identifying as a lesbian, again not fitting, and then deciding to live as a man and switching to testosterone and undergoing a mastectomy. All along the way he finds he does not fit and feels like an imposter.

McHugh points out that both Piper and Beck are harmed by imposed passing, and feeling that they are imposters and fraudulent. Imposed passing includes being judged as trying to pass (e.g., Piper seen as trying to pass as black) and being forced to pass (e.g., Beck as having to pass as either male or female).

Before going on I would like to express my appreciation for McHugh for highlighting the harm that is caused to individuals, where the passing is, in the case of Piper, unintentional and passive, or, in the case of Beck, forced on the person by a sharp, binary categorization where he clearly falls between the two alternatives. In my argument I focus on passing where some intention is involved and where typically it is done to avoid some harm, seek some gain, or out of shame. I do mention a moral culpability of society with regard to people having to decide whether or not to pass and being forced to make moral compromises. But I emphasize there being some moral cost on the part of the individual. But in Piper's case she has found herself in difficult situations through no fault of her own because of some thinking she's claiming to be black to take advantage of affirmative action policies, and others feeling somehow deceived by her when they find out she is black. And Max Beck, also through no fault of his own, has gone through much suffering and confusion because of not fitting the sharp male/ female distinction that society holds to be of great importance. These are cases of passing and harm I did not consider, and which it is important to include in a project on passing.

The source of this problem is identified by McHugh as essentialism, seeing identity as being fixed and stable, combined with a culture that wants these categories to be clear and binary: black or white, male or female.

The examples involve categories that are visible, or generally visible. Piper is black, but does not look black and people are disturbed when they find out. Beck feels he must pass or present as either male or female. Trying to live androgynously as an intersexual freaks people out. And these experiences cause feelings of shame in both Piper and Beck.

It must be remembered that many cases of passing involve categories that are invisible or not always visible. Probably most gay and lesbian people are not identifiable on sight. Many Jewish people are not visually identifiable. Some categories which have been related to negative treatment of people are not visible at all, such as illegitimacy. So we must supplement visual identification with what we might call, following Adrian Piper, *cognitive identification*. Piper says:

> What joins me to other blacks, then, and other blacks to one another is not a set of shared physical characteristics, for there is none that all blacks share. Rather, it is the shared experience of being visually or cognitively *identified* as black by a white racist society, and the punitive and damaging effects of that identification. (Piper 1996: 267)

This is similar to Kurt Lewin's observation noted by me earlier that it is not similarity of individuals "that constitutes a group, but interdependence of fate" (see Chekola, this volume). Cognitive identification covers a variety of things, such as being informed by the individual or another, making judgment on the basis of a name (e.g., regarded as typical to a certain group, such as American Indians or Jewish people), etc.

McHugh notes the strong interest in clear boundaries with regard to categories such as black/white and male/female. This is shown in Max Beck's case, where the sharp distinction between male and female does not fit his biology, and there are efforts by medical people and his parents to make him fit one or the other. And because he does not, he feels like an imposter, and even a "monster."

The interest in clear boundaries, and the existence of sexism in connection with this can also be observed in people's discomfort when it is not clear whether someone is male or female in terms of their name when making a telephone call to the person. And misidentification of sex is often upsetting to people misidentified, especially when a male is misidentified as female, such as when sent a message to "Ms. X," when their first name is one typical to females, or when contacted by telephone and their voice is high-pitched and sounds like a woman's voice.

McHugh attacks these problematic categories of identification by claiming that they are based on a belief in essentialism and the existence of stable, fixed categories of identity. She also mentions an emphasis on essences being visually identifiable. I think we have to be careful, because, as I noted earlier, there are many categories regarded as significant that are not, or are not always, visually identifiable.

I am not exactly sure how essentialism would be defined here. It seems to be a metaphysical view, a view about the nature of the world. With regard to identities of persons "Outward appearances are thought to be sure indications of the inner, essential, timeless self" (see McHugh, this volume). As an alternative, we have Ladelle McWhorter's discussion of how being a Christian, which is in her home state of Alabama seen as a key part of one's identity, is a constructed and chosen identity (see McHugh, this volume). The rejection of essentialism then seems to be a commitment to constructionism, viewing categories as being constructed, not found. But this binary of essentialism vs. constructionism may be too sharp and fixed.

If we set aside the question of exactly what our concepts refer to we can note that in our living and acting in "the world" we do need to organize what we experience under concepts. Among the basic concepts that have emerged we have sex, with a distinction between males and females, and race, which has included black and white. In the case of sex, it does seem to be the case that the living beings we encounter include largely males and females and that the majority of people fall under one or the other with a fair degree of clarity. In the case of race, things are less clear. In the case of black and white, historically people have made the distinction, and have often used skin color as at least an initial basis for it. With regard to both male/female and black/white there is something in experience that is the basis for our basic shared concepts.

But extra things get added to the basic concepts, such as connecting certain roles and behavior to each sex, and valuing one more than the other, and regarding the distinction between black and white as including properties, "natures," that differ, with one being valued more than the other. These could be seen as socially constructed layers or additions to the basic concepts. In the case of male/female, when it is discovered that there are some beings, a relatively small minority, who do not fit, such as intersexuals, people may be at a loss as to what to do. One possibility is to regard these cases as something like mistakes of nature, "freaks," and then hide them away or ignore them. As medicine developed and offered some possible interventions with surgery and hormones, a fix was available that seemed to offer a way to "save" these people by getting them into one of the two categories of sexes. In the case of race and black/white, cases of people such as light-skinned blacks not being clearly identifiable presented the problem of how to keep the distinction, which had become important through constructed additions to the concept because of the devaluation and exploitation of blacks. Thus the various determinations and distinctions we now find absurd (e.g., "octaroon," the "one drop rule") came into being.

It does seem that we have to have some basic concepts with which to start. In the discussion of Max Beck, in identifying him as intersexual it is noted that he has mosaic (XY and XO) cells, and a "rudimentary phallus." So there are some things "in the world" noted that show he does not fit the standard male and female categories. It would seem to me that this part, the basic concept, is not "socially constructed" in a way that would enable us to say it is dispensable. But the accretions, such as the sharpness of male/female, allowing nothing in between, and connecting roles and behavior and wanting those to be fixed, as fixed as having XY or XX cells, do seem to be socially constructed and dispensable. The categories that come up in the discussion of passing, sex, race, sexual orientation, etc., are based on some basic concepts that are not socially constructed and chosen as is being a Christian. One can imagine not having the concept of being a Christian, but it is harder to imagine not having the concepts of male and female.

It would seem that the injustices and harms to people arise from what I call the constructed accretions to the basic concepts. Drawing attention to this and asking people to keep in mind what the basic concepts really seem to be and to realize that the sharpness of the male/female binary does not seem to be true to the facts, when you consider examples such as intersexuality, and that the importance given to clarity about being male and female and being or the other is not as important and necessary as often thought could be the start of a change that could lead to much greater well-being for future Max Becks. With regard to race, given that there has been a good deal of progress in showing the irrationality as well as injustice of racial distinctions, Piper's experiences show us how deep racism still is in the culture.

I believe Adrian Piper in "Passing for White, Passing for Black" holds a view close to what I am arguing for here. She is critical of people presupposing "an essentializing stereotype into which all blacks must fit" (Piper 1996: 238). This is a criticism of an addition or accretion to the basic concept, not a claim that there is no basic concept at all. When her parents suggests she not identify as black on her graduate school application in order to be sure that be judged only on her merit, she responds, "But that would be passing … That would have been a really, authentically shameful thing to do" (ibid.: 240). Some in her family had passed, and dealing with this was painful for her and her parents.

Comments on Chekola's "The Moral Dimensions of Passing"

Nancy Arden McHugh

In the "Moral Dimensions of Passing" Mark Chekola provides an incisive argument regarding the moral integrity of passing, focusing on how passing can lead to a compromise in one's morality. He begins by pointing to the role of passing in our cultural narratives, such as fairy tales, and moves on to point to situations in which successfully passing can be a matter of one's survival. His argument is an attempt to get to the heart of the ethics engaged in passing. He points to several examples in which passing may be practically expedient, such as Billy Tipton's passing as a man in order to succeed as a jazz musician and writer Anatole Broyard, who passed as white in order to not be viewed as black writer, but as just a writer.

Chekola draws the reader through the moral complexities of passing by challenging the expediency of passing. He develops the "master/multiple identities argument" that troubles the idea that passing is an innocent denial of incidental features of who one is. Chekola argues that many people engage in passing because they view the feature of themselves that they are trying to hide—their race, their sexuality, etc.—as an incidental feature of who they are, that what they really are is so much more. The author is careful to point out that there is something to this claim, but that it is also highly problematic. The fact that one feels the need to hide this part of her or his identity indicates that this feature is anything but small. As the he points out "this is something that one cannot avoid: one is a member of the category, the group, by virtue of a shared life. It is not a small part of you. Society, by its reactions, does not let it be just a small part of you" (see Chekola, this volume). The need to deny one's race, gender or sexuality only serves to show how culturally significant these characteristics are. With the cases of Anatole Broyard and Billy Tipton Chekola argues that while their passing "may have been a plausible" choice early in their careers, after they became highly successful in their careers, the choice becomes a moral compromise because the extent to which they had to lie in order to continue on with the pass seems to outweigh the dangers of what may happen to their careers if they were discovered to be other than they have presented themselves to be.

Chekola also points to more troubling cases in which people pass in order to merely survive, such as Jews passing as Aryans in order to not be exterminated or light skinned blacks passing as whites in order to not live with the very really dangers of living in a racist culture (which could have played in to Anatole Broyard's desire to pass as white, though he seemed to have a relatively safe life in Greenwich Village where his race was known), or gays and lesbians passing as straight to survive and succeed in a heteronormative, homophobic culture. This second set of cases shows how morally troubling passing is because, on the one hand, an individual certainly has a moral right to pass in order to live safely. Yet, on the other hand, even in doing so, the individual's self becomes compromised. To deny one's blackness in order to pass as white erodes one's individual integrity, one's self, even when one does it out of necessity. Further, as Chekola points out, passing under these conditions forces one to engage in the "tools of one's own oppression" (see Chekola, this volume). and, perhaps even more troubling, to further the oppression of others in one's "community" that may not have the privilege to pass or who choose to not pass. Thus, even though passing may be a necessary means of survival, it comes at costs on both an individual and social level, thus the compromise. The nature of passing is such that most people do not do it lightly. Not only does it involve a loss of the self on several levels, it also involves the loss of others from one's life, as in the case Anatole Broyard, who lost contact with much of his family while living his white life. He also sacrificed a level of intimacy with his children and their knowledge of their heritage. His passing became their forced and unknown pass.

These cases of passing make passing appear to be a selfish act, thus compounding the moral compromise, but passing can also serve as a mode of protection for one's family or community. During the Jewish holocaust a person living as a German Christian who had Jewish ancestor would not only be ensuring one's own survival if she or he was able to successfully hide her or his heritage; she or he could also be successfully ensuring the safety of other family members. The same would have held for a light skin black person during Jim Crow—the ability to "pass on" one's light skin privilege to one's children by passing as white allowed these families to not only have the benefits of whiteness, but also to live without the threat of racial oppression, which literally endangered black lives. This does not mean that passing in these instances is not morally problematic. It means, as Chekola pointed out early in his argument, it is very complex, and one has to make an evaluative decision regarding her or his moral priorities and obligations. If the choice is the safety that could be obtained by passing or the daily threat of a racist culture, it is not surprising that those that could pass during Jim Crow did so.

Though Chekola states clearly he is not seeking "to blame the victim" in his analysis of the moral complexity of passing and I do not think he is blaming the victim, I also think that passing as a survival or practical skill says more about our culture than it does about any one individual attempting to pass. The fact that we live in a racist, sexist and homophobic culture in which it can be physically and psychically dangerous to be black or LGBT, says so much about just how morally problematic U.S. culture is. Chekola does point to this issue, but it is not emphasized in his argument. From my view of passing it says so much more about how we function culturally than how we function individually. The fact that people feel the need to pass for their safety is a cultural and political moral failure.

One challenge I had with Chekola's line of reasoning was how to interpret "moral compromise." Some of that challenge may be evidenced in this response. At times I read "moral compromise" as if he was arguing that an individual's morality was compromised, as in a loss of one's moral integrity. At other times I read "moral compromise" as one is negotiating two competing moral obligations and having to compromise by choosing one over the other. In the end I treated the argument as if he was using the term in both senses because I thought it fit what his goals of the argument were: to indicate the eroding of self that occurs when one chooses to pass and to indicate that one is deciding between competing demands. In many ways my struggle to interpret the term made the argument very interesting because it helped illustrate the complexity of the compromise that is taking place when one engages in passing—that in compromising competing values one compromises oneself.

Chekola's and my contributions to this volume are in many ways sympathetic arguments but initiate from different directions. While Chekola's line of reasoning focuses on the intentional pass and how these individual's may morally compromise and be compromised via the act of passing, my argument focuses on the unintentional pass and how we may be morally compromised and morally culpable as a culture by forcing people to pass. Approaching the issue of passing from these two trajectories paints a complementary picture that illustrates the ways that passing leads to moral compromise on multiple levels and points out just how deep and wide the stakes are in passing. Passing is about what individuals do and about what cultures do and expect. A full analysis, which of course is not possible in a single article, is required to understand the complexity, nuances, and dangers of these two types of passing.

"The Moral Dimensions of Passing" raises important questions about the moral complexity of passing and highlights that passing requires significant moral occlusions that shape and reshape individual and cultural identities. Even when done out of necessity passing has high moral costs that are carried both individually and culturally. Mark Chekola provides an important and necessary analysis of the moral significance of passing. I appreciate his attempts to not provide a morally simple answer to what is an incredibly complicated and nuanced practice that has so much historical and contemporary significance.

A Response to McHugh

Mark Chekola

Nancy McHugh's and my discussions of passing show various aspects of its complexity. Her discussion focuses on passing as a cultural phenomenon and how various types of discrimination (racism, sexism, homophobia, etc.) indicate a moral failure of the society. My discussion focuses on the moral costs involved in passing and claims that a person's having a reason for doing it, such as avoiding discrimination or avoiding being reduced to a certain category is not sufficient for regarding the passing as morally justified without qualification.

I agree wholeheartedly with McHugh that passing is done largely to avoid stigma and discrimination in cultures in which certain groups of people are oppressed and that the existence and continuation of these oppressions are a moral failure of these cultures and the citizens and leaders who permit this to continue.

Since the culpability of the culture is clear it may seem that those who pass are free of any moral culpability. But when we as individuals in minorities pass our hands are not completely clean. The culpability depends on the situation and the reasons.

Let us consider the homosexual closet. Conditions in the United States for lesbian and gay persons are certainly much better now than they were in the past. But many still remain closeted even when there seems to be little reason for it (consider tenured college teachers, successful prominent people, celebrities). People are notoriously weak at risk assessment and often misjudge what family members, friends, and colleagues will think and do. It also seems that for many their passing as heterosexual is rooted at least in part in shame. And I have argued that shame-motivated passing amounts to servility to an oppressive society. For some the passing is a habit. For some their passing may have been justified in the past (when conditions were worse, or when they were young in a homophobic family) and the tangled web of the secret makes it complicated and awkward to now be open.

McHugh pointed out that passing is sometimes done for the protection and benefit of others, such as family and community. An example is Jews living as Christians during the holocaust in Germany. In my discussion, I had not included examples where the passing is done for the sake of others, and I thank McHugh for adding this to the discussion. Passing motivated to promote the survival and thriving of one's children in Nazi Germany seems clearly morally justified and its being done for the sake of others adds a positive moral dimension to it.

But even cases such as this end up not being so simple. They do support the oppression, though in situations as extreme as Nazi Germany one could not weigh this heavily. And they do often lead to tangled webs. Fairly regularly there are reports in the news of people discovering that parents or grandparents were Jewish (for example, Madeleine Albright's) or a light-skinned black person, and passed. It is difficult to know how to reveal the truth after the conditions motivating the passing have changed. Heirs sometimes feel deceived or betrayed upon learning the secret. And, as McHugh points out, the ancestor's pass becomes their forced and unknown pass.

If it is wrong to treat people poorly because of their race, sex, intersexuality, sexual orientation or religion then it is wrong to expect people to hide these features of themselves. And if they do, they are complying with the discrimination and supporting it. But sometimes the society expects people to do this. In 1993, voters in Cincinnati passed an amendment to the city charter prohibiting any protections on the basis of sexual orientation. A United States Court of Appeals upheld this amendment in part because homosexuals are not an "identifiable class" and noted that many homosexuals successfully conceal their orientation. In other words, if you can pass, you do not need protection (Chekola 1996: 142-4).[8]

There is a moral perversity here. It is common for many people to suggest that if you can protect yourself or benefit by passing you should do so, and if you are open and honest and suffer, you have asked for it. In this case, a federal appeals court, a prominent United States legal institution, basically made the same argument. Passing has moral costs, and expecting people who can pass to do so is burdening them not only with dealing with discrimination, but with having to lie, perhaps act on shame, and hide information about themselves from neighbors, co-workers and others that may limit their relationships. This is a common method by which a culture supports discrimination and oppression: coerce the minority to support the structure of its own oppression. While the society or culture is morally culpable, it coerces individuals to behave in ways which involve moral compromises, incurring some level of moral culpability as well.

McHugh's discussion of how to interpret "moral compromise" in my argument nicely captures what I had in mind, and I thank her for this. Sometimes it is a compromise where one is deciding between competing demands. For instance, one wants to be open, but being open will jeopardize someone else (a family member, friend, partner) who has a strong reason to pass, such as facing a real and serious risk. But sometimes it involves compromising one's own morality, such as where the passing is motivated by timidity, shame, or irrational estimates of risk, basically a failure to be honest, truthful without good reason.

It is a moral failing for individuals when this happens. But the culture's in effect placing them in a situation where they are forced to have to figure out what to do because of its racism, sexism, anti-Semitism or sharp binary conception of sex burdens them in a way in which others are not burdened. We must do what we can to eliminate these conditions.

A Response to Chekola

Nancy Arden McHugh

I want to begin by thanking Mark Chekola for his response to my argument. We agree upon most major points in relation to passing, even those where I think Dr. Chekola sees us differing—the salience of the essentialism vs. constructivism debate that has pervaded much of academic life for the past 20 years. In my

---

8   The Appeals Court ruling was overturned by the U.S. Supreme Court in 1996, after *Romer v. Evans* overturned Colorado's Amendment 2 which similarly banned protections of homosexuals.

argument, I discuss what I call folk essentialism, the type of essentialism held by most lay people, which entails that there are readily identifiable categories in which most of us naturally fit. Folk essentialism has a long history in U.S. race and gender relations and views both race and gender as purely naturalized categories that tell us certain things about individuals within groups. This essentialism can be tied to some physical characteristics, such as bodies, but it is the broader beliefs that we attach to these bodies where the substance of folk essentialism comes in to view.

The challenge presented by someone like Max Beck is our folk essentialism fails with him. It points out the ways in which though our beliefs about sex and gender are attached to bodies, these beliefs cannot account for people whose bodies do not readily meet our reasoning about sex and gender. This serves to challenge the fixity of such categories as well as the normative claims that are more than implicit in our folk essentialism. Folk essentialism would have Max Beck be different from whom he is, a more easy fit. Yet the lack of the ability to provide an easy fit is the problem. Max Beck tried the easy fit. As did his parents for him as an infant. But the easy fit was no fit. Thus, though he may be part of a rather small minority, we certainly have an obligation to intersexed people to challenge the rigidity of our categories and to exercise more metaphysical and ethical creativity in conceiving how we can make room for intersexed people such that they are not forced to pass. This may mean being willing to challenge our narrow conceptions of male and female, which I have to agree with Chekola, are rather convenient categories, but they are not categories that should be wielded. Many intersexed people agree with the broadening of the categories of male and female such that intersexed people have a sexual identity within these categories.[9] On the other hand, some members of the transgendered community would prefer to have more categories than male and female.[10] Either of these strategies could be effective, but we need to move in one of these directions or we are going to continue to use narrow categories that are convenient only to those that benefit from them.

One of the ways in which I really appreciated Chekola's argument and my argument fitting together is the move from questions about categories, ontological categories, to questions about morality. We both are attentive to the importance of the need to initiate conversations about what our obligations are whether it regards ethical problems raised by passing, as Chekola's line of reasoning develops, or ethical problems raised by a culture that forces some people to pass. We are both clear that we do not believe that enough attention has been paid to this component in passing. I also appreciated the ways in which our arguments departed from each other. Even though we both were raising questions regarding ethics, our reasoning complemented each other in this sense in that they were dealing with two different categories of passing, Chekola with the intentional pass and my argument with the imposed pass. With my argument focusing on the imposed pass I paid much

---

9   See for example, the Intersexed Society of North America http://www.isna.org/

10   See for example, Kate Bornstein's now classic *My Gender Workbook* (New York: Routledge, 1997).

more attention to the way in which a broader culture was failing individuals who were forced to pass. With Chekola's emphasis on the intentional pass he was much more attentive to how the individual may be failing society. Each of these lenses is important and valuable in considering the myriad of ways that people pass. Furthermore, engaging in conversations about what we ought to do from a plurality of perspectives is valuable in getting people engaged in these discussions and creating change. For example, Chekola and I both point out the ways in which each of our ethical concerns, his on the individual and mine on culture, can also be applied to the other's examples. Society and individuals are frequently mutually responsible, though the extent to which they are responsible may vary given the particular case. Opening conversations, such as those engaged in by the reader response practice modeled in this book, is necessary for making change.

References

Anonymous, 1989. A secret song. *Time* [Online], February 13. Available at: http://www.time.com/time/magazine/article/0,9171,956936,00.html [accessed: October 26, 2011].

Anonymous, 1989. Musician's death at 74 reveals he was a woman. *The New York Times* [Online], 23 February. Available at: http://www.nytimes.com/books/98/06/28/specials/tipton-obit.html [accessed: 26 October 2011].

Beck, M. 2001. My life as an intersexual [Online]. Available at: http://www.pbs.org/wgbh/nova/gender/beck.html [accessed: October 26, 2011].

Berger, R. 1992. Passing and social support among gay men. *Journal of Homosexuality*, 23(3), 85-97.

Bok, S. 1989. *Secrets.* London: Vintage Books.

Bornstein, K. 1997. *My Gender Workbook.* New York: Routledge.

Chekola, M. 1996. Equality Foundation v. City of Cincinnati: Invisibility and identifiability of oppressed groups. *Law and Sexuality*, 141, 142-4.

Davies, P. 1992. The role of disclosure in coming out among gay men, in *Modern Homosexualities*, edited by K. Plummer. New York, 75-83.

Frye, M. 1983. *The Politics of Reality: Essays in Feminist Theory.* New York: The Crossing Press.

Fuss, D. 1989. *Essentially Speaking: Feminism, Nature, and Difference.* New York: Routledge.

Gates Jr., H.L. 1996. White like me. *The New Yorker*, June 17, 66-81.

Gilman, S. 2001. *Making the Body Beautiful.* Princeton, NJ: Princeton University Press.

Ginsberg, E.K. 1996. *Passing and the Fictions of Identity.* Durham, NC: Duke University Press.

Goffman, E. 1963. *Stigma: Notes on the Management of Spoiled Identity.* Englewood Cliffs, NJ: Prentice Hall.

Hill Jr., T.E. 1977. Servility and self-respect, in *Sex Equality*, edited by J. English. Englewood Cliffs, NJ: Prentice Hall, 170-80.

Inness, J. 1995. Passing in Europa, Europa: Escape into estrangement, in *Philosophy and Film*, edited by C.A. Freeland and T.E. Wartenberg. New York: Routledge, 218-32.

Kant, I. 1963. Ethical duties toward others: Truthfulness, in *Lectures on Ethics*, translated by L. Infield. Indianapolis, IN: Hackett Publishing, 226-7.

Kessler, S. 1998. *Lessons from the Intersexed.* New Brunswick: Rutgers University Press.

Lewin, K. 1948. Jewish self-hatred, in *Resolving Social Conflicts: Selected Papers on Group Dynamics.* New York: Harper & Brothers, 186-200.

McWhorter, L. 1999. *Bodies and Pleasures: Foucault and the Politics of Sexual Normalization.* Bloomington, IN: Indiana University Press.

Oxford English Dictionary. 1989. 2nd Edition. Oxford: Clarendon Press.

Piper, A. 1996. Passing for white, passing for black, in *Passing and the Fictions of Identity*, edited by E.K. Ginsberg. Durham, NC: Duke University Press, 234-70.

Rich, A. 1993. Compulsory heterosexuality and lesbian existence, in *Adrienne Rich's Poetry and Prose*, edited by B.C. Gelpi and A. Gelpi. New York: W.W. Norton & Company, 203-24.

Robinson, A. 1994. It takes one to know one: Passing and communities of common interest, *Critical Inquiry*, 20, 715-36.

Stramel, J. 1996. Gay virtue: The ethics of disclosure. Dissertation, University of Southern California.

West, C. and Zimmerman, D.H. 1987. Doing gender, *Gender and Society*, 1, 125-51.

Wilson, G. 1970. *Passing for White: A Study of Racial Assimilation in a South African School.* London: Tavistock Publications.

Chapter 2

Complicating Reason(s) and Praxis for Coming Out

Dennis R. Cooley, Alice MacLachlan, and Susanne Sreedhar

Introduction

In this chapter Dennis R. Cooley, Alice MacLachlan, and Susanne Sreedhar discuss the ethical demands of passing in regards to reasons vs. emotions, ideals of flourishing, and the cost to the lives of individual LGBTQ persons. The ethical demands placed on outing oneself are complicated in the case of queer femmes who may authentically find that their gendered self-expression more readily produces a façade of passing, whereas greater attempts at visibility may feel inauthentic.

Is There a Duty to be Out?

Dennis R. Cooley

Andrew Sullivan, a gay, conservative commentator, claimed that "all gay people have a moral duty to be out" (2009). His reasoning might be nuanced to a greater degree than presented here, but the primary justification I see for his position is that the more people who are out about their sexual orientation, the greater positive impact in changing people's minds about homosexuality. Basically, Sullivan's argument is utilitarian with (perhaps) a hint of Kantian self-respect thrown in. What makes it a bit different from basic cost-benefit analysis is that for Sullivan, it is not carefully crafted arguments appealing to reason that will convince people, but "a slowly rising tide of familiarity" which will drown out "people's disgust, revulsion, and deep-down aversion to 'the other.'"[1] Therefore, there is a duty for each homosexual—and I assume, non-heterosexual—person to be out for the betterment of the oppressed group as a whole.

Sullivan's rejection of reason's power over that of emotion is a plausible position to maintain on several grounds. First, there is a vast gap between the beliefs people claim to hold and whether they act in accordance with those mental states. For example, according to surveys, a large number of people believe in

---

1 These are one of Sullivan's readers' words, but Sullivan agrees with the characterization of his position.

the benefits of recycling and claim that they recycle. However, the very same individuals cannot state basic facts about how they recycle, including their daily and weekly practices, or how the community in which they live and work recycles (Tonglet et al. 2004, Tudor et al. 2005, Tudor et al. 2007). The strange forgetfulness about asserted everyday activities shows that the respondents' beliefs do not align with their actions in recycling and possibly other areas. This and similar examples show that reason does not have the compelling force that Kant and others like him thought it did. Moreover, when matching action with rational thought increases the cost to the moral agent, then there is even less incentive for the agent to do what she thinks she should. Hence, Hume's insistence that reason is the handmaiden of the emotions appears to be closer to the truth of what determines how a person will act and what the person will truly believe, if by that term we mean a belief that will cause corresponding behavior. Therefore, if we want behavior and social conventions to change, we must first change people's relevant emotions.

Second, a Gallup poll on gay marriage[2] supports Sullivan's contention on familiarity breeding acceptance rather than contempt. Nationally, 40 percent of respondents were in favor of same-sex marriage legalization, while 57 percent were against.[3] When the figures were broken down by whether the respondent knew a gay or lesbian person, the findings were significantly different. For those acquainted with at least one homosexual person, 49 percent favored legalization and 47 percent were against. For respondents who personally did not know a gay or lesbian individual, only 27 percent were in favor of legalization, while 72 percent were against. Moreover, from those surveyed, being comfortable around a homosexual person is markedly different for those who know homosexuals compared to those believe that they know only heterosexuals—88 percent and 64 percent, respectively (Morales 2009).

With this relatively thin empirical evidence, what are we to conclude about a moral obligation for all gay people to be out to the public in general or in particular? I will make a philosopher's radical claim that the answer is a big "It depends upon the circumstances."[4] At times, the answer is a resounding yes. At others, a cacophonous no. And for a number of cases that fall somewhere in the murky grey, the answer is maybe, maybe not. For the most part, my argument will focus only upon the duties someone has to out herself to strangers, but what is said about this can also apply to outing oneself to those with more intimate ties to the moral agent.

---

2   It is more accurate to label this same-sex marriage.

3   The figures I am using for each question do not add up to 100 percent. All I am interested in showing is that familiarity leads to acceptance, which does not require those who are neutral or who refused to answer the question.

4   John L. Cox has raised the issue of age and maturity in coming out. The duty, if there is one, might become stronger as the person ages, and her sexual orientation becomes more solidified within her identity.

When there is not a Duty

I will begin with clear cases of when there is no duty to out oneself. If the actual or reasonably perceived risks attached to coming out will cause significant harms to the outed person's life, i.e., the person will lose something of comparable moral worth,[5] then, in general, the person has no duty to come out (Singer 2006). In the mid-20th Century United States, for example, many homosexuals worked hard to pass as heterosexual so that they would not lose their jobs, be subjected to increased police surveillance, or suffer any other severe negative consequence resulting from being thought homosexual or "swishy" (Loftin 2007: 1). Anyone whose sexual orientation was questioned was treated as less than full persons by mainstream society, regardless of their actual sexual orientation, which caused a significant cost to their lives. Instead of being free to flourish as they permissibly were as persons, they had either to suppress essential or important characteristics of their identity or be subject to being unethically harmed in their communities, work environments, or other areas of human interaction necessary for an objectively and subjectively satisfying life.

In today's more enlightened society, there are dangers to social interactions, careers, mental and physical health, and even the lives of those who differ from the heterosexual norm. For example, hate crime legislation has been passed to increase the sentences of criminals whose illicit conduct was caused in part by antipathy toward homosexuals. However, there are few federal or state laws against discrimination based on sexual orientation in housing, employment, or other basic areas of everyday life. Therefore, non-heterosexual individuals may legally be injured merely on the grounds of another person's unwarranted prejudices. Although it might not be as obvious as it once was, there is still a lot of hate in certain communities that will cause sufficient harm to those who are out of the closet to make their lives unable to flourish.

Less tolerant societies or sub-societies in the developed and developing world pose even greater risks to homosexuals and other non-heterosexuals including violent attacks and murder. Certain hate groups target gays and lesbians; so being out in a particular community is imprudent because of the general threat. Uganda's proposed death penalty for homosexuals, which was thankfully abandoned under international pressure, fundamentalist Islam's persecution of homosexuals in Iraq and elsewhere, and hate crimes in more developed countries are examples of social hate toward homosexuals' lives and well-being (FBI 2010).[6] This danger can be sufficient in many cases to show that being out-in-general, which means

---

5   I borrowed this phrase from Peter Singer's work. Given the difficulty in determining whether this is an objective or subjective determination, the procedure's complex details to evidence weighing, and lack of consensus on what should count, I will leave "comparable moral worth" as vague as he does.

6   The United States Federal Bureau of Investigation (FBI) noted a rise in hate crimes based on perceived sexual orientation between 2007 and 2008. Although the increase might

that one lives one's life as an out person to everyone within the entire community in which the person interacts, does not maximize one's agent-utility nor is a moral obligation.[7]

The potentially excessive burdens of outing oneself override any *prima facie* duty to be out. The reason why should be clear: we know that it is unjust to the innocent and disrespectful of individuals to require them to pay severe costs in their own person merely to maximize utility for society as a whole, or to improve people's perceptions of homosexuals. That is, another Matthew Shepard case could be useful to advance laws that will offer protection to non-heterosexuals, or make society or a sufficient number of its members more tolerant in general—thereby improving social utility to a sufficient degree—but the person who will bear the burden of being another Shepard is not required to take the risk. Of course, on the grounds of respecting personal autonomy, if innocents want to be moral saints by being out in general or particular in these precarious situations, then that is their prerogative, but we cannot expect them to sacrifice themselves for the greater good.

It is here that we see the benchmark by which we can measure if an injury or potential harm is significant enough to preclude any duty to self-out. If the potential injury suffered is undeserved and it is reasonable to believe that it will prevent or terminate the outed gay, lesbian, or other non-heterosexual agent's life flourishing, then there is at least a *prima facie* justification for the claim that the agent has no duty to be out. As Michael Bayles states, "The only ultimate test for the value of a life is whether at its end it is found to have been worth living" (1994: 130). A flourishing life is an existence in which at least one's basic physical and mental needs are met in a way that is sustainable and good for the person's well-being and happiness.

Flourishing is relevant both to individuals and to communities or societies, which are comprised of individuals and the cohesive relationships they have to each other within their environment. Since we need some way to explain why we should lead one life rather than another; why one life is better than another, why we should act one way rather than another, we require some standard by which we can measure the things we want to evaluate. Flourishing is as plausible a benchmark as any of its competitors; in addition to appealing to the values that most people already have. Hence, arguments incorporating it are more likely to have justificatory force than ones based upon less accepted moral factors, principles, or standards.

Whether something is flourishing is determined by both subjective and objective factors, such as the environments in which we are raised and live. For example, every moral agent *qua* moral agent has to fulfill universal characteristics in order to be a flourishing moral agent. If the person's life is more painful than

---

have been caused by greater reporting of such incidents, the central point that being perceived as having a non-heterosexual orientation can be dangerous even in the Developed World.

7   A person can be out in different ways and to different communities. For example, the person can be out to friends, but might judge it unwise to be out to his or her family.

pleasurable, then it would be difficult at best to classify it as a life worth living. In addition, if the person's intrinsic value is never recognized, that is, he is treated as a mere object all his life, then flourishing is impossible for the agent. Societies objectively flourish when they allow their citizens to thrive sustainably.

Individuals and societies also have some freedom to choose what counts as flourishing. For example, assuming that each moral agent needs good work of the Marxian variety in order to thrive, there is nothing that states that each agent must have the same type of work or career to flourish. If an individual can have a life worth living by choosing to be a teacher, accountant, line worker, or nurse, then whichever work the agent chooses for himself is ethically justified. That he must flourish is not up to him because it is a species' requirement for all moral agents, but how he does it within the parameters of the objective limitations is wholly dependent upon him.

The combination of the objective and subjective realities that create the standard of flourishing for a particular person or group can be seen in Alice MacLachlan's contention that:

> Our sexuality is composed of many strands: these include desires, practices, orientations, self-presentation, gender identities and our many aspects of our lived, physical embodiment. Each of these can come to play a more or less significant role in my sexuality, depending on how I—or others—infuse them with significance ... It matters to our flourishing that we "get these right". (MacLachlan 2012a: 1-2)

As MacLachlan recognizes, there are universals about people that can be worked out in different ways for individuals. Part of our flourishing is determined by us through the goals we set for ourselves, our attitudes, reactions, character traits and all other factors over which we have control. However, there are objective factors here, as well. An agent might not want her sexuality to be important in her existence, but it could be important in some way regardless of what she wants. If other people make those characteristics significant, then they are significant.

Provided that remaining closeted in very dangerous circumstances is necessary for obtaining or maintaining a flourishing life, Sullivan is mistaken about an actual moral obligation that *all* gay people have that would require too much self-sacrifice. A high enough probability of death, serious physical harm or mental injury that would make their lives not worth living would be enough, *ceteris paribus*, to undermine any claim that a person must intentionally risk coming out due to the benefit others might receive from such an action. Moreover, even in the absence of a severe incident, if being out leads to chronic negative states of affairs that adversely affect a person's life to such a degree that the person's flourishing is sufficiently compromised, then being out for that individual cannot be morally required. So a universal generalization that there is an obligation to be out is false, but is an existential quantifier more appropriate for Sullivan's claim?

When there is a Duty

Sullivan might be correct that there is a duty to be out if the situation is altered sufficiently. For the first case, suppose that a closely closeted politician, for his own profit, has made a career of outing people, with callous disregard for the injuries it would likely cause them. He crusaded against non-heterosexuals to appeal to his base and other bigoted voters, and win office, power, and additional benefits for himself. In this case, the closeted politician has a moral duty to out himself, even though it will severely restrict his ability to flourish in his chosen career. The injury to his flourishing is part of the punishment he deserves for illicitly destroying others to further his self-interests. On the grounds of Aristotelian justice, if likes should be treated alike, his exposure of those who were in the same situation as he is demands his self-outing otherwise he is an unjust hypocrite who disrespects his own morality, as well as the autonomy of others. In order to flourish, he must eliminate his debt and begin the process of becoming a better person.

Sullivan's claim seems strongest in a more likely set of circumstances than punishing closeted politicians. Basically, let us focus on average people, who happen to be homosexual, or non-heterosexual, for that matter, in average society. For these individuals, a moral obligation to out themselves exists if the following two conditions are met.

First, if being out does not pose a significant danger to a person's flourishing life, then there is *prima facie* reason to think that the duty to out oneself exists for the person. The good generated for herself or others would help justify her loss of privacy and the negative consequences that result to such a degree that it would be reasonable to believe that utility—both social and agent—is being served. For the first, society would be better off than it otherwise would be. For the second, she is better off than she would have otherwise have been. That is, coming out would be of higher value, all things considered, than remaining in the closet.

In many cases, being out will enhance the person's flourishing by allowing her to create and nurture caring relationships that would otherwise be denied to her whilst she is closeted. For example, finding a significant other or other partners who are compatible with an agent's sexual orientation can enhance the person's web of personal relationships in a positive way that being closeted cannot. This is especially the case if the closeted individual enters a male-female relationship to create the appearance of being heterosexual. In addition, being out allows an agent to share an important, if not essential, characteristic with others so that true friendships and other positive relationships can be built on the trust and communication that is denied to those who are closeted or veiled. Instead of having to disseminate and deceive those for whom the person cares, he can be honest. Moreover, outed people enjoy more relational goods, which are "goods that arise in our relationships with others in personal non-instrumental ways and we recognize that they are important components of our well-being" (Chekola 2009: 3).

Other benefits can be uncovered. Among them, the sheer relief gained by eliminating the mental strain caused by maintaining a closeted life, e.g., having to ensure never giving oneself away in conversation or other actions, and remembering which lies were told to which people. More importantly, there is an end to denying one's identity, the latter of which causes shame, degradation, and inadequate self-esteem and integrity. By being honest, the benefits can go a significant way in improving a person's happiness, and therefore flourishing. Mark Chekola argues that the loss of privacy from being out is more than compensated for by the elimination of worthlessness' implications (Chekola 1994: 67). Furthermore, being able to show publicly who one is and the relationships the person has, instead of hiding them out of fear, allows an individual to be more of a community member, who can receive the full benefits of being in a community. Closeted individuals are always a bit of the Other because they have to be so careful not to reveal something that is damaging to them. The deceit makes it more difficult for them to have honest interactions with other community members. There has to be a perpetual distance that does not allow the closeted individual to share his narrative as non-closeted people can, and do share. Hence, if coming out is beneficial enough to the agent, there is good reason to do it on the grounds of ethical egoism and utilitarianism.

There can still be adequate reason to require being out even in particular situations or in general in which a person's overall flourishing is reduced as a result. Granted that many in society now accept non-heterosexuals and non-heterosexual lifestyles, there is still a vast social element that makes their lives less worth living than it does for heterosexuals in the same circumstances. Besides negative comments, looks, exclusions, stereotyping, and other common low level nastiness, this social group issues more serious threats to mental or physical safety, such as being emotionally or physically attacked. However, as long as non-heterosexuals can have flourishing lives, these devaluations are insufficient to preclude a duty to be out. Living as one truly is in an overall tolerant and nurturing environment is better for each gay and lesbian person than having to maintain a stifling personal façade, which denies important or essential elements of who the person is. Even in a society that barely tolerates non-heterosexuals, it is better to be out in many cases so that the out person can have the benefits above described.

If we take a more Kantian perspective, then outing oneself and living "out" allows an individual to respect himself and others as each truly deserves to be respected. When a person tries to pass, then he is performing an action of deceit. As Kant states, a lie is "an insult to the person to whom it is made, and even if this were not always so, yet there is always something mean about it" (1989: 229). Being closeted insults not only other people, but the person who is closeted. Deceit is unethical on its own because "lying is 'mean and culpable' and ... truthful statements are preferable to lies in the absence of special considerations" (Bok 1989: 30). It is only when living as the person truly is will sacrifice something of comparable moral worth that deceit of this type can be justified. Instead of denying who the person is in an important, and I think, essential way, a person who outs himself takes control of his life and lives honestly with himself and others. He is authentic, which will help him create his own life affirming narrative, and he respects other's autonomy to make the best decisions for themselves by providing them information they might need to live their lives authentically. That being said, the person should at least acknowledge the truth about himself to himself so that he knows who he is.

The self-outing duty's second necessary condition requires a reasonable chance of success in influencing people in the correct way. More specifically, being out must make it more than likely that at least one person will become more accepting of homosexuals than if the person remained closeted. The justification for this condition is obvious. No one has an obligation to endanger or reduce her flourishing unless there is adequate reason to do so. Since there is risk of injury attached in some situations to homosexual activities or being known as a homosexual, there is no need to threaten oneself for a dubious beneficial outcome to another or society. Perhaps being out will help the "slowly rising tide of familiarity" which, in turn, will drown "people's disgust, revulsion, and deep-down aversion to 'the other.'"[8] But if there is no reasonable chance of success, then there is no adequate justification for risking one's flourishing or society's utility.

Although it might seem rather a low standard to be able positively to influence at least one person or make homosexuality become more familiar even if it is only infinitesimally better, the condition is apt. Given that the other criterion is that the person does not have to sacrifice anything of comparable moral worth, the improvement in another's moral character or the environment for those who are different in morally irrelevant ways is a worthy goal to pursue, especially in societies in which homosexuals are members of one of the worst off social classes.

As the potential for impact becomes greater, perhaps through the sheer number of people affected, the degree to which they are affected, or by some other practical measure, then so too does the strength of the duty to out oneself.[9] If coming out is likely to help further the social acceptance of homosexuals as full-fledged community members, then the case for the duty's existence move toward being absolute. No particular outing is likely to change a large number of people's minds, but much like a pile of sand, each little grain adds to the overall whole, as well as possibly helping individuals grow in their particular understanding and tolerance. In the end, these small alterations to the *status quo* can eventually build to significant changes in social mores and beliefs that will improve the society as a whole, and the individual lives of many of its citizens.

---

8   These are one of Sullivan's readers' words, but Sullivan agrees with the characterization of his position.

9   Of course, how a person should out himself is also determined by these two conditions. Outing should be done in such a way that success is more likely than if the person outed himself in a different way.

Complicating "Out": The Case of Queer Femmes[10]

Alice MacLachlan and Susanne Sreedhar

Since being taken up by activists in the early days of the gay and lesbian liberation movement, usage of "out" terminology has spread. It is now applied to the disclosure and ongoing expression of other stigmatized identities that are not necessarily or obviously visible: those with psychiatric disabilities, addictions, survivors of abuse, and so on. From within the arena of queer politics has emerged a new call for self-disclosure and an emphasis on the power of visibility. To live an authentic life and to resist the false values of oppression, queer and "queered" persons must actively and intentionally identify themselves as such to others, making their difference visible against a horizon of social expectations: i.e. the expectation that one is heterosexual, cisgendered, physically, psychologically, and neurologically typical, and so on. These disclosures are often difficult and costly, but they are also often personally and politically liberating.

There are undoubtedly complex moral and political issues facing all those for whom out or not-out, passing, covering, or "being loud and proud" all exist as possibilities, and choosing between them is often very difficult. For philosophers interested in the ethics of queer identity and visibility, it is tempting to find and frame the relevant ethical questions in terms of this choice: whether and when we hold a duty to come out, whether life "in the closet" is ever morally defensible, and so on. But there are those for whom the primary difficulty of coming out is not found in the choice or decision but in the communication itself. The value of coming out lies partly in its purported connection to authenticity—in disclosing her queerness, the individual reveals some significant part of her "true" self that was previous hidden; that is, she comes out of the closet as the person she "really" is.[11] But the power of this revelation depends, at least in part, on audience uptake— and thus acts of coming out are vulnerable to misunderstandings, ignorance, and confusion of others. Moreover, some queer identities face greater risks of misunderstanding than others.

In this chapter, we take up some ethical questions surrounding passing/ outing—specifically, as they arise for those with queer femme identities. We argue that for persons perceived by others to be female, and who have queer sexual identities and feminine or "femme" gender identities, choice between the various possibilities listed above may be complicated in morally significant ways.[12] For example, what it means for a femme to "pass" or "cover" is not always distinguishable—conceptually or in practice—from living authentically

---

10 Our sincere thanks go to Christina Konecny both for her superb research assistance and for her philosophical insights into these issues.

11 For more discussion of how controversial this argument is, see Harbin 2011: 77-93.

12 The issues and experiences that form the basis of our *particular* discussion are, we believe, limited to femmes whom others are likely to read by others as biologically

and resisting heteronormative identification: i.e. the conditions of being "out." In some ways, these conflations *privilege* queer femmes; in others, femmes find themselves implicated in a political double bind. We contend that this example complicates the political and ethical demands that are typically taken to arise from the question of passing or coming out.[13] We conclude by briefly exploring what it means to live queer femme identity *responsibly* and what this means for the ethics of sexual identity more generally.

Philosophers on the Ethics of Queer Visibility

In recent years, a debate over the ethics of queer visibility—that is, the moral significance of coming out, of remaining closeted, and of outing others—has arisen among moral philosophers in the analytic tradition.[14] While queer theorists in other disciplines have challenged the very existence of identities stable enough to be disclosed, analytic moral philosophers have focused on arguments concerning whether, how, and why to "come out of the closet" by first publicly disclosing one's queer sexuality or gender identity, and then by living openly and visibly as a queer or genderqueer person.[15] Richard Mohr, for example, argues on Kantian grounds for a universal duty to come out, held by all lesbian and gay people, as well as a corollary duty to out others with or without their consent. Mohr grounds this duty in dignity, arguing the following: since there can be no good reason short of immediate physical danger *not* to come out, failing to do so expresses acceptance and even endorsement of the supposed need for secrecy that has enforced queer stigmatization. Choosing to remain closeted thus endorses the stigma itself (that a queer identity is bad, wrong, unnatural and should be hidden), and so disrespects the personhood of *all* queer persons.[16] Coming out—and even outing others who fail to come out—is an assertion of dignity. Almost all philosophical attention to the ethical responsibilities of queer persons *as* queer persons has centered around the ethics of coming out.[17]

Why has this particular act of self-disclosure come to take such a central role in queer ethics and politics? Historically, silencing, enforced secrecy and even outright denial—in other words, the social conditions taken up and conceptualized

---

female (i.e. those, in a heterosexist context, whose bodies lead to social expectations and enforcement of feminine gender roles).

13   Many of the ethical and philosophical issues associated with queer femme identity and visibility that we raise are insightfully discussed by Brennan (2011: 120-34).

14   Prominent examples include Mohr 1992, Card 1995, Stramel 1997, Halwani 2002, Halwani et al. 2008, and see Cooley, this volume.

15   For a recent philosophical discussion of the metaphysics of personal identity and sexual agency implicated in queer theory, see Wilkerson (2009: 97-116).

16   See Mohr, *Gay Ideas*.

17   Notable exceptions to this rule within the analytic philosophical literature on queer visibility include lesbian-feminist philosophers. See Card 1995, Calhoun 2000, as well as Halwani et al. 2008.

as the "closet"—were effective methods for maintaining heterosexism. Since the 1970s, queer activists have rallied around the power of communities increasing in number, in visibility, and in voice. In present-day activist circles and in wider public discourse, it is typically assumed that being out is always, or almost always, better than being not-out and, further, that coming out is a necessary condition for living a queer life *well*—not to mention participating in queer communities.

The moral values of living a good or flourishing life and of resisting and repudiating oppression are not insignificant. And certainly, we do not deny the connection between these goods and the ability to live freely and openly, without hiding or covering significant relationships, desires, and identities. Whether and when these result in a moral duty to come out is another question—and one that we take up elsewhere.[18] Here, our interest lies with the ethical complexities of visibility, recognition, privilege, and passing that continue once the choice to come out has already been made—complexities that are overlooked when we focus too entirely on that choice alone. Furthermore, as we demonstrate, these complexities can serve to weaken the correlation made between visibility and authenticity presumed by advocates of a duty to come out. To get at these dilemmas, we turn to the experiences of queer femmes.

The Case of Queer Femmes

Like so many signifiers of queer identity, "femme" has multiple, overlapping meanings, several of which have shifted over time. At its root, the title "'femme" indicates some relationship to femininity, that is—to the appearances, attitudes, roles, and social positions expected of women in a gendered, heterosexist society. The term also has a queer history; it entered popular discourse as part of the butch/femme dichotomy, once taken to represent constructed or assumed gender roles within lesbian communities.[19] Just as butches reject the trappings of feminine gender identities and instead adopt a masculine gender identity, femmes embrace, exaggerate, and occasionally parody their own femininity, leading to the appellation "high femme"—implying that femme femininity is a distorted, excessive, or *queered* femininity. Nevertheless, on a daily basis, queer femmes are far more likely to be mistaken for conventional, "straight" women than other lesbians and bisexual women.

The association with femininity makes femme an interesting and complex identity for those within lesbian and feminist communities. After all, femininity represents a problematic social norm in the eyes of both communities, associated with the control, diminishment, objectification, exploitation, and even infantilization of women. And, at the same time, since femininity is a social norm that continues to be enforced by the wider society, it is both imposed upon and expected of *all*

---

18   For an extended argument *against* a duty to come out made by one author of this chapter, see MacLachlan (2012a).

19   For further discussion, see Nestle (1992).

those who are female-identified. Successfully performing oneself as both female and feminine—"pulling it off," so to speak—is a social achievement, and one that comes with rewards. Such rewards include acceptance, praise, and sexual desire, or even the sheer relief of being socially intelligible to others, however costly these rewards might be to the bearer. Femininity in these cases expresses sexist oppression and—at the same time—*hetero*sexist privilege.

It is hardly surprising then that, as Angela Pattatucci Aragon (2006) notes, lesbian communities have historically had what she describes as a "love/hate relationship" with femmes, subjecting them to public vilification and private fetishizing—a femme might provide social status or bragging rights for her butch partner, even while the femme's own membership in the queer community is viewed with suspicion. Lurking beneath these attitudes is the belief that embracing rather than rejecting femininity is "a less noble pathway to lesbianism," that femmes "reify the patriarchal oppression that *real lesbians* were fighting to end." Aragon points out that even now, "feminine women tend to be seen as less genuine lesbians and are viewed with constant suspicion (e.g. that they only are interested in sexual play and might run off with a man at any moment)" (2006: 14, footnote 13). Suspicion of femme identity can be found in academic circles too. Even in queer theory, the editors of *Femme: Feminists, Lesbians and Bad Girls* note, "little has been written about women's use of femininity as queer, subversive or radical" (Harris and Crocker 1997: 4).

Perhaps in response to this disapproval, recently there have been some concerted efforts to remake and reclaim femme identity as wholly, properly, and necessarily queer—and thus to challenge the reduction of "femme" to "feminine" (Harris and Crocker 1997, Rose and Camilleri 2002, Burke 2009, Dahl and LaGrace 2009). In *Brazen Femme: Queering Femininity*, Rose and Camilleri, insist that femme is "a way of being that cannot be described as quintessentially feminine. Instead, femme might be described as 'femininity gone wrong' … we are not good girls—" while two contributors reverse the conceptual dependence, by decrying femininity as a "debased and fallen form of [femme] itself" (2002: 13, Duggan and McHugh 2002). Similarly, *Femme's* editors individuate femmes by remarking, "femme queerness is a sustained gender identity, a chosen rather than assigned femininity" (Harris and Crocker 1997: 5). Today, some femme-identified lesbians highlight *queerness* rather femininity by adopting the hyphen "femme-dyke." One femme-dyke defends the move as an effort to distinguish herself from "the vile assimilationist politics of what I mark as lipstick-lesbian culture, in which being seen as 'straight-acting' is taken as a high compliment" (Rugg 1997: 175-89).

These reclamations have a common goal. They all aim to retain rights to the trappings of femininity (expressed through fashion, comportment, modes of embodiment, sexual roles, voice etc) while stripping them of whatever patriarchal meaning they might hold—in particular, messages of submission, weakness, and the status as object (and not subject) of desire. Yet, given how much of what we understand by femininity depends on exactly these meanings, such separation is always provisional, unstable, and even tentative—and is certainly capable of being misread. Put simply, one person's brilliantly subversive high femme is another person's classy (straight) lady, walking down the street in heels, lipstick, and a sweater set. Furthermore, judgments of masculine and feminine—and in particular, of being "feminine enough"—are always contextual. As one frustrated femme laments, "Why am I a femme when I play in the queer community and a tomboy when I play in the straight community?" (VanNewKirk 2006: 75).

Where does this leave queer femmes, when it comes to the ethics of passing and coming out?

In the first place, the successful act of coming out—and certainly, the sustained, consistent state of "being out"—is often especially *difficult* for queer femmes. "Coming out" has been described as a choice and as a revelation, but for many queer and genderqueer persons, the choice is made for them and the revelation hardly surprising. As LGBTQ visibility grows—especially in mainstream popular culture—many people are now familiar with certain stereotypical markings of queer difference. In urban centers and among younger people, in particular, the strong, athletic woman and the gentle, artistic man may simply be presumed gay until proven otherwise, and the suggestion that two same-sex adults sharing a small apartment are "roommates" treated as laughable. As Ivan Coyote (2009), a queer and genderqueer storyteller and activist, puts it when reflecting on Coyote's own, visible, queerness: "I never get the chance to come out of the closet, because my closet was always made of glass." In some ways, only those who *lack* the visible markers of queerness face the dilemma that coming out was traditionally meant to present—or at least, the dilemma in its starkest, most accentuated form. That is, only those who *can* pass are able to choose between a life of (fraudulent) heterosexist privilege burdened by the moral and psychological costs of secrecy and compartmentalization, on the one hand, and the risks of reneging privilege by committing to living openly and in solidarity, on the other. Those who can access more privilege in the first place have more to lose by renouncing it.[20]

It might seem that while queer femmes are among those most likely to face the dilemma of coming out in its starkest form, the basic choice between visibility and privilege remains consistent—but the picture is more complicated than that. Consider the following point: coming out is an act of disclosure and being out a state of visibility. Both disclosure and visibility require audience uptake and interpretation; for me to show and tell, you must see and understand. For me to successfully come out as queer to you, without my performance misfiring, you must understand what I mean by "queer" and believe me when I tell you that I am. If you have no idea, or take my words as a practical joke, as delusion, or as simple nonsense, there is a very really sense in which I have not *come out* to you; certainly, I am not visible to you as queer.

This is the second way in which coming out is made difficult for queer femmes. Because they do not appear gay or queer to many people's eyes, femme

---

20   Coyote implies as much, by going on to say, "But you do it for me. You fight homophobia in a way that I never could" (Coyote 2009).

disclosures and performances of queerness are far more vulnerable to misfire. A queer femme who uses a subtle cue to demonstrate her queerness is more likely to be misunderstand—references to her "girlfriend" may be heard as "female friend" rather than "romantic partner," for example. Even her direct, unambiguous claims ("Mom, Dad—I'm a lesbian" or "Actually, no, not 'he'—my ex is a woman") are likely to be taken *less* seriously. She may be seen as experimenting, rebelling, going through a phase, or finding herself temporarily "between men" after a broken (heterosexual) heart. Her queerness is subject to challenge in a way that others' may not be; it can be contested, disputed, and may require defense or proof. Robbin VanNewkirk captures this sense of contested queerness nicely when she recounts a conversation with another lesbian who assumed VanNewkirk was straight, and made a joke on that basis. Forced to explain herself, Newkirk notes, "there is no quick, clever response I've found for being shoved back into the proverbial closet. I corrected her arrogation along with a nervous laugh, to which she replied, 'Gee, I really didn't get that vibe from you'" (2006: 74).

The challenge to VanNewkirk's sexual identity (at the time, she was an out, lesbian, academic, working in women's studies) is double. First, she is presumed to be straight—and this presumption comes from someone within the queer community. Second, once this presumption is corrected, VanNewkirk's now-stated *queer* identity is again undermined. She lacks the appropriate "vibe" or marker; she does not register on the other (unquestioned) lesbian's gaydar. Now, a skeptical reader might respond that VanNewkirk is in danger of oversensitivity here. Her conversationalist did not directly doubt her, but only expressed surprise (and possibly embarrassment). This is *not*, the skeptical reader might conclude, a terribly big deal. But such skepticism overlooks the social significance of "vibes" and "gaydar," of markers and difference. The now commonplace notion of a gay vibe, accessed through the radar of those in the know, suggests that there exist criteria for queerness—or at least for real, legitimate or (as Aragon puts it, above) *noble* queerness—which someone who sincerely expresses queer desires and who identifies as queer might still fail to meet. Claiming an identity for which you lack the appropriate markers has "the implication of fraudulency" (VanNewkirk 2006: 79). At the least, it suggests that your loyalties and your staying power remain in question.

VanNewkirk's anecdote illustrates an additional way in which coming out is made difficult for queer femmes: it is a task to be performed over, and over again—to each new audience, or to the same audience multiple times: "it's not just the clueless straight man who assumes I must be straight and therefore sexually available according to my femininity, but also members of my own community and their assumptions about my femininity that requires a constant re-telling or coming out" (2006: 76). Coyote (2009), too, describes this repetition and acknowledges the burden of it: "I want to thank you for coming out of the closet. Again and again, over and over, for the rest of your life. At school, at work, at your kid's daycare, at your brother's wedding, at the doctor's office. Thank you for sideswiping their stereotypes." While the ability to pass (and thus escape confrontation) might once have been envied for its pragmatic advantage, in a world where "out" has become an expected norm and visibility the primary measure of queer pride, Coyote is right to acknowledge that for some, meeting this norm requires daily attention and thus extra effort.

Not only is the performance of "coming out" potentially more arduous for queer femmes, but also, the goods it is meant to achieve may be more tenuous. The act of coming out is praised, in part, for the recognition and visibility it is meant to secure; while the closet person must compartmentalize their existence and bifurcate their identities into public and secret, the out person achieves authenticity and wholeness. In coming out, he or she loses privilege but gains community. Yet for some queer femmes, these may be fragile, ephemeral and even unattainable goods. Indeed, Coyote (2009) puts it best: "Sometimes you are invisible. I have no idea what this must feel like, to pass right by your people and not be recognized. To not be seen." Queer femmes may fail to be recognized as such—both by members of their own community, and by those outside it.[21]

Furthermore, once queer femmes succeed in make themselves known as such, the "femme" aspect of their identity may be taken to detract from their queerness, rather than qualifying or even (or partly) constituting it. This can create tensions within the individual's own agency and sense of identity, if the queer femme herself internalizes the belief that her femininity, her *femmeness*, is somehow at odds with her queer sexual identity—as she is likely to do, given the prevalence of that message, within and beyond queer communities. Indeed, she may feel forced to choose between these aspects of herself, hiding or masking her femmeness in order to prove she is (i.e. "pass" as) truly or properly queer. Many lesbians and gays are still expected to "cover" (that is, to minimize and play down their queer identity) for the comfort of straight acquaintances, while equally, feeling pressure to conform to homo-normative standards *within* the community in order to belong. The newly out may well force the mannerisms they perceive to now be expected of them.[22] Queer sex columnist, Susie Bright, gives an account of early attempts to "pass" within the queer community:

> At the height of my college cruising, I was attending Take Back the Night meetings dressed in Mr. Greenjeans overalls, Birkenstocks, and a bowl haircut that made me look like I'd just been released from a bad foster home. There is nothing more pitiful to look at than a closeted femme. (Quoted in Walker 1993: 866)

---

21 As Brennan notes, the isolation of invisibility is also experienced by other queer women who may not meet the social and fashion norms of large, urban queer communities—this includes many working class, older and rural queer women (Brennan 2011).

22 Again, VanNewkirk, a femme lesbian, describes "the insecurity I feel when I am not deemed real enough to be gay, and ... the gratification I feel when I can pass for gay, again with the underlying assumption that in passing I am not intrinsically real" (VanNewkirk 2006: 79).

In highlighting the especial difficulties and fragilities of coming out, as experienced by queer femmes, our intention is not simply to bemoan the plight of the queer femme, to argue that their struggles are uniquely difficult—or indeed, to suggest that queer femmes should not engage in the sometimes daily effort of coming out at all. Instead, we wish to highlight how the ethical significance of queer identities and visibility, passing and not-passing, do not begin or end for femmes (and indeed, as we will show—for many others) with the question whether to come out. Rather the convoluted visibility of already—out queer femmes can leave them implicated in a political double bind.

We have already shown how identifying as a queer femme can leave someone in the peculiar situation of feeling as though she must "pass" as what she already is (i.e. queer). The queer femme identity brings with it a presumption of fraudulence or inauthenticity. Indeed, this is not unlike a milder version of Talia Bettcher's (2007) description of the inhospitable dichotomy transpeople face, when accused of being either deceitful or fraudulent. Certainly both groups have faced marginalization and ostracization within lesbian communities. But unlike transpeople, queer femme identity also functions as a source of (complicated) privilege for those who possess it. As we noted earlier, queer femmes voluntarily adopt many of the feminine gender markers that heterosexism demands of women. Most queer identities, once open and visible, preclude those who possess them from accessing heterosexual privilege—at least at the same time as they express and make visible their queer identity. But such privilege remains available to queer femmes. Not only can they comfortably enter gender-segregated institutions (e.g. public washrooms) without risk of challenge, but femmes are less likely to be seen as deviant, sexualized, or predatory. They may find it easier to access the confidence and trust of straight women, that is, to present as "one of them" and—if they choose—femmes can appeal to the heterosexist chivalry and flattery of heterosexual men. Indeed, they may not be able to avoid it. In situations where being obviously queer might lead to serious confrontation and even physical harm, the *invisibility* of queer femmes takes on the advantage of camouflage, rather than the burden of explanation.

A relatively banal experience illustrates this point. While we were writing this paper, one of us found herself negotiating the cost of repairing a cat-damaged armchair with a male business owner. On learning his estimate, she explained that the cost was high enough that she'd need to talk it over with her partner (whom, she indicated, was a woman). The male shop-owner noted her pink sundress but missed her pronoun, and immediately assumed the partner in question was a husband—and further, that this husband was responsible for both filling and controlling the purse strings. His demeanor changed from haggling to sympathetic and flirtatious, as he dropped the price to "help her make her case" while he (along with several other customers) proceeded to offer advice for how to flatter and cajole her fictional husband into giving her what she wanted. Is this an example of misbegotten privilege or subtle oppression? On a very practical level, this author clearly benefitted from her femme gender expression—she received a lower estimate, and the good will of everyone in the shop. On the other, this advantage comes first at the cost of being misread—she was left feeling guilty and complicit for not once again clarifying what she had originally stated. Further, her small financial gain in this particular transaction depended on the shopkeeper's sexist assumption that, as a woman, she was financially dependent, naïve, willing to manipulate her male partner—and in need of a strange man's advice about how to best do so. That is, her small gain came at the larger cost of the power he exercised, when he insisted on providing it.

Conclusion

The experience of queer femmes suggests that not all queer identities are created equal. The point we have made is not simply that queer femmes will necessarily find it easier to "pass," where passing is understood to entail accessing heterosexual privilege. Presumably many queer people could and can successfully pass, whatever their most comfortable mode of gender expression. Rather, queer femmes are distinctive in that it is their queer identity itself—their own, authentic expression of their individual sexual identity—that provides access to privilege. Indeed, fully reneging on that privilege by working to demonstrate, even *prove*, their queerness to others—if that requires they cover or minimize their femmeness, to do so—may end up feeling less authentic, and more akin to passing, than the alternative. In this way, the two goods highlighted by philosophical arguments for coming out—the political importance of queer visibility and the personal importance of feeling authentic and wholly *oneself*—come apart for queer femmes. Instead of choosing these goods over problematic privilege, they find themselves forced to choose between the two of them, in scenarios where all possible options seem to implicate them in complex and uncomfortable forms of privilege. Queer femmes may feel unrecognized or invisible—even fraudulent—within supposedly safe spaces (i.e. queer communities) at the same time as they feel alienated from the comfort they are assumed and even expected to feel within wider, heteronormative ones. It is for this reason that we described queer femmes as facing something like a double bind, when it comes to the ethics and politics of queer visibility.

To be bound is to be restrained, and even disempowered. The double bind facing queer femmes, on the other hand, comes with a special sort of power—one that has not gone unnoticed. In choosing to "thank" queer femmes, for example, Coyote calls attention to their unique ability to disrupt people's assumptions about both gender and sexuality. In other words, queer femmes are uniquely positioned not only to *pass*, but also to *disrupt*. The fact that femmes have to come out constantly means that they are constantly in a position to challenge people's stereotypes—stereotypes that depend on heteronormative and sexist assumptions and in particular, the association of female femininity with heterosexuality. That queer femmes may find themselves feeling like an "insider-outsider" in both straight and queer communities also provides them with an informed and critical voice, a voice that contributors to *Femme, Brazen Femme* and other recent femme manifestos have begun to adopt. Undertaking this task appears to require that queer femmes not only be visible—the clarion cry of queer politics—but that they be *responsibly* visible, navigating the discomforting combination of being both recognized and misread, with an eye to the power that a queer girl in a sundress may possess.

Comments on Maclachlan and Sreedhar's "Complicating 'Out': The Case of Queer Femmes"

Dennis R. Cooley

Although Alice MacLachlan and Susanne Sreedhar raise a number of interesting points, I will confine myself to the two I think are most important to the ethical issue of passing. First, in one author's personal narrative of initially, unintentional passing at a furniture store, the issue of guilt is useful in understanding whether the passing was ethical. Second, the queer femmes' general characteristics and unique difficulties can best be understood as an example of moral luck, which privileges them on one way, yet severely disadvantages them in another. I will consider each in turn.

In the personal narrative, the author mentioned feeling guilt as a result of passing in a store even though she did not intend to do so. She had outed herself to the salesperson, but he seems to have misheard what she was saying, and then made an assumption that was unwarranted given the information that had been provided to him. The result of his "deafness" was a reduction in the price of a piece of furniture, in part, because the salesperson thought that her "husband" would prevent her from buying it if it was too expensive.

But why would someone feel guilt in the situation? Using what is probably illicit armchair psychology, I would hazard to guess that the author felt that she had done something wrong, if we assume that guilt is caused by a self-recognition of some sort that the agent has failed to act ethically in some way.

Guilt can be subjective or objective. Subjective guilt occurs when an agent has done nothing objectively wrong, but still feels as if she has violated some personal principle that does not tip the action into being immoral (Conee 1982). An example of this might be when a person passes because the situation's circumstances entail a considerable danger to his ability to flourish. He permissibly remains veiled but feels guilty because he has not done the supererogatory.

Objective guilt, on the other hand, is appropriate in situations in which whatever the agent did broke some objective moral principle or code. In this case, the author might not have lived up to her free choices of who to be as an individual, as well as one or two that are general to all human persons as persons. Since she has decided to be out, then the situation ended when she was not authentic to whom she is as a person, and hence, interfered with her own flourishing.

Being out is, in my view, one of the more important life goals a person can choose. In order to find a plausible mechanism for justifying that one life goal is more central to thriving than another—and hence, is more valuable—it is necessary to consider whether there are general features that all human persons have as persons. As stated above, flourishing is the standard by which to judge the value of any person's life. What constitutes flourishing is universal for some aspects of being a human person, such as the absence of debilitating pain, presence of enough pleasure to make life have positive utility, creative work, possession and use of autonomy, and so on. These aspects make whatever has them fall under the general category of *being a person*. There are also goals that are under the control of each agent, such as whom the person dates, whether to have children, whether to work here rather than there, and where to set up one's abode. These aspects help make the person a particular individual.

Although being a particular individual is important, its value is dependent upon the more fundamental characteristic of being a thriving person. By necessity, when flourishing's universal conditions, e.g. being authentic, are not met, then the individual's life cannot flourish. When particular goals of a particular person are unmet, then there is no automatic lack of flourishing. People can be stymied in their attempts to fulfill their idiosyncratic choices, e.g., jobs they select in order to obtain the financial resources they need for a good life, but that does not entail that they will lead a bad or significantly worse life. They can fail in their individual goals and try something else. However, if they fail to fulfill the basic requisites, then they cannot have a thriving life. The best analogy to use here is to show that each person has to have her basic physical needs met in order to survive. These needs are comparable to flourishing's universal requirements. On the other hand, individual choice can affect thriving, but tends not to be able to make the life not worth living in the manner that lacking one or more of the essentials can, unless that choice affects an essential.

So where does passing fit into this division between types of characteristics and goals? I would say that passing when a person is out is linked to being authentic to who the person is. More specifically, in situations in which it is unnecessary to pass, then remaining veiled, even if it is the result of other's misinterpretations, assaults the very identity of the individual passing, if it is allowed to go unchecked. The person feels as if she has betrayed who she is as a person. Being out allows people to be authentic and to act and think in ways that satisfy their basic needs as the persons they are, even if it costs them something to do it. There are many ways this openness enhances their flourishing as a species being and an individual, but the most important might very well be that they are not deceivers. By being authentic they are being as they truly are.

My commentary's second component focuses on MacLachlan and Sreedhar's central position. Queer femmes have unique opportunities and difficulties precisely because they are queer femmes. First, queer femmes have more to lose since they can pass better than those who have stereotypical queer features. Second, their coming out is often not believed by their audience, and the former often have to come out to the same individuals again and again. Third, queer femmes, when they can make clear their identity, are often ostracized from both the heterosexual and queer communities for a hurtful, wrongheaded view about the queer femmes' authenticity: both communities assume that queer femmes are not really queer. Fourth, and most importantly:

> queer femmes are distinctive in that it is their queer identity itself—their own, authentic expression of their individual sexual identity—that provides access to privilege. Indeed, fully reneging on that privilege by working to demonstrate, even *prove*, their queerness to others—if that requires they cover or minimize their femmeness, to do so—may end up feeling less authentic, and more like passing, than the alternative. In this way, the two goods highlighted by philosophical arguments for coming out—the political importance of queer visibility and the personal importance of feeling authentic and wholly *oneself*—come apart for queer femmes. Instead of choosing these goods over problematic privilege, they find themselves forced to choose between the two of them, in scenarios where all possible options seem to implicate them in complex and uncomfortable forms of privilege. Queer femmes may feel unrecognized or invisible—even fraudulent—within supposedly safe spaces (i.e. queer communities) at the same time as they feel alienated from the comfort they are assumed and even expected to feel within wider, heteronormative ones. (see MacLachlan and Sreedhar, this volume)

This argument is right, but it also shows us where moral luck plays its role in power, sexual identity, and being out.

Moral luck exists in the disparity between queer femmes and other groups of individuals, whether the latter are oppressed or not. Moral luck refers to unearned or unmerited advantages and disadvantages that people have in their lives. For example, some individuals are born into a life of wealth and privilege, while others have to contend with poverty merely because they were born into a poor society. These unearned positives and negatives can affect the moral evaluation of people and their actions. If we are committed to treating people as equals *qua* moral agency, then there is a feeling that moral luck produces unfair situations and defective evaluations, especially for individuals lacking the opportunities afforded to those with privileged power. In this case, queer femmes are forced to choose between being authentic and being politically visible, while other non-heterosexuals can have both.

Fortunately, the perceived unfairness is merely an illusion, once the larger circumstances are considered. Moral luck is not as lucky as some would like to believe. Some privileged characteristics, included among them are sexual identities, might be experienced as a burden rather than an advantage. Consider the related alleged moral gap between the wealthy and the poor. People assume that being born into wealth is an example of good moral luck that allows the powerful person to have an advantage over the person with less access to power.

But there is no reason to believe that claim. Although the duties are determined by the same moral principles, what must be done will be decided in part by the person's actual situation, including the power the agent has. First, people with greater opportunities have more alternatives from which to choose because their power allows them to do things that those without power cannot. Hence, those with more power will be obligated to do more, while those with less are obligated to do less. In situations in which those privileged in the queer community by being politically visible and authentic have a duty to help those who can achieve only one of the two, until that time in which those who are more vulnerable become equal.

People with privileged sexual orientations—and I am including heterosexuals here—have the general duty to help those with disadvantaged sexual identities achieve a reasonable opportunity to have a flourishing life. In the face of opposition, privileged people have to work to change the cultural mores, social norms, laws, and so on that allow for oppression. The reason for this general duty is based, once again, upon flourishing. What kind of person enjoys a privilege without realizing what it costs others who have less power than he does? What kind of person will do nothing to alleviate the suffering of others when it will cost the privileged little? It would be akin to someone seeing a car accident with victims in need of help, who does nothing to render assistance, even when it will cost him little in comparison. In order to flourish, the privileged must use their power in an appropriate way to help those less powerful, possibly giving up power so that they and those around them are equal as persons with equal opportunities. To begin this process, those with privilege must sensitize themselves and others to what it is to be a queer femme, not treat people according to harmful stereotypes, show disapprobation for other's wrongful actions, such as discounting someone when she does not fit a stereotype of being a lesbian, and do what is within their power to allow everyone a fair chance at a flourishing life.

But I do not want to give the impression that queer femmes are helpless victims who need others to act paternalistically toward them. As MacLachlan and Sreedhar recognize:

> queer femmes are uniquely positioned not only to *pass*, but also to *disrupt*. The fact that femmes have to come out constantly means that they are constantly in a position to challenge people's stereotypes—stereotypes that depend on heteronormative and sexist assumptions and in particular, the association of female femininity with heterosexuality. (See MacLachlan and Sreedhar, this volume)

Given the deep fear people have of challenges to the very essence of their conventional identity and morality, queer femmes have the ability to less painfully change ideologies in both the heterosexual and non-heterosexual communities. That is power.

Comments on Cooley's "Is there a Duty to Be Out?"

Alice MacLachlan and Susanne Sreedhar

The title of Dennis R. Cooley's argument poses a question (is there a duty to be out?), which, to paraphrase his own words, he answers with a strong and steadfast "it depends." Yet this somewhat rueful self-assessment does Cooley's very thoughtful discussion a disservice. Cooley not only argues for a duty to come out that holds in some, but not all, cases; he also provides a single ethical standard or benchmark—namely, the Aristotelian value of *flourishing*—which both grounds the general duty and provides the explanation for when and why that duty is absent or overridden. In doing so, he makes a significant contribution to the growing philosophical literature on the ethics of coming and being out. Previous analyses of a duty to come out have typically argued for a universal duty, holding in all situations save the most grievous risk of harm to life and limb, or have adopted a pluralist and occasionally piecemeal approach, for example by pitting the broader utilitarian benefits of coming out (e.g. visibly gay public figures) against the rights of the individual, or by measuring the values of dignity and honesty against other significant concerns, like compassion, friendship, and loyalty. In advocating a moderate version of the duty to come out *and* providing a single rubric for assessing that duty, Cooley's analysis draws eminently reasonable conclusions, and also leaves the reader optimistic that we might—at least in theory—account for all the relevant ethical variables, when spelling out the crucial details of that "it depends."

In our response, we will focus on what is novel in Cooley's treatment, namely, the central role he gives to the concept of "flourishing". Cooley's argument hinges on his acceptance of the claim that the concept of flourishing represents the best standard by which to make ethical evaluation; that is, that "the only ultimate test for the value of a life is whether at its end it is found to have been worth living" (Bayles 1994:130, cited by Cooley, this volume). Like other Aristotelians, Cooley takes flourishing to be an ethical concept, including both subjective and objective factors; we do not flourish when we happily partake in ill-gotten benefits that come at an unjust cost to others, for instance. Cooley connects flourishing to the more specific question of coming out in two stages. First, he suggests that—all things being equal—coming out *adds* to an individual's flourishing, both through its effects on her life and character, and for its likely effects on the attitudes and emotions of others. Thus, when these conditions obtain, we always possess ethical reasons to come out, unless there exist other reasons *not to*. What might reasonably count as a reason *not* to come out? Again, we turn to individual flourishing: we should come out whenever doing so does not sacrifice something of comparable moral significance, and such significances are weighed against each other by their relative contributions to individual flourishing.

In some sense, it is impossible to disagree with Cooley's main claim. If there is an act that will improve someone's life in significant ways, for example by "allowing her to create and nurture caring relationships that would otherwise be denied to her" and by granting her significant relief from self-denial, shame, degradation, and "mental strain," and if this act will—at the same time—improve the moral attitudes and behavior of others, it certainly seems as though it ought to be undertaken. If that act can be undertaken without sacrificing anything of comparable moral worth, then *of course* it ought to be undertaken. We might want to caution that this is not yet sufficient reason to *enforce* such a duty through coercion or social pressure, but—at the least—the case as presented gives the agent very good reason, and most likely overriding reasons, to take such an action. But perhaps there still lurks some small devil or two in the details, which may well complicate the duty to come out as Cooley describes it. Indeed, we might ask when (if at all) such fortuitous conditions obtain—that is, how often does coming out lead to the flourishing Cooley describes, in practice?

Consider the benefits to the individual achieved by coming out. Cooley claims that the out individual gains access to relational goods and to psychological relief. Let us focus on the latter, and recall that Cooley is concerned with "the duties someone has to out herself to strangers". Does coming out to strangers lead to relief, as well as "an end to denying one's identity … shame, degradation, and inadequate self-esteem and integrity"? The process is not always, or immediately, so affirming. Coming out is a performative speech act, in which one person discloses something of herself to others. What she succeeds in disclosing depends, in part, on her audience's uptake—how they hear, understand and interpret her—and in this case her audience are strangers. Thus, the dependence on audience uptake can leave the person who comes out extremely vulnerable. She risks having her life and her identity "excerpted", as Claudia Card (1995: 212) puts it: that is, reduced to her sexual self in ways that do not feel authentic or truthful and may well be self-alienating. Judith Butler expresses a little of this alienation when she remarks that it is not clear "what or who [it is] that is "out", made manifest and fully disclosed, when and if I reveal myself as a lesbian" (1993: 309).

Furthermore, the strangers to whom she discloses herself are members of a wider culture that is both sex-obsessed and relatively sex-phobic. No matter how much activists remind us that coming out discloses an identity, not specific sex-acts, those who may most need their attitudes changed are likely to hear "sex" when told "sexuality." And Cooley agrees with us that sexuality is composed of many strands, which include desires, practices, and orientations as well as fantasies, imaginings, identities, and embodiments. Coming out reveals queer sexual desires, and it does so against a social background in which sexual desire is highly regulated. As even a cursory glance at contemporary American pop culture reveals, while we are not strangers to sex, we have strict expectations about who, exactly, is a subject of desire, who is an object of sexual desire, and who is assigned as asexual comic relief. Sexual and erotic desires that match these expectations are so completely normalized as to become invisible: they belong in commercials for beer, yogurt, real estate, or household cleaners, or become the stuff of casual jokes. Queer desires, in contrast, are startling, and may appear exaggerated as a result. Choosing to come out may mean accepting a public identity that is not only problematically excerpted from her broader self-concept, but is also disproportionately sexualized.

We mention the dangers of excerption and sexualization because these do not seem like external costs to be weighed against the moral value of coming out (itself taken as a *prima facie* moral plus)—as risks to family relationships, career, citizenship, and life would be. Rather, sexualization and excerption are potential complications *internal* to the meaning of the act. Coming out, or even "coming clean" about one thing, i.e. that one is gay, lesbian, bisexual or transgendered, may clear up some misperceptions and misidentifications and thus bring some relief, but in doing so the act itself may create others. This is especially true for those who fall short of audience expectations in other ways, perhaps by failing to meet wider, admittedly problematic, gay stereotypes. We focus on one such case in our argument, and suggested that—among other things—queer femmes feel pressure to keep closeted the "femme" aspect of their identity in order to successfully come out as queer. Similarly, there are those who experience their sexual identity as fluid, as a history of choices and relationships over time, or as a trajectory of unfolding possibilities. It may be that they cannot provide what feels like a truthful account of themselves ahistorically. A duty to come out—where coming out refers to discrete acts of disclosure—may leave such individuals struggling to translate their own, experienced, sexuality into a set of facts that is wholly discernible and communicable to others at a given point in time. Reframing the duty as a duty to come out over and over again (once for each identity) is also problematic; the duty becomes more burdensome, for one thing, and second, the language of "coming out" implies what is revealed was first denied or hidden. If someone comes out first as lesbian, then as genderqueer, and then as a transman, others may take her subsequent disclosures as evidence that her coming out as a lesbian was partial or provisional—or even mistaken (this may well be true—but it is certainly not necessarily so).

Should the complications we have raised concern Cooley? In some sense, these are extensions or further illustrations of his basic claim, that applying the duty to come out always involves an individual calculus of enhancements to and detractions from flourishing. But, as illustrations, they suggest that the calculus is far from straightforward. Rather than being a *prima facie* addition to one's level of flourishing, whose contribution may be lessened when weighed against external costs and considerations, the act of coming out looks like a calculated risk; a willingness to correct one decidedly problematic set of misperceptions and mis-readings by others even in the knowledge that doing so may well lead to another set, one that cannot be determined before engaging in the act. Both possibilities are uncertain, and both depend on interpretive moves by others, moves over which the agent has little control. Sometimes, the risk is slight and the benefits are great: these are the cases where, with Cooley, we agree there is likely overriding reason to come out. Once we include the more complex cases, though—such as those with fluid or less recognizable queer identities—we wonder if talk of a "duty to come out" can best capture the moral variables in question, even in "all things considered" cases. So, our first question is, how often does Cooley envisage the duty obtaining, in practice?

Certainly, we *can* account for the more difficult cases in the framework of a duty to come out, either by denying they have a duty, admitting that it's not clear whether or not they do, or by reframing that duty as a duty to come out over and over again. Doing so starts to lessen the strong connection Cooley makes between the duty and the individual's own flourishing. The objective benefits (i.e. improvement to others' attitudes) remain, but the subjective experience becomes 'burdened' in ways that, phenomenologically, bear little resemblance to any picture of *eudaimonia*.[23] We invite Cooley to consider, first, whether the duty remains (in weakened form) when the psychological benefits of coming out are compromised, in the ways we describe.

On the other hand, someone committed to *eudaimonia* might propose an alternate framework, one that would shift the focus from a single, or more likely, a set of discrete communicative acts, to think instead about the values these acts are meant to communicate and enact. It might also allow us to explore duties of sexual selfhood that emerge *before* or *after* the act of coming out, as well as duties held by heterosexuals and cisgendered persons, for whom coming out is not an issue. After all, we agree that openness about oneself, self-esteem, pride, willingness to connect with the like-minded and like-selved, community membership, honesty and affirmation are all qualities likely to enhance individual flourishing. We worry that while sometimes these are best achieved by the act of coming out, too close a focus on a duty to perform that act risks excluding both persons and considerations of moral value. In introducing the value of flourishing, Cooley is perhaps more radical than he acknowledges; rather than limiting the question of flourishing to the act of coming out, we might ask what a broader ethics of sexual flourishing would look like.

A Response to MacLachlan and Sreedhar

Dennis R. Cooley

I want to start considering MacLachlan and Sreedhar's claim that whether or not someone should unveil himself will be based on "something like an ongoing series of provisional principles and guidelines for responsibly navigating a series of

---

23   Feminist Aristotelian Lisa Tessman claims that under conditions of oppression, virtue and flourishing come apart. Tessman hypothesizes the existence of 'burdened virtues', virtues that "while practically necessitated for surviving oppression or morally necessitated for opposing it, carry with them a cost to the bearer." These virtues are *burdened* because they "have the unusual feature of being disjoined from their bearer's own flourishing" (Tessman 2005: 5).

messy trade-offs, and compromises" (see MacLachlan and Sreedhar, this volume). That's right; ethics is a lot messier than some might have us believe. Pluralism is necessary to capture morality's complexities because our intricate reality cannot be classified by one absolute, abstract principle. Not everything fits cleanly into a single box, and we should recognize that fact.

However, there are certain duties that are flexible enough to account for the vast majority of exceptions. More specifically, the duty to flourish, if one exists as I think it does, is not overridden by even the most pathetic of circumstances.

In an example suggested by Raja Halwani, suppose that a person is in the closet to his mother. Due to a physical illness, she needs long-term care that requires her son to live with her. If she knew about his sexual orientation, then her flourishing would be significantly compromised. His orientation will make her extremely unhappy to the point that her life will no longer be worth living. Even if he does not tell her, if he attempts to live as the gay man he is, some gossiper will relay the information to her. Revealing himself will also cause injury to both because their relationship will be severely harmed. If nurturing, sustaining relationships with our parents is part of their and our flourishing, then we should care for them as they want to be cared for. Moreover, the son's flourishing benefit can be enhanced even after his mother is dead. By remaining closeted, he will know that her end of life was much better than it would have been. He can then achieve closure in a way denied to those who realize their parent's life ended in strife. Therefore, if they do not want to know that their child is non-heterosexual, and it will affect their care if they know, then there is at least a *prima facie* obligation to remain in the closet.

There are two responses to this example. First, people, who decide to reproduce and raise children make the decision to bring a sentient, potential person into being, thereby creating an obligation for themselves to seek their offspring's flourishing. The self-created duty might require great sacrifice on the parents' part. However, parents cannot create a debt for their children unless the children take the burden on themselves (English 1995: 300). Children do not choose to be born to particular parents; hence, the former have no gratitude duty that outweighs their individual obligation to flourish. In fact, gratitude, when done right, is part of an individual's flourishing.

Second, flourishing can show that being out to one's loved ones, even if it harms them, can help justify an obligation to be out. We must recognize that those who are injured by the knowledge that their loved one is non-heterosexual are unwarrantedly hurting themselves because there is nothing inherently wrong with acting non-heterosexually or evil by being non-heterosexual. Bigotry should not be rewarded. Therefore, the immediate reduction of flourishing is self-inflicted and unethical, which is not the child's responsibility. Moreover, since parents willingly take up the burden of having offspring whose flourishing they must foster, they have a moral obligation through their entire lives to assist in their child's flourishing as long as doing so sacrifices nothing of comparable moral worth. Given that sexual orientation is an essential component to a child's identity, and sexual orientation is neither morally good or bad, then parents have the duty to accept their children's orientation no matter what it is. Doing so is necessary for the child's flourishing because it recognizes who the child is *as* the child is. That is, it allows the child to be authentic and to have authentic relationships with those for whom she cares.

Of course, outing oneself to those for whom we care and who will be harmed is more ethically complex than examined here. Although the impact on flourishing is the key criterion for whether there is a duty to be out, there seem to be different moral principles at work for different types of outing. Outing oneself to oneself— odd though the notion may appear—seems to be something that respecting one's intrinsic value, virtue ethics, and even ethical egoism cover best. Outing to family and friends can use the same principles, but involves more ethical factors. Care ethics has to be one of the principles because of the caring relationships we need to develop and nurture. Outing to others, such as acquaintances, might use utilitarianism, respect for all persons, a bit of care ethics depending on what the relationship is, and the principles for outing to oneself. Outing to others with whom we have less intimate interactions, such as strangers, might use utilitarianism, respect for all persons, and the principles for outing to oneself. Basically, as the connection's intimacy weakens, more general principles focusing on what is good for society or persons in general take greater weight in the evaluation, while those based on more intimate relationships are less applicable. How all of these principles work for every case is beyond the scope of this response, but it is important at least to recognize the complexity in play. Doing so does not harm the argument that there is a duty to out oneself; it only shows that the duty exists under a pluralist theory of morality based on actual circumstances.

A Response to Cooley

Alice MacLachlan and Susanne Sreedhar

We are grateful to Dennis R. Cooley for his thoughtful and constructive response to our argument. Cooley appears to agree with many of our substantive commitments—and also with our concluding thought, that is, that the particular dilemmas faced by queer femmes are ultimately tied to the *power* they possess: that is, "the ability to less painfully change ideologies in both the heterosexual and non-heterosexual communities." Indeed, rather than disputing our core claims, he extends our analysis further and in new terms, suggesting that our paper's focus reveals "where moral luck plays its role in power, sexual identity, and being out."

It was not our original intention to identify and delineate specific ethical obligations adhering to queer femme identity. However, Cooley's analysis—when applied to our original observations—raises a series of interesting questions, namely: does the power we have ascribed to queer femmes give rise to specific obligations? If so, is the obligation to be visible as a queer femme—where possible—among them? Given his remarks on the importance of challenging problematic stereotypes and ideologies, and his emphasis on the close relationship between visibility and flourishing, it would seem that Cooley believes this is the case. Indeed, read at its strongest, the claim that queer femmes have relatively unique power to contribute to ideological change, when taken together with Cooley's analysis of moral luck and attending obligations, implies that queer femmes who do *not* take advantage of every opportunity to challenge stereotypes, or at least those with little personal cost, are not unlike witnesses who walk away from minor accidents without stopping to assist. Put simply, this gave us pause.

At the same time, we struggle with the question of how this claim should be put into practice. Maintaining a requisite level of visibility would presumably entail more than simply being out in one's personal life, since, as we argued, for queer femmes simply being out does not always lead to being visible as such. In fact, in some cases, any further obligation might fall afoul of "ought implies can," unless we understand "visibility" as a willingness to utter and re-utter direct, clear, and impossible-to-misunderstand statements, reinforcing them until they are understood (e.g. "No, I am a lesbian. A lesbian. Yes, I'm sure." "No—you misheard me. My partner is a woman. Yes, my sexual partner—not my business partner." "No, while I am married to a man, our marriage is not heterosexual, as neither person in it is heterosexual. I am bisexual and so is he."). And certainly, when compared to legal or physical harm, material loss or alienation from family and community, an ongoing commitment to daily enactments of such conversations does represent relatively little personal cost. But neither does it appear, to us, to contribute to one's level of flourishing.

And ultimately, visibility and disruption may come apart. Let us return to our original example of the author and the shopkeeper. Here, our sympathies lie with Cooley; this does seem like an excellent opportunity to exercise what we have called the subversive power of queer femmes. But is direct and immediate visibility (perhaps an immediate, insistent correction of pronouns) the best way to do so? There would be little cost beyond immediate awkwardness and the loss of a (sexist) discount on furniture, and the moment might well have been educational. Yet, as it turns out, an alternative, longer-term strategy is even more effective. The author's inadvertent short-term invisibility led to a conversation with the shopkeeper about the vagaries of relationships, budgets and interpersonal negotiation—though this conversation suffered from the sexist and heterosexist assumptions, on his part, about the relationships in question. Through civility, a connection was formed. The potentially disruptive impact of the author's return several days later—along with her female partner—was thus even greater, given this connection, which in turn depended on the unfortunate happenstance of her temporary invisibility. Indeed, we suspect that the ubiquity of such situations is partly why we did not draw specific conclusions about what concrete obligations queer femmes hold, in practice.

Cooley's general challenge to us is well taken. Assessments of someone's power to do good raise important questions about their attendant responsibilities: i.e. how and when to take up that power. If my identity, in and of itself, contradicts harmful stereotypes, then being visible as the person I am represents one way to disrupt these stereotypes. Nevertheless, a general duty to disrupt remains importantly distinct from a general duty to visible—and this is especially true when the call to disrupt is understood as a call to disrupt strategically or effectively, and when the visibility in question remains fragile and easily misread. Thus, while we are grateful that Cooley's reframing has pushed us to consider how we might best articulate the practical consequences of the power we have attributed to queer femmes, we suspect that accurate analysis of these consequences—beyond the basic injunction to use it responsibly—will likely resist formulation as a set of general obligations. Rather, it will resemble something like an on-going series of provisional principles and guidelines for responsibly navigating a series of messy trade-offs, and compromises. Enumerating these remains a task for another day.

References

Aragon, A.P. 2006. Introduction: Challenging lesbian normativity. *Journal of Lesbian Studies*, 10(1, 2), 1-15.

Bayles, M.D. 1994. Marriage, love, and procreation, in *Philosophy and Sex*, edited by R. Baker and F. Elliston. Amherst: Prometheus Books, 130-45.

Bettcher, T. 2007. On evil deceivers and make-believers: Transphobic violence and the politics of illusion. *Hypatia*, 22(3), 43-65.

Brennan, S. 2011. Fashion and sexual identity, or why recognition matters, in *Fashion - Philosophy for Everyone: Thinking with Style*, edited by J. Kennett and J. Wolfendale. Oxford: Wiley-Blackwell, 120-34.

Burke, J.C. 2009. *Visible: A Femmethology Vol. 1 and 2*. Ypsilanti, MI: Homofactus Press.

Butler, J. 1993. Imitation and gender subordination, in *The Lesbian and Gay Studies Reader*, edited by H. Abelove, M.A. Barale and D.M. Halperin. New York: Routledge, 307-21.

Bok, S. 1989. *Lying: Moral Choice in Public and Private Life*. London: Random House.

Card, C. 1995. *Lesbian Choices*. New York: Columbia University Press.

Calhoun, C. 2000. *Feminism, the Family and the Politics of the Closet: Lesbian and Gay Displacement*. Oxford: Oxford University Press.

Chekola, M. 1994. Outing, truth-telling, and the shame of the closet. *Journal of Homosexuality*, 27(3, 4), 67-90.

Chekola, M. 2009. *Happiness, Relational Goods, and an Invisible Minority: The Effects of Negative Views of Homosexuality*. Paper to the Happiness and Relational Goods Conference, Isola di San Sevolo, Venezia, June 11-13, 2009.

Conee, E. 1982. Against moral dilemmas. *The Philosophical Review*, 91(1), 87-97.

Coyote, I. 2009. Hats off to beautiful femmes. *Xtra Magazine* [Online]. Available at: http://www.xtra.ca/public/national/hats_off_to_beautiful_femmes-7215.aspx [accessed: 12 July 2011].

Dahl, U. and Volcano, D.L. 2009. *Femmes of Power: Exploding Queer Femininities*. London: Serpent's Tail Press. Burke, Jennifer Clare. 2009. *Visible: A Femmethology*, Volume One and Two, Homofactus Press.

Dahl, Ulrika and Del LaGrace Volcano. 2009. *Femmes of Power: Exploding Queer Femininities*. Serpent's Tail Press.

Duggan, L. and McHugh, K. 2002. A fem(me)inist manifesto, in *Brazen Femme: Queering Femininity*, edited by C.B. Rose and A. Camilleri. Vancouver: Arsenal Pulp Press, 165-71.

English, J. 1995. Why do grown children owe their parents? in *Philosophical Perspectives on Sex and Love*, edited by R.M. Stewart. New York: Oxford University Press, 300-3.

Federal Bureau of Investigations (United States of America). 2008. *Hate Crime Statistics* [Online]. Available at: http://www.fbi.gov/hq/cid/civilrights/hate. htm [accessed: June 18, 2010].

Halwani, R. 2002. Outing and virtue ethics. *Journal of Applied Philosophy*, 19(2), 141-54.

Halwani, R. 2008. What is gay and lesbian philosophy? *Metaphilosophy*, 39(4, 5), 433-71.

Harbin, A. 2011. Sexual authenticity. *Dialogue: Canadian Philosophical Review*, 50, 77-93.

Harris, L. and Crocker, E. 1997. *Femme: Feminists, Lesbians and Bad Girls*. New York and London: Routledge.

Kant, I. 1989. On a supposed right to lie from altruistic motives, in *Lying: Moral Choice in Public and Private Life*, edited by S. Bok. London: Random House, 267-72.

Loftin, C.M. 2007. Unacceptable mannerisms: Gender anxieties, homosexual activism, and swish in the United States, 1945-1965. *Journal of Social History* [Online]. Available at: http://www.articlearchives.com/society-social/sex-gender-issues-gays-lesbians/1662209-1.html [accessed: June 2, 2009].

MacLachlan, A. 2012a. Closet doors and stage lights: On the goods of out. Forthcoming in *Social Theory and Practice*, 38(2).

Mohr, R. 1992. *Gay Ideas*. Boston, MA: Beacon Press.

Morales, L. 2009. Knowing someone gay/lesbian affects views of gay issues. *Gallup* [Online]. Available at: http://www.gallup.com/poll/118931/Knowing-Someone-Gay-Lesbian-Affects-Views-Gay-Issues.aspx [accessed: June 4, 2009].

Nestle, J. 1992. *The Persistent Desire: A Femme-Butch Reader*. Boston, MA: Alyson Publications.

Rose, C.B. and Camilleri, A. 2002a. *Brazen Femme: Queering Femininity*. Vancouver: Arsenal Pulp Press.

Rose, C.B. and Camilleri, A. 2002b. Introduction: A Brazen Posture, in *Brazen Femme: Queering Femininity*, edited by B. Rose and A. Camilleri. Vancouver: Arsenal Pulp Press, 11-14

Rugg, R.A. 1997. How Does She Look? in *Femme: Feminists, Lesbians and Bad Girls*, edited by L. Harris and E. Crocker. New York: Routledge, 175-89.

Singer, P. 2006. Famine, affluence, and morality, in *Applied Ethics: A Multicultural Approach*, edited by L. May, S. Collins-Chobanian, and K. Wong. Englewood Cliffs, NJ: Prentice Hall, 253-62.

Stramel, J. 1997. Outing, ethics and politics, in *Same Sex*, edited by J. Corvino. New York: Rowman & Littlefield, 284-88.

Sullivan, A. 2009. Why marriage equality is winning, ctd. *The Daily Dish* [Online]. Available at: http://andrewsullivan.theatlantic.com/the_daily_dish/2009/05/why-marriage-equality-is-winning-ctd.html [accessed: June 4, 2009].

Tessman, L. 2005. *Burdened Virtues: Virtue Ethics for Liberatory Struggle.* Oxford: Oxford University Press.

Tonglet, M, Phillips, P.S. and Read, A.D. 2004. Using the theory of planned behaviour to investigate the determinants of recycling behaviour: A case study from Brixworth, UK. *Resources, Conservation and Recycling*, 41(3), 191-214.

Tudor, T.L., Barr, S.W. and Gilg, A.W. 2007. Linking intended behaviour and actions: A case study of healthcare waste management in the Cornwall NHS. *Resources, Conservation and Recycling*, 51(1), 1-23.

Tudor, T.L., Noonan, C.L. and Jenkin, L.E.T. 2005. Healthcare waste management: A case study from the Cornwall NHS. *UK Waste Management*, 25(6), 606-15.

VanNewkirk, R. 2006. Gee, I didn't get that vibe from you: Articulating my own version of a femme lesbian existence. *Journal of Lesbian Studies*, 10(1, 2), 73-85.

Walker, L. 1993. How to recognize a lesbian: The cultural politics of looking like what you are. *Signs*, 18(4), 866-90.

Wilkerson, W. 2009. Is it a choice? sexual orientation as interpretation. *Journal of Social Philosophy*, 40(1), 97-116.

Chapter 3
Power, Oppression, and Passing

Daniel Hurewitz and Kelby Harrison

Introduction

Daniel Hurewitz and Kelby Harrison examine issues of ethics and power in passing in oppressive systems. Harrison considers the role of power through a feminist, Foucaultian, and critical race theorist lens. Hurewitz shares his investigation into a crime that seems to be at its very heart a disguised case of homosexual activities that violated U.S. laws in the late 1930s. His interaction with the one of the men's sons raises an interesting question about the responsibility of someone who possesses the secrets of a man who passed to keep the subterfuge going so that the survivors can keep intact their memories of the deceased and what he meant to them.

Visiting Our Sins

Daniel Hurewitz

Janet Malcolm has famously insisted that journalism is a profession steeped in deceit and disloyalty. "Every journalist who is not too stupid or too full of himself to notice what is going on," she once wrote, "knows that what he does is morally indefensible. He is a kind of confidence man, preying on people's vanity, ignorance, or loneliness, gaining their trust and betraying them without remorse" (1990: 3). It is clear, however, that historians share the same capacity and desire for betrayal—if not a greater one. We dream of revealing the secrets that our subjects kept hidden, of publishing the letters they wanted no one to see, of explaining the dark motives they never would reveal. That is our hope: to explain the seemingly inexplicable mystery of other people by uncovering the secrets that they kept.

To do so, we practice reading and listening against the grain—looking for the hidden subtext or secret code. Particularly in the realm of LGBT history, we are always listening for the things which are not fully being said, and always trying to read between the lines to find them. Trying to discern whether two men sharing a bed in an Illinois storefront or two women writing passionate letters in a "Boston marriage" were just friends, or were involved in a rich sexual and affectionate relationship (Rupp 2002). Our work transpires in an arena of secrets that have, more often than not, been well guarded for years—and the task we have assigned ourselves is to expose those secrets. We do it with a belief that uncovering these truths will bring insight and liberation of some kind. And yet, as Malcolm makes clear, the moral terrain is slippery at best.

Several years ago, I stumbled upon a criminal court case involving the arrest of nearly 20 men who, in the late 1930s, had attended a cabin party on the outskirts of a West Coast ranching and military town, and had been accused of drinking, dancing, and having sex with one another while there. I was captured by various pieces of the story—the extraordinary effort the police made to witness them having sex, the terrible way they were vilified in the trial, and the fact that the majority of them were sent to a maximum security prison for several years after their conviction. Their case seemed to scream, "Injustice!"

I was captivated by the work of the police, who knew about the party a week in advance and spent that time preparing the cabin for a stake-out. They popped out knots in the wooden walls, so that they could look in and see what was happening. They placed a mattress inside a custom-made wooden cupola on the roof and then pushed apart some of the wooden slats, so that the police could be both comfortable and hidden as they looked down at the party below. And for several hours, stationed in the bushes, in a ditch, and up on the roof, seven police officers watched as the drinking, dancing, groping, and sex ensued. By 1:00am, having seen enough, the police converged on the cabin and arrested the men.

The riveting eye-witness testimony of the police officers who took the stand to describe every sexual event they witnessed proved powerful in the courtroom. Their descriptions were supplemented by physical evidence—namely the men's shirts, underwear, and bed sheets, all of which were analyzed and found to be spattered with semen. With a few more hostile witnesses, the district attorneys built a fairly solid case.

The defense, by contrast, built almost no case. The defense attorney objected and objected, sometimes strenuously, but never in a meaningful way. His only real challenge to the prosecution's narrative was to put all the partygoers on the stand and have them declare, in nearly uniform and unconvincing language, that they neither saw nor participated in any untoward behavior. By the laws of 1937, these men appeared guilty, and their attorney shielded them almost not at all from the punishment the law chose to mete out.

And punished they were: all who pled not guilty were found guilty and sent to prison for indeterminate sentences of several years. One 18-year-old high school student who testified against the other men was forced to leave the state and live with his grandfather. With only a few exceptions, very little leniency was offered these men.

My heart broke over these men as I read their trial transcript. I identified with them. I admired their daring and their innocence. For no clear reason, I was especially smitten with the lead plaintiff, a hair stylist named Joseph Erickson. I cringed as he insisted on his innocence on the witness stand, and cringed again when his lawyer referred to his mother—with whom he lived and who was there in the courtroom during his testimony. And my heart truly sank when the district attorney called up his trump witness, a young man direct from juvenile hall who described the many times the hair stylist had sex with him. There was, I felt certain, no denying their likely guilt at that point.

Yet despite their "guilt," the case felt like an injustice. I wanted to reach into the transcript, into the courtroom, and wring the neck of the defense attorney for so poorly protecting these gay brothers, and then bash in the teeth of the scornful judge and assistant D.A.s for attacking them so mercilessly, and then somehow comfort the hairdresser and his friends, so victimized in this way. If I could, I wanted to undo the past. That felt like my moral goal.

Last spring, after I read through the trial transcript, I began to research the men online, particularly using ancestry.com. Though the trial record shined a bright light on these men, it did so for only a tiny portion of their lives—from the time they went to the party, until they went to prison. I wanted to use the census and other documents to think about how this episode fit with the rest of their lives.

The census proved only a limited resource, but ancestry.com proved a fascinating tool. As you gather research materials on ancestry.com, the site automatically formats your findings into a family tree, assuming (no doubt, correctly) that most people are using the site to research their own family histories. As you focus in on a particular individual—Joseph Erickson, say—the site tells you who else has placed Erickson in their family tree and invites you to look at their tree. This makes sense: if Erickson is your great uncle, then finding another tree that includes him means finding a new branch in your own tree, and hence more relatives. And to encourage that kind of family-finding, ancestry.com allows you to send messages to the other tree builders: "I see you're researching Joseph Erickson. He was my great uncle through marriage. Who was he to you?" And suddenly you're chatting with cousins you never knew you had living on the other side of the country.

For me, I had very little expectation about this family-connecting function of ancestry.com. First of all, it seemed clear to me that most of the men I was interested in were gay. They would be, therefore, dead-ends on their family trees, and likely not that interesting to the genealogical hounds who were tracing cousins and marriages and offspring. What is more, I suspected, some of those hounds would wish to erase any trace of their gay relatives. This view was confirmed for me in an exchange I had about Erickson, the hairdresser, with a cousin of his I found through the family tree system. Even though the cousin responded to my inquiry, writing that it was "so exciting to hear of long forgotten relatives," he could tell me almost nothing about Erickson, other than that he "spent some time in prison" and was "caught up in the San Francisco lifestyle." While he was eager to tell me about other relatives, when I pressed him for more details about his cousin, he stopped responding to me. He closed the door on our "exciting" communication, either because his gay convict cousin was not that interesting for him, or because he felt it best that his life be left unremembered. And in general, that is what I thought the family-focused ancestry.com would offer me in my search for gay men: very little.

Of course, I was wrong about that and wrong in my thinking about these men.

Working my way through ancestry.com and Google, I tracked down the birthplace and nearby burial of one of my other convicts, Alexander Florentine, a soldier who had been arrested at the party. Florentine was from a small town in Mississippi and was buried near there. His name was so unusual and his hometown so small, that when I found a living Florentine, one Jackson Florentine, in roughly the same location, I thought he must be a relative—a cousin or nephew—and sent him an email message. I explained that I was a historian, working on a court case from the late 1930s which involved several people including Alexander Florentine who served several years in prison. I did not specify the details of the case, fearing that if I did, I would trigger some reflexive homophobia that would also lead this nephew or cousin to slam the research door on me. I wanted to see how much I could learn about Florentine before having to navigate my way around the potential obstacle of "the San Francisco lifestyle." Instead, I simply wrote, "It's clear to me that the case involved a real miscarriage of justice, and so I'm trying to research it and understand how and why it happened."

Jackson Florentine wrote me back in the middle of the night that night and his reply stunned me. I imagined that he had stayed up late mulling over my email, thinking about how to respond. His reply forced me to re-imagine what I was doing, both in terms of what story I was looking for and what role I was playing by trying to uncover it. He wrote:

> I am Jackson Florentine, born in Jan of 1942 and the oldest of three sons born to Alexander Florentine of whom you speak. I have no direct knowledge of the events you mention but some years after Dad passed away in 1969 from cancer I remember my mother mentioning this to me and I resented her divulging such a thing to me that Dad had put behind him before I was even born and was no longer here to defend himself. I remember her saying that it had to do with the rape of a woman and that Dad's life-long friend, Alex Cobb had gone to prison with him … I know nothing of his guilt or innocence or any other details of that time. I'd be glad to fill you in on other details of his life.
>
> Needless to say, I was very surprised to hear from you regarding this period of Dad's life as I have never spoken to anyone about it or had anyone speak to me about it except the time my mother (also deceased) mentioned it to me.[1]

The email ended abruptly, without a sign-off, and I interpreted that abruptness as a flash of anger. It certainly felt like a direct blow to my previous thinking. First and foremost: one of my men had married and had a son! He had not lived "the San Francisco lifestyle" the way I have and built an identity around that. Being at that cabin party in 1937 was not part of some readily legible gay life trajectory: perhaps it was a single episode, perhaps it was a phase in his younger years, perhaps it was

---

1   Jackson Florentine to author, April 10, 2010.

part of his secret life. Whatever it was, its meaning and its relationship to his self-determined identity, it now became clear to me, was far from apparent. If I thought I was pursuing the victimization of gay men in history, I was mistaken: this was a more complicated tale.

Secondly, however secret his homosexual activities were, they were not his only secret. His imprisonment was also a secret. He was an ex-con who went to his grave without revealing that fact to his son. So if I was going to be unearthing secrets, I needed to recognize that sexuality was just one secret arena, perhaps one of many.

Third, these secrets were emotionally loaded. Jackson had been infuriated by his mother's posthumous revelation and had, it seemed, never pursued the topic again. For me to mention that his father was a criminal was no small thing. It was volatile in ways I could not fully imagine.

Finally, while Jackson had been given some inkling of his father's secret criminal past, the keeper of the secret had lied about the central fact of the case. Florentine had not been arrested for raping a woman: rape was never one of the accusations, and no women attended the party. That secret version of events was a fiction that Florentine had likely invented. Indeed, I came to imagine that as soon as Florentine walked out of the prison gates, he never again told the truth about why he had been there. He buried his secret past with a combination of silence and distracting fabrication.

And then suddenly here I was, possessing some piece of that secret, and I was interested in bringing the secret to light. I wanted, quite nobly I thought, to reach into the past and make what happened to these gay men somewhat better by identifying what had occurred, describing it, making it real so as not to be forgotten. That was the vindication I wanted to achieve.

But I can now see that from another perspective, perhaps from the perspective of Alexander Florentine himself, what I wanted to do was stir the pot. I wanted to stir up a host of secrets that he and perhaps several people in his family had worked hard to keep hidden. I wanted to undo the work they had done to make their lives and their family function. Clearly that work involved lies, but those lies contained emotional power that I could not begin to imagine. Was it really my place to shake that power loose?

I was no longer sure where my research was going to take me, or where I should—and should not—allow it to go. Nevertheless, I did not turn away.

I quickly wrote back to Jackson, and immediately apologized if I had "upset" him by "referring to [your father's] past the way I did." I accepted his offer to learn more about his dad, and "learn whatever details you feel like sharing with me." And then in terms of the court case, I added, "we can discuss as much or as little of it as you like. We can ignore the case entirely and not discuss it at all. Or I can tell you the limited details that I know — whatever feels most comfortable to you.

Most importantly, I have no desire to create a situation that feels uncomfortable for you."[2]

My honest hope was that he would opt for us *not* to discuss the case. I feared his reaction to the news, and feared that he would shut the door on me and our communication, feeling that this was a chapter in his father's life that he did not want to know about, let alone discuss with some stranger.

Eventually, Jackson agreed to speak with me on the telephone, though with no great enthusiasm. "I'm not sure that I look forward to this exchange of information," he explained, "but I'm willing to talk with you." He wanted there to be more told about his father than his criminal record.

> As I said before I have no knowledge of his guilt or innocence or any details of the case but feel as though the exemplary life he led from that point on certainly stands for something and either way should be a part of any record or story. Dad was a very loving, caring father to us three sons and a good husband and provider to our mother up until his death.[3]

I could not imagine how the story in my head fit with this story in Jackson's. One of the court officers had described Florentine at sentencing, writing, "His conduct at this party and his aggression ... were characteristic of a constitutional homosexual." Even if I scorned the judicial officials in general, I believed that assessment, and the story Jackson offered, even in brief sketch, was already for me the false story. His was the grain against which I was reading, the fiction against which I believed I held the truth.

Jackson and I spoke on the phone about ten days later. We were both a bit nervous at the outset, and maybe throughout our conversation. I apologized again for "raising issues that you'd rather not have raised," and he reiterated how he had "resented Mother ever bringing that up long after Dad had died ... since Dad wasn't there to ask questions of and defend himself."[4] But then we settled into conversation, skirting the central issues of the court case, perhaps happily for both of us, as he began to unfold for me his memories of his childhood and his father.

After getting out of prison, Florentine met his future wife, married, had children, and eventually settled back in Mississippi. By the time his oldest son was ten, Florentine had become a traveling salesman, selling dental supplies to dentists across the south. He was away from home a lot, for two, three, four weeks at a time, and his wife took care of the three boys, ran the house, paid the bills. Otherwise, they were a normal family—church-going, card-writing, holiday-celebrating. Easter meant huge egg hunts with all the cousins. Fourth of July, there were washtubs filled with soda and watermelon and nonstop barbecues and fireworks. "Christmas time, as soon as he would come in off the road, anytime

---

2   Author to Jackson Florentine, April 11, 2010.
3   Jackson Florentine to author, April 11, 2010.
4   Jackson Florentine, interview with author, April 21, 2010.

from November through January he would stop at the coffee table in the living room, sit down, and start looking at all the [holiday] cards ... He would sit down and read every word of every card, and ask Mother had she sent these people a card." Jackson sobbed a little as he remembered these sweet moments with his father, and he assured me that he'd had, "a wonderful mother and dad, and a great life."[5] I could not imagine arguing with that.

But early in our conversation, Jackson began telling me about Alex Cobb, and a new level of dissonance overwhelmed me. I felt like I was watching the kind of play in which you know one character is being deceived, and all you can do is watch—fascinated but powerless—as the deception unfolds. Literary scholars refer to it as "dramatic irony," when the audience knows that Oedipus is killing his father and marrying his mother, even though Oedipus himself does not. Every tidbit that Jackson began to tell me felt like the hidden code for a totally different narrative. I heard a story he did not realize he was telling.

Alex Cobb was the "life-long friend" Jackson had referred to in his first email to me, the one he thought had gone to prison with his father for committing rape. Jackson told me that he had subsequently forwarded our email exchange onto his younger brother, and his brother explained that Cobb had told him that he had not gone to jail with their father, but had met him there—having been locked away a few years earlier for manslaughter. Then from prison on, Cobb and Florentine became "life-long friends." "That's really all I knew about it," Jackson explained.

> That they were friends for life. We traveled around the country together. He and Dad both were in various sales jobs, and a lot of times, we lived in the same house or same apartment. He had twin girls, Hope and Violet, that were my age, and they were like sisters. And we moved around the country. God we lived in Houston, and San Antonio, in Los Angeles at one time, Kansas City ... all over the area, till Dad got a job ... and sort of settled down as far as the traveling.[6]

For Jackson, this was the portrait of a friendship; but to me, already imagining his father as gay, it sounded like something else, maybe not a Boston marriage, but something similar, something profound.

Cobb, in talking with Jackson's brother, confirmed and elaborated what their mother had said about their father's crime. Namely, he repeated that Florentine had gone to prison for rape, but elaborated that it was for statutory rape. Cobb apparently told his brother "that Dad was at some type of party, and there was a young lady there that he hooked up with ... and she ended up being underage." Her age eventually came to light, and Florentine went to jail. So Cobb confirmed a sex crime, yes, and did so with a sense of greater revelation, of somehow taking the brothers closer to the truth. And in truth, there was an 18-year-old, then considered a minor, at the original party and his presence added to the opprobrium that was

---

5   ibid.
6   ibid.

heaped on the arrested men. But fundamentally, Cobb kept their father's lie intact. The crime he had concocted to tell them was not the true one, the one I knew to be the source of Florentine's imprisonment.

Nonetheless, Cobb told Jackson's brother—who was also named Alex—one more piece of half-truth. He explained then when their father got locked away, Cobb "had protected him in prison. That some particular faction there … had come after Dad, and Alex Cobb went to bat for him. I do not know if it involved physical violence or what, but he protected him, and that is where the relationship formed."[7] Of course, homosexuals in prison often needed protection because they were frequently victims of sexual assaults and other violence. But that protection often came as part of a sexual relationship between a stronger man and the would-be victim: I now began to imagine Cobb and Florentine as prison lovers.

Jackson told me that Cobb was still in prison when his father was paroled, but that in some manner Florentine waited for him. And then the two spent the next several years living together and traveling the country together, even as they married and had children. That was the picture in my head by the end of my conversation with Jackson: of his father going to prison and finding there a sort of life partner—a man with whom, in prison and then out, he fashioned a life, even if under a cloak of incredible "Brokeback Mountain"—like secrecy. Cobb, I was convinced, was Florentine's lover, unacknowledged even after both their deaths, and their secret story was not just one of injustice, but of romance.

That night, I typed Alex Cobb's name into various search engines and found the basic newspaper outline of his crime. He had gone to prison for killing a man, that much was true. But while the newspapers were far from explicit, the story they sketched was of a gay pick-up gone awry. Cobb, then a sailor, was out with another sailor and they ended up in a vacant lot with a third man. Something sexual occurred and then Cobb and his friend turned violent, beating the other man unintentionally to death.

Clearly, Cobb was no gay hero. More likely, he was conflicted about his sexuality and in the moment after, exploded into violence in a familiar "gay panic" attack. Yet once imprisoned for that crime, he then took steps to protect another gay sex criminal in his prison. And then he began to fashion some kind of life with him.

Jackson and I were on the phone for nearly an hour and a half, before we started running out of steam. As I felt the end coming on, I offered again to tell him "more about the case, if you like. Or I can save it for another conversation if you feel like." And Jackson, likely hearing the wish in my voice to get off the phone without having to shatter his vision of his father, said, "Alright, we can save it till a later date."[8] I was, admittedly, relieved.

Before he hung up, Jackson emphasized to me that whatever crime his father had committed, he was willing to forgive him. "There's nothing, I don't think, that

---

7   ibid.
8   ibid.

I wouldn't want to know," he said. "If he was some terrible person that brutally raped somebody and killed them in the aftermath, well, that was another life, and another person, and it's not the Dad I have known and loved for all these years."[9] But he cried when he said that to me, and I took his sobs to be more honest than his words. Even as I assured him that his father's crime was nothing so heinous, I felt powerfully how much I did not want to tell him what he did not yet know. I was developing a story in my head of his father's life that was radically different from the picture he possessed. Perhaps my story was wrong, but I could see no way to explore it with him without doing violence to his treasured stories. And who was I to destroy his memories?

In truth, I had come to fear the very power that as a historian I had set out to possess. I knew Florentine's secret, but even if I had the power to fix, in some tiny historical way, a criminal injustice done to him, in some other way, I had taken on a new power. It felt like I had traded places with the local sheriffs. Now *I* was the one telling stories from behind the cabin wall, insisting, "He told you he was just going out with friends, but let me tell you the truth about him!" And while I was not going to send the father to prison again, in some way, I was on the brink of causing a new harm. With just a few sentences, I could smash the stories of Jackson's life and family and childhood that had given him security and stability for all these years.

Jackson's father and Alex Cobb had constructed their lives out of secrets for reasons that made sense to them, and reasons that they believed in. Perhaps they were right to do so. Perhaps they had done what was best by lying to their wives and children for all those years. Certainly they gave Jackson the gift of a childhood that he still cherishes. And rather than take that gift away from him, maybe my moral obligation—not as an LGBT historian but as a person—is to honor them by honoring their commitment to deception. Keep their secrets, let their beautiful illusions stand.[10]

Power Over The Passing Subject: Creating Ethics Under Oppression

Kelby Harrison

The problem of sexual identity passing does not make sense in a world without power. There would be no implicit or explicit benefits to be derived from hiding an aspect of one's identity. There would be no hierarchy of preferred behaviors in relation to sexual identity, gender, religious belief, class status, or race without a structure of power to define who and what constitutes privilege. It seems to me, that in order to think through the layers of intersection that produce communities of individuals that have reason to pass in relations with others, and a subjectivity

---

9   ibid.

10   The names in my section, except for that of the author, are invented.

capable of restricting its authentic expression, we must consider aspects of power as it is theorized by feminists, Foucaultians, and critical race theorists. Moreover, passing involves a certain ethical posturing to power, one that is complicit with the dehumanizing flaws inherent in the structure of passing. A theory of power capable of explaining the phenomenon of passing that can also inform our understanding of ethics will be one that considers power that constructs subjectivity through psychic forces and through infusion into bodies. But as the lived experience of most sexual minorities will demonstrate, power is most actively felt through its ability to oppress. This chapter will also explore what happens to our lived experience of morality and our theories of ethics under oppression.

Constructing Subjectivity through Psychic Forces

Oppression is systematic power-over particular communities in line with cultural ideologies of privilege. For those who are oppressed, oppression creates a sense of alienation. Passing can mask this alienation, as passing can attempt to mitigate the insidious psychological effects of oppression, and especially in the case of sexual identity: shame. Franz Fanon *Black Skin, White Masks* exposes the experience of psychological alienation; it is an alienation that has immediately recognizable social and economic realities. This psychological alienation manifests itself as an inferiority complex that is comprised of two components: primarily economic, and secondly the internalization, or what he says better yet, is the epidermalization[11] of this inferiority (Fanon 1967: 14). I found three basic themes in his exploration of alienation: relation to self inside the structure of power, relation to whiteness through language and desire, and the experience of lack of reciprocity that defines subjugation in all its emotional and psychological discomfort. I will briefly mention two alongside their insight into the case of the sexual identity passer.

The dominant power relation for Fanon is the white power-over black race relationship, which constructs the subjectivities of black men through white privilege. He states clearly, "what is often called the black man's soul is a white man's artifact" (Fanon 1967: 154). The internal self-referencing of the black man, the residing location of his soul, is a product of his relation to the white man. He states, too, that this psychological problem is elevated to the level of the ethical.

> When the Negro makes contact with the white world, a certain sensitizing action
> takes place. If his psychic structure is weak, one observes a collapse of the ego.
> The black man stops behaving as an *actional* person. The goal of his behavior

---

11   Epidermalization is medically defined as "the transformation of glandular or mucosal epithelium into stratified squamous epithelium." Glandular/muscosal epithelium is the sensitive, porous, and moist skin that constructs internal cavities like the mouth, esophagus, vagina, or anus. Stratified squamous epithelium is the skin that constructs the external body. As a metaphor, one might think of this as literally transforming the sensitive interior into the rough exterior.

will be The Other (in the guise of the white man), for The Other alone can give
him worth. That is on the ethical level: self-esteem. (Fanon 1967: 154)

This relationship to the Other, and the capitulating of self to the gaze and the
power of the Other is thematic throughout his text and the clearest of motivations
for the passing individual. Attempting to construct one's soul for the happy uptake
of one's oppressor and ignoring one's sense of self-esteem in contorting this image
of self has deep ethical implications that run counter to existential virtues such as
authenticity.

The lack of reciprocity is that which produces the psychological and emotional
discomfort of subjugation. The experience of reciprocity that the black man can find
with others of his race differs from the reciprocity he finds with the white Other.
This can take the form of different behavioral modalities, objectification, ontological
resistance, continual conscious awareness, or an enduring but futile plight for
recognition. In accordance with the title of his work, Fanon (1967) announces
that black men behave differently with white men and with black men. These two
behavioral modalities illustrate that certain aspects of his persona the black man
knows he cannot experience reciprocity with the white man. So he must alter his
behavior for sociality and social recognition. Black skins under white masks is a
perfect image for racial passing. An attempt to regain the psychological benefits
of reciprocity would explain why those of sexually minoritized status, particularly
given their increased access to instrumentalized identity mobility through the relative
invisibility of queerness (compared to race), would choose to pass.

What Fanon calls "psychic alienation" is the most pronounced experience of
minoritization as the internalization of the socializing forces that define, produce,
and maintain the power differentials between groups of people. Subordinates
must appropriate a society's perspective—engaging their subordinated role,
with minimal psychic investment, or they must, alternatively, maintain a critical
perspective on the sociological pressures, constantly combating the urge to
submit. This is to say that one's sense of self results not from an internal source,
but rather through the appropriation of the gaze of the oppressor. So oppression
is the product of a more fundamental subjective phenomenon: psychological
oppression.

Psychological oppression is the appropriation of and dominion over the self-
esteem of an individual. It is the capacity of a broader society's narratives to produce
the experience of self and self-regard in a way that is destructive, either subtly or
overtly. Psychological oppression, Sandra Bartky argues, is "institutionalized and
systemic," it reinforces the structures of power that keeps it in place by making
the domination easier. It breaks "the spirit of the dominated by rendering them
incapable of understanding the nature of those agencies responsible for their
subjugation" (1990: 23).

Psychological oppression blinds people to the forces that replicate and inscribe
the sociological structures that maintain the oppressed subject's location within a
system of oppression. The myth of inferiority is just that, a myth: but the forces

of psychological oppression instantiate the myth through its literalization within the subject.[12] The oppressed subject must engage the system for the oppression to operate.

Very much related to this concept of psychological oppression is what we might think of as a pervasive sense of shame. Not the shaming that occurs in a moment of moral failure, but the shaming that helps to construct someone's entire sense of self. It is the kind of shame having "boundaries [that] are blurred; [because] it is less available to consciousness and more likely to be denied. This shame is manifest in a pervasive sense of personal inadequacy that, like the shame of embodiment, is profoundly disempowering" (Bartky 1990: 85). One way that Bartky wants us to begin thinking about, and categorizing shame is as a "species of psychic distress" that is "occasioned by a self or a state of the self-apprehended as inferior, defective, or in some way diminished" (ibid.).

When we think about psychological oppression, and shame as constructing of identity we think about it in relation to socially recognizable identities. Both Fanon and Bartky considered their model of psychological oppression to be applicable in cases of transparent identity markers: namely, gender and race that are easily readable by others in society. Of course, there are few forms of shaming as powerful as forms of sexual shaming.

Passing, by the very nature of its phenomenon, erases the readability of the identity markers involved. This, I think it is fair to argue, complicates the psychological pressures experienced by the subject. Perhaps, for some, it magnifies the psychological pressure given the inherent isolation that passing demands, and perhaps alleviating pressure for others given that passing inhibits the subject from experiencing the psychological pressure directly.

Passing, one might argue, doubles the experience of isolation: isolation from the group in power and isolation from one's subjugated community. In addition, passing is only singularly alienating in that one sustains a connection to the group in power by building distance from the subjugated group. But in the second argumentative structure, distance from self must also be inserted if we can assume a common sense understanding of an authentic self.

Power Infused Through Bodies

Infusionary and bodily constructing models of power are most often attributed to, and appropriated from Foucault. His conception of power and the literature that engages these models of power takes one of three forms: 1) what is called the "docile bodies" thesis or the notion of "biopower" that refers to the state regulation of bodies. 2) the agonistic model of power; where power relations are viewed as always already containing resistance, and 3) where power is seen as constructive of sex identities, and is that which is the proliferation of the subjectifying discourses on sexuality.

---

12   I conceptually borrowed a productive myth's literalizing from Judith Butler (1990).

Postmodern feminist literature often appropriates these conceptions of power and its construction of subjectivities with grave political results. The subject is constructed by and trapped within the power system. Resistance is constructed by that system, through the very infusionary forces (discourse, state institutions, etc.) There remains a residue of the perfect sense of no escape. Any attempt to usurp this system to empower oneself against it is fundamentally futile.

I am interested in thinking about how the first conception of power (which is utterly intertwined with the third sense of power—though I wish to emphasize the third definition's subordinate position to the first sense of power) can be appropriated for an explanation of the concept of passing without trapping us in a politically inefficacious grave.

Modern power, for Foucault is centrally located around the principle of discipline. Sex is the primary force around which discipline and normalization systematize bodies into categories that separate off the delinquent, the insane, the hysteric, and the homosexual. Through this disciplinary process, the body becomes the political field upon which power relations inscribe themselves. The centralizing mechanism in Foucault's work that maintains the normalization of bodies through an unseen observatory force is his metaphor of the "panopticon." Referring to a building structure employed in the construction of prisons, where all prisoners can be viewed from a centralizing tower, the panopticon is used by Foucault to describe a ubiquitous sense of authorial social observations in disciplinary regimes. Feminist scholars appropriate this concept to explain female capitulation and acquiescence to patriarchal standards of femininity.

The conceptual shift in models of power that I wish to glean from Foucault and to sustain as helpful for a model of power that is explanatory of the phenomenon of passing is his focus on power's ability to be *constituitive* of subjectivity. Foucault's agonistic model of power is the version of power that undermines and fails to provide us with a sustainable notion of agency.

Because this model of power conceptualizes resistance as inherently intertwined with power, the subject is unable to extricate herself from the system. This eradication of agency, Deveaux argues, leaves feminists (and by feminist here I wish to expand the notion to include any politically motivated gender, race, or sexuality based thinker) unable to articulate the "inner processes that condition women's sense of freedom" (1994: 234) The most problematic Foucaultian argument in relation to power for my overall project is his discussion of power in relation to sexual identity. It is readily recognizable by queer scholars that Foucault's conception of power in relation to subjects and sexuality is contradictory to the political aspirations of queer activism. Foucault warns against the uncritical appropriation of queer identities given their production through discourse that establishes them "through the isolation, intensification, and consolidation of peripheral sexualities" (Foucault 1985: 48). His primary concern, it seems, is in the unwitting and uncritical appropriation of the discourses that establish queer identities and utilizing them as a stable identity for political activism. Instead, he wishes for the rallying point of sexual politics to be "bodies and pleasures" rather than discursively established subaltern identities like "gay," "lesbian," "bisexual," or "queer."

Celia Kitzinger argues that "power is implicated in the 'doing' of sex, such that both heterosex and sex between two people of the same gender is constructed of eroticized power differentials" (1994: 194). All sexuality is the embodiment of power; power infuses the very act itself. Here again we can see the directly constructive nature of power in bodies through the power exchange of sexuality.

Gender, then, becomes the product of sexuality—its "molding, direction, and expression." It is that which organizes society around two sexes—women and men—which division underlies the totality of social relations. This is the most prominent aspect of heteronormativity: the social construction of moral obligations and relations around gender bifurcation. Sexuality is power, and "sexuality is that social process which creates, organizes, expresses, and directs desire, creating the social beings we know as women and men, as their relations create society" (Mackinnon 1982: 516). Power, filtered through sexuality, becomes the regulatory manifestation of power on the body.

Power, then, and its infiltration into the body's construction through sexuality also creates the homosexual body. The power behind sexuality constructs the bifurcated gender pair of male and female, then places the identity of homosexuality beneath the identity of heterosexuality. The homosexual has no choice but to appropriate the shaming components associated with the infusion of power through sexuality into the body that privileges the heterosexual body over the homosexual body. Homosexual bodies are bodies infused with power. Homosexual bodies that are passing as heterosexual bodies are infused with power and bodies are reactionary or perhaps completely absorbent of the oppressive regimes of psychological oppression.

Ethics under Oppression

If power based relations are constructive and destructive of human psychology, subject embodiment, and social relations, it also makes sense that power can be constructive and destructive of our moral lives. In this section, I will explore ways of thinking about our sense of morality under systemic oppression, and will primarily draw from the moral lives of concentration camps' prisoners in Nazi Germany. I will draw connections here with sexual identity passing, that while under more ambiguous regimes of power, also must thrive within significant oppression. There is no ambiguity regarding the totalizing systemic nature of oppressive forces inflicted upon the Jews by the Nazis. In this regard (its totalizing nature) I think it is the cleanest model to establish a theory of what happens to our ethics under oppression. I will be working with two theories: Claudia Card's adaptation of Primo Levi's moral grey zones and Trvestan Todorov's understanding of heroic and ordinary virtues. Both theories work with different aspects of life in the camps, and at face value seem to be incommensurable with each other. In the end, however, I argue that the concept of supererogatory duties helps us to bring both models together, and that this might be the best way to remove the theories from the concentration camps and apply them to our lives under ordinary oppression. Finally, I will begin to articulate a normative structure of the moral responsibility of queer folks under ranging degrees of oppression.

Moral Grey Zones

Claudia Card appropriates Levi's concept of moral grey zones to describe complex demands of morality under systemic oppressive structures, like the ones found in concentration camps. She wants to apply this moral framework to help us think through ethical problems under ordinary (non-war) states of systematic oppression: namely, regimes of gender oppression under patriarchy, racial, class, and sexual identity oppression. The guiding premise of her exploration is that "oppressive social structures are an unfavorable context for flourishing or developing good character, whether we are favored or disfavored by those structures" (Card 1999: 3). Levi and Card both agree that under systemic oppression moral agents are necessarily subject to moral compromise, moral ambiguity, and complicity. Card, at least, does not present us with another option.

First a bit about Primo Levi's grey zones. The grey zones he discusses have three definitional features: 1) "their inhabitants are victims of evil," 2) "these inhabitants are implicated through their choices in perpetuating some of the same or similar evils on others who are already victims like themselves," and 3) "they act under extraordinary stress" (Card 1999: 9). Levi's grey zones primarily refer to Kapos, or camp guards that were selected from the population of prisoners. These individuals served the interest of their captors, while in turn receiving favors and pardons. A significantly higher percentage of Kapos survived the camps then did traditional prisoners. What is clear in the case of grey zones is that Kapos are both innocent in that they were victims of unbelievable oppression that they did nothing to deserve, and also implicated in evil they have chosen to perform given the degree of voluntariness in their actions. Here, perhaps we can begin to see the moral paradox of the sexual minority passing for heterosexual. The analogy is even more effective if we consider that individual as living in one of the seven countries[13] that currently has the death penalty for homosexuals. For Card, grey zones are "neither gratuitously nor willfully evil but nevertheless implicate choosers in perpetrating, sustaining, or aggravating evils" (ibid.: 14). In a non-war context, individuals in a moral grey zone for Card would include women who under extreme patriarchy inflict wounds on other women, or closeted gay politicians who vote for anti-gay legislation.

Card wants to be perfectly clear in the ability to still place moral blame on individuals in grey zones. She argues, "we lose innocence in becoming responsible for other's suffering, even when we make the best decision under the circumstances" (Card 1999: 7). Innocence's loss demands responsibility for our

---

13 As of July, 2011.

actions, even when the extraordinary stress pushes us beyond our natural sense of right and wrong. But, this blame is mitigated. Card argues, "the involvements of grey zone inhabitants are not of the same order or extensiveness as that of perpetrators who are not victims" (ibid.: 9).She does seem to want to place the displaced blame somewhere, and does so by condemning oppression. "One of the greatest evils," she says, "threatening victims of oppression is the danger of becoming evil oneself, becoming complicit in evils perpetrated against others" (ibid.: 3-4). The oppression is the evil's instigator, and the locus of its origin.

Moral grey zones, at a considered glance, appear to be a functional analytic tool for an ethics of passing, if a sensitive mitigation of moral responsibility is what we desire. Passing suggests a hostile (oppressive) context, where the damage inflicted on oneself (if it can be argued that passing inflicts damage on the self) and on others, is rendered less severe—in terms of our moral judgment—in light of the compromising circumstances. Systemic pressure on a certain aspect of identity that encourages the individual to forge a new identity that can more easily maneuver (or even survive) within a social context shares this ethical structure. I do not, however, think that this model of ethics under oppression (and therefore as an ethic of passing) captures the full extent of the moral story, nor what should be the full range of intuitions about the moral complexities that arise. Resolving to adjudicate the oppressed subject in light of his/her experience of oppression is not the only ethical option, nor is it the only way that the impact of oppression on the ethical subject has been theorized.

Heroic and Ordinary Virtues

Trvestan Todorov's *Facing the Extreme: Moral Life in the Concentration Camps* explores the impact of oppression on the ethics of individuals under a totalizing system. It does so in the manner of a theorizing historian, taking into consideration memoirs and personal accounts of the ways in which moral lives were shaped under the influence of daily pressures and horrors of life in the Nazi Germany concentration camps. His basic argument is that ordinary virtues, and ordinary vices are amplified to the realm of heroic and monstrous, respectively.

For Todorov, the ordinary virtues are: dignity, caring, and intellectualism. Under extreme oppression, such as the circumstances of the camps, these ordinary virtues become amplified. Dignity, for example, might refer to the acceptance of corporeal punishment or starvation or even death for the sake of protecting oneself against humiliation. Caring might involve the sacrifice of well-being for the comfort of others. The ability to maintain this virtue is one that Todorov argues is "to render oneself especially vulnerable, for in addition to one's own suffering, one takes on that of the people one cares about" (Todorov 1996: 90). Suffering is ample and to maintain caring connections is to leave open to amplified suffering one's emotional self. Where intellectual pursuits are considered valuable under circumstances of ordinary social relationships; under circumstances of oppression (extreme or otherwise) the tenacity to pursue a life of the mind demonstrates its heroic quality. The scholar is just as easily terminated as the most inconsequential prisoner in the camps, but the mind's persistence becomes notable by withstanding the oppressive regime. Here we have a moral analogy to the type of heroics we see in LGBT activists who are currently living in regions where they are facing potential death. Take for example David Kato, the recent martyr/activist of Uganda who was assassinated for being openly gay and seeking equality for his people. His displays of dignity, caring, and intellectualism were all heroic.

The ordinary vices include: fragmentation of behavior (or the disconnection of conduct from conscience), depersonalization, and the enjoyment of power. In any given profession, Todorov argues, professionals are required to accomplish a certain amount of fragmentation from the work that they do. And while he defines this as a "vice" one might readily counter by arguing that this fragmentation is necessary, and when contextualized, and often one of the most virtuous things that professionals can do (think for a moment of a doctor who can—without conscience—cut open another person in a professional capacity, while clearly doing so under any other context would seem appropriately abhorrent). But in the context of extraordinary oppression, or in a scenario of extreme dehumanization, the fragmentation of behavior can be viewed in a light that is truly monstrous. This would include the types of camp roles that Card alludes to: prisoners who are employed to implement torture or death upon their fellow prison-mates. Depersonalization and enjoyment of power (in its insidious manifestations) become the corollaries of the fragmentation of behavior that can result in truly monstrous consequences. Stepping into "professional" responsibilities within a war camp that employ the abilities to depersonalize and enjoy positions of power was evidenced to produce millions of deaths. Here we can imagine an analogy with the closeted despot, or more commonly, the closeted preacher, who condemns to death, or at least eternal damnation of his/her brethren, while likely at the same time enjoying sexual concubinage with one or more members of the same sex.

Clearly in the application of an analogy of Nazi War Camps to ordinary social regimes of social oppression, hegemony, and other structural inequities, we must be careful in too readily assuming the same type of moral corrosion, even in lesser degrees.

But the dual interpretations of the moral life of prisoners: on the one hand as positioned within a moral grey zone where ordinary judgment must be mitigated, and on the other where all moral qualities (both virtues and vices) are amplified presents us with a basic incongruity of how to conceive of the impact of oppressive or hostile circumstances on our moral lives.

What I wish to suggest is that this incongruity does not necessarily force us to choose one model over the other. There might be compatibility if we blend our understanding of moral grey zones and heroic virtues while thinking about the latter as supererogatory, as David Heyd defines the supererogatory.

Heyd argued that an action is supererogatory if and only if all the following four conditions hold: The action is neither obligatory nor forbidden; its omission is not wrong and does not deserve sanction; it is morally good; and it is done voluntarily for the sake of someone else's good (Cudd 1999: 199).

Let us take a look again at Todorov's "ordinary virtues turned heroic" of dignity, caring, and intellectualism. In a moral grey zone, all three virtues (particularly the last one) are beyond what the situation demands. Given that the grey zone presents a scenario where ordinary expectations of human morality is lessened, ordinary virtues are no longer obligatory and their absence no longer wrong. (Therefore, the first two criteria are met). They remain virtues (the third criterion is satisfied) and they must be done voluntarily in accordance with the second virtue primarily for the well-being of others. (Therefore, the final criterion is met).

Why is it valuable to think in terms of ordinary virtues turned supererogatory virtues in moral grey zones? As a result of serious considerations on the varying degrees of genuine social hostility that encourages scenarios of sexual identity passing, the result cannot simply be to reduce moral culpability for passing individuals, nor can the increased cost of ordinary virtues of the openly queer individual under the same degree of oppression be overlooked either. So what the combination of Card and Todorov allows us is a model of ethics under oppression, where we must on the one hand think of moral culpability as somehow mitigated and on the other hand be able to lift up instances of ordinary virtue as supererogatory.

Comments on Harrison's "Power Over The Passing Subject"

Daniel Hurewitz

What are our ethical obligations when living under a system of oppression? That, for me, is a powerful and fascinating question. But to clarify Harrison's assessment of it, I have needed to infuse it (perhaps predictably) with more of the historical and concrete. The place to begin seems to be with a clear definition of "passing" and a sharpened image of actual "passing subjects." Without Harrison to guide me in that, I have conjured several definitions and images in my head. Initially and with little reflection, I considered passing as a widely-practiced, sometimes pleasurable, sometimes anxious, almost-victimless crime—an act of some kind of identity deception. The concrete realities I recalled from my own history were of me passing when I deepened my voice to buy tickets for some movie that I was not actually old enough to attend. I was passing when I mentioned "Christmas presents" in such a way as to let people imagine I celebrated Christmas. And, yes, I was passing when I let all those airplane passengers sitting next to me imagine I was straight.

When I look beyond myself and think more seriously about passing, particularly in a framework of sex and identity, I think historically about all those women who carved lives for themselves more similar to the lives they dreamed of by passing themselves off as men—like the women who fought in the American Revolution as men. Or I think of Billy Tipton, the jazz musician and bandleader. Or I think of some transgender individuals who are trying to find their way to a differently sexed body.

But as I look over my limited array of concrete examples, I realize that I imagine "passing" as a wide-ranging activity taken up by individuals whose oppression and ethical quandaries do not necessarily jibe with the framework Harrison has mapped. From an oppression perspective alone, take the women of the Revolution: while they were clearly oppressed in some of the ways Harrison described and would likely have fought as women if the system of gendered power had not been in place, were they necessarily coming into the revolution from a Fanon-like position of shame and inferiority about their womanhood? That would be much harder to argue. Or take the transgendered individuals who are navigating the terrain of bodily reconstruction to become embodied as the male or female person they feel themselves to be: is there really a system of power that could be removed or eradicated that would then eliminate their desire for transformation?

Not only do these experiences of passing not actually fit Harrison's model, it is not at all clear that these various passing subjects' decisions and actions really demand a new ethical framework. In fact, I suspect that Harrison would concur that despite the broad framing of her argument, these multiple passing subjects are not the ones that worry her. The average passing queer person—and the ubiquitous endless presence of passing in daily and nightly queer life— is not the focus of Harrison's concerns. Despite the fact that the average queer person might experience our lives as lived under a system of colonial oppression such as Fanon described, and despite the fact that we may well need some ethical guidance in such a world, Harrison is not yet constructing an ethics for us.

The individuals whose passing ethics most troubles Harrison, it would seem, are a more narrowly defined group: the James Wests, Ken Mehlmans, and Ted Haggards: the secretly gay people who rise into political or ecclesiastical power on a platform of homophobia. They, Harrison explicitly indicate, are the Kapos of our LGBT people. And it is their presence in our lives that seems to demand an ethical frame: Harrison is inviting us to view their actions through an ethical lens. That seems a valuable goal, and that effort on Harrison's part raises additional fundamental questions.

Central among them is the question of forgiveness. What becomes apparent, with Harrison's borrowed revisions of Fanon, is that the pressure to pass is enormous. As she says, the internal suffering of psychological oppression can be enormous, and therefore, "An attempt to regain the psychological benefits of reciprocity would explain why those of sexually minoritized status … would choose to pass" (see Harrison, this volume). If the impetus to pass is explainable or understandable, then, as long as no harm to others is done, it seems to me it must also be forgivable.

But with Harrison's particular examples, passing has been accompanied by the wielding of power against our own people. And to think about the ethical implications of that behavior, Harrison asks us to think about Jews who acted as Nazi surrogates against other Jews. Clearly, Kapos were not passing as anything than what they were. Nevertheless, Harrison suggests that there is something to learn from them. On the one hand, it seems, we might follow Primo Levi's lead and determine that no judgment can be made against people struggling to survive in the ambiguous moral gray zone of an evil empire. But Harrison implies that we would do better to follow the analysis of Trvestan Todorov and view their actions as truly "monstrous." Levi would let us forgive; but Todorov would have us condemn. And at the end of the day, Harrison remains unwilling "to reduce moral culpability for passing individuals." Maybe "eternal damnation" is not the decree she would issue, but neither, it seems, is forgiveness.

History, of course, does not disagree with Harrison entirely. Many a Kapo—among the few who survived the war—stood trial afterward as war criminals: they were held accountable for their actions and condemned. On the other hand, Ted Haggard, the evangelical minister who finally confessed to his homosexual encounters, was on the cover of the gay magazine, the *Advocate*, last spring under the very headline "Can You Forgive Ted Haggard?" And according to the article, some people are starting to do just that. Similarly, Ken Mehlman, who masterminded the Bush administration efforts to defeat same-sex marriage is now trying to use his skills, talents, and connections to help LGBT causes, and people are slowly accepting his assistance: they are, in a sense, forgiving him.

Why are they forgiving when Harrison seems unwilling? Perhaps because the harms they caused were less specific and less directly fatal than those of the Kapos—though as Harrison rightly reminds me, homophobia really does kill. Perhaps they are being forgiven because they were just one voice among many shouting out the phrases and policies of homophobia, and people are unwilling to hold them alone responsible for that whole edifice. Or perhaps they are being forgiven because enough people are willing to believe that the pressures of an oppressive regime are, for some—just as Harrison suggests—too great to resist.

I can see why we do not forgive the passing gay-basher for the clear harm they do. But perhaps these people are correct, that we should forgive the passing hate-speaker. If Ken Mehlman came to Harrison and apologized and said he was wrong, that he was weak, that he could not resist the pressure to fit in and be a homophobe, but that he was sorry—could Harrison not forgive him? Must he be viewed as monstrous? Should we not have an ethics that forgives the failure to resist the almost irresistible?

I feel like that question matters mostly not for Ken Mehlman's sake. Surely, he is not concerned about Harrison's or my dollop of forgiveness. No, the question matters because of how much the rest of us are engaged in similar small acts of deceit and disempowerment. Despite the implication that Harrison is only interested in the passing preacher or politicians, her assessment of passing still ultimately implicates all of us. And if Harrison does not forgive the Mehlmans, I wonder if she will forgive any of the rest of us.

In Harrison's framework, the hate-speaking Haggards and Mehlmans cannot be the only Kapos. What about the Jodie Fosters or Rosie O'Donnells or Rock Hudsons? They rose to incredible heights of economic, social, and cultural power while promulgating the very heteronormative lessons that replicate heterosexism and drive LGBT individuals into the grip of shame. In this way, they can be viewed as Kapos as well: the price of their ticket to fame was the continuation of a cultural system that kept the rest of us oppressed. Their work at keeping that system alive can be seen as a comparable ethical failing. Do we really wish to condemn them for it, or can we forgive them?

But really, if we view them as moral failures, in truth, have we not all failed along the same moral lines—all of us LGBT folks in the audience, who have laughed and cried and paid for their heteronormative movies and shows? In those moments, we too have supported the cultural systems that celebrate heterosexuality and denigrate us. We have joined them in their work. And no doubt we have failed more regularly than that. Every time we simply do not speak out against the systems of heterosexual power we have helped sustain them: every time we pass into silence we are helping the oppressors remain in power. In our silence, given Harrison's ethical framework, we too have become kapos.

But in our silence, in our frightened passing silence, the condemnation of Harrison's Todorov feels too heavy. I want an ethics that forgives our moral failings, if that is in truth what they are.

There is a brief final thought in Harrison's argument that I find encouraging: it is the suggestion that under a system of oppression an ordinary effort at authenticity is not just valuable, but perhaps heroic. Authenticity, she implies in the last moments, might be viewed morally as above and beyond the call of duty—a supererogatory virtue. To take that view is to suggest that being authentic—not passing—should not be expected of all of us, all of the time: it cannot be. We are not all moral failures for our moments of inauthenticity and hiding. We may lack a certain kind of courage in those moments, but we are also deeply human.

In fact, if Harrison had asked me, prior to reading her contribution, to think of an analogy between passing queers and Jews in Nazi Germany, I would not have considered kapos. Instead, I would have made an analogy to the Jews who, under the early laws, went out without their yellow stars on or their identifying papers. They were truly passing. Some of them passed to find food or necessities and bring them home. Some of them passed to escape. And some of them passed to join a resistance effort. All of them, though, seem incredibly daring and even heroic to me. Their willingness to hide their authentic selves toward some other purpose deserves a rich ethical appreciation.

The limitations of these analogies with the Holocaust highlight for me a final and subsidiary issue in Harrison's argument. Although her piece is aimed at thinking about sexual identity passing, it rests on analytic foundations drawn from studies of race and ethnicity—in particular, thinking about the experiences of blacks and Jews. I find myself wondering if race and ethnicity are really so parallel to sexuality that we can effectively think about passing as white—or more likely, being oppressed for being black—as being the same as passing for straight or being oppressed for being gay. The same questions hold about Jews. Are these really our best analogies?

Perhaps the answer is "Yes," these are the best *analogies*, but they are still only analogies. To develop a theory of sexuality oppression in Ted Haggard's world we likely need to develop an analytic framework that takes us well beyond Fanon's Algeria. Thinking about the policing that Ken Mehlman did as similar to what kapos did gets us close, but not close enough.

We know, from a political perspective, that LGBT activists in the U.S. have encountered a fair bit of resistance when they have described their political goals as "civil rights" or when they have made parallels between, say, the effort to achieve same-sex-marriage equality and the fight over interracial marriage. Those agendas have been perceived by some African-American activists as fundamentally different. And perhaps we should take that to heart, and start to imagine that sexual identity oppression is deeply different than other forms of oppression. To theorize about the shape and meaning of sexuality oppression we need to focus on our particular oppression. We need to begin with the historical and concrete ways that oppression has shaped people's lives, and build from there.

Comments on Hurewitz's "Visiting Our Sins"

Kelby Harrison

It is clear to me that Hurewitz is experiencing a scholarly moral dilemma. His values are conflicting as researcher and investigator with his general decency and emotional sensitivity to those he is interviewing, which means he has found himself caught between two prongs in this dilemma: posthumous justice vs. family secret keeping. It is also clear that Hurewitz did not conceive of the possibility of the second prong in this dilemma and so its existential implications for his sense of himself as morally responsible investigator vs. a social justice driven historian have come into direct conflict. I want to try to untie the knots of this conflict and affirm Hurewitz's scholarly pursuit and show him the way out. I also want to offer some potential reinterpretations of facts he has encountered. I, of course, am only limited to the facts he re-presents here, and so his fuller data means I must admit that his intuition is more thoroughly informed than mine.

After reading his argument, I decided to do a quick google investigation of Daniel Hurewitz, and imagined myself as the recipient of his email late one night inquiring about a deceased family member. I checked Hurewitz's credentials (as I'm guessing anyone in such a position would do). I was pleased to discover he is a faculty member at a reputable institution, with a Ph.D. from a very good institution, that he owns a couple of animals that he clearly adores (giving him good sensitivity points), and that he— indeed—teaches "queer history, and the politics of sexuality" and researches the "emergence of a gay rights movement and the politics of homophobia." Now, even if I were uneducated in the nuances of gender, sexuality, and LGBT history, I could certainly piece together from who Hurewitz is as a history scholar that he is interested in tracking the lives, experiences, and political climates of homosexuals. His publications, indeed, suggest that anything he is researching has a compass somewhere that leads back to the gays. I think it is fairly safe to assume that Jackson Florentine knew this about him.

I also think that children who live in a family that contains secrets—especially ones of this kind of magnitude—know at some level of their psyche, however sublimated, that something is amiss. This may explain Jackson's interest in continued conversation with Hurewitz, Jackson's defensiveness about the conscious stories of his father as loving heterosexual dad and fiscally supportive husband, and even his resentment of his mother for bringing up his father's involvement in the trial so many years ago. Some part of him knows there is a greater truth here that can unravel the fabric of his psychological assumptions of how his family is pieced together which may reveal some truths about his own life and relationships that he does not want to fully face. And this seems to be the very crux of Hurewitz's second prong. By being the instigator of previously un-faced truths he is suddenly responsible for someone else's psychological well-being, however temporarily, however possibly needed, however more authentic and real and "true," and Jackson may not be psychically prepared for this. Hurewitz feels responsible. He wishes to do no harm.

But, Jackson is delicately walking the path with Hurewitz. He certainly could have shut down the conversation, or chosen to ignore Hurewitz and this altogether. Jackson certainly resents his mother. He could have protected his father's memory, and shunned Hurewitz. Hurewitz is not in a position to betray Alan Florentine's memory, his son is in that position. Hurewitz has carefully, graciously, even perhaps pastorally, offered to sketch out that memory more fully, to etch the greater details with better clarity for a son that should want to know the true struggles of his beloved gay dad who was loving to him, his brothers, and his mother.

However, I think the primary restriction to Hurewitz's moral thinking is the limited parameters of the social justice goals of his research. He clearly is invested in bringing the stories of our people into greater relief, excavating the history of secrets of lives that we are now struggling to live open in a more hospitable—yet often still hostile—climate. In the exposing of these lives, we find greater spiritual strength within ourselves. The discovery that we are not alone finds depth and richness within history in the same way that coming into our contemporary communities removes the pangs of isolation so indicative of many of our adolescences. Doing LGBT history provides groundwork for our liberation from the manifold sources of our oppression. The full breadth of that work extends beyond finding the hidden stories that our contemporary souls crave from individuals who, yes, might be rolling over in their graves.

That being said, I have to imagine that Alan Florentine, as Hurewitz calls him, would not wish to have lived the double life Hurewitz (and I) think that he lived. He clearly had enough strength and desire to find a community for his sexual expression. He was victimized at an early age by a legal system that perpetuated extreme injustices on the desiring bodies of gay men, and a social climate that marked those bodies with perpetual shame unless they could find respite in an ideology of family and heterosexuality that seamlessly concealed that shame. I want to acknowledge that Alan's ability to create and sustain heterosexual family speaks to a certain kind of strength, one I'm sure he would have preferred not to have to employ, but I'm also sure was sincere on some level and not quite the "sham" Hurewitz describes it to be. Given that the depth of his shame was always a secret to be revealed just beyond the horizon amplified by his legal case and prison time, the respite he found from his psychic pain surely provided feelings of gratitude and affection for his wife, even if his loins were not encouraging the depth of connection and soul love affliction that we lesbian and gay folks know is only possible with those of our own sex/gender. I have to imagine that Alan would have preferred the resolve of a split life by living openly with Alex Cobb, in his relationship of romance and passion, without separation and other obligations. I have to imagine that Alan would have preferred to have not been arrested and publicly shamed for his youthful sexual explorations. I have to imagine that like most contemporary queer folks, he would have preferred to live a life advocating the pride he feels for himself and his love connections. He would have wanted to be an out and proud "constitutional homosexual," and to have his children— should he have chosen that family composition—love him as such.

Hurewitz begins his argument with thoughts about the inherent betrayal of journalism, and history as a protracted form of journalism. I do not believe Hurewitz has betrayed the spirit or the soul of Alan Florentine. In the former's writing, Florentine can live the life he was not free to live while alive. We— contemporary queers—can be granted greater insight into the difficult choices we have been forced to make under difficult circumstances. We can see the greater legacy and depth of our oppressions and struggles through his cultural and legal victimization. But, I do not think this is Hurewitz's concern. I think he is mostly concerned about betraying a son who was the innocent victim of the ideological crime of passing and a set of deceits that buttressed that crime. But, I want to contend that while Jackson may have been the innocent victim in his childhood, if he remains fearful of his father's homosexuality and the truth of his passions, if he feels disgust at the idea that his father could have been in love with men, had sex with men, fantasized about men perhaps even during the sexual encounter with his mother that made for his conception, then Jackson becomes a perpetuator of these ideological crimes making victims of others. Familial homophobia is a nasty, nasty moral beast, as all queer folks can attest. Familial homophobia is the kind of systemic oppression, shunning, and rejection that the ideology of "family values" as necessarily heterosexual perpetuates. Those to whom we are most deeply vulnerable perpetuate it: our parents, siblings, grandparents, children, nieces, nephews, etc. It is not so subtle implications are that straight people are more important than LGB/Q people, straight people are real members of a family/ real participants on the family tree, LGB/Q people are its dead-ends and its dark secrets. Familial homophobia is gravely immoral, it is a death-dealing ideology (how many LGBTQ folks commit suicide after rejection from their families?) And the conclusions of familial homophobia are simply not true. LGBTQ people are equally important as their straight counterparts. LGBTQ people are important participants in a family tree whether they produce biological offspring or not. LGBTQ people extend families in important ways. Alex Cobb and his children are part of a family that could not be part of the Florentine family in any other way. But the deep cultural roots of familial homophobia are so extensive, rhizomatic even, that we cannot see it fully. Queer folks help perpetuate it. Even Hurewitz seems loathe to really expose familial homophobia for what it is in this Florentine family.

While I contend that Hurewitz may have an interpersonal moral obligation to respect a boundary and not to tell an adult child facts about a deceased parent he or she has expressly or in this case implicitly requested not to know, Hurewitz certainly does not have a moral obligation to hide this information from the world to protect that adult child. Jackson Florentine is aware that his father was involved in a court trial and did jail time. He knew this before Hurewitz talked to him and never pursued more information. Presumably he was always free to do the research that Hurewitz did to find out details. Now there is an even easier method for him to find out this information, he can simply read Hurewitz's argument in this anthology and know the true details of the miscarriage of justice his father suffered. He has good reason to want to see what Hurewitz writes: loving curiousity towards his father's life. He might have personal reasons of self-care not to read what was written: protecting his father's memory and the rosy perfected image of a childhood completely shrouded in heteronormativity. But, if he reads the argument, I hope that all can agree that he has a moral obligation to accept the fuller image of his father—one that includes same-sex desire, sexuality, and romance—without letting that fuller image tarnish his love for the man who raised him. He has a moral obligation to his father to provide this continued affection and accept his gay dad; this moral obligation has political and social implications for the social justice plight of all our people. Jackson Florentine is the son of a gay man. That is a wonderful thing to be.

My final set of comments for Hurewitz are about how he interprets the case facts he reveals in his argument about Alex Cobb. Hurewitz determines that his murder was either the result of violent homophobia, or a "classic gay panic attack." But what seems incongruent with this version of his crime is the life-long relationship that Alex engages with Alan. Perhaps the violent homophobe was the man who was murdered. Alex and his gay sailor buddy are drinking at a bar, they meet a third, and they all go to a parking lot for sexual activity. I find it hard to believe that two guys could be "lured" into a gay panic attack, but certainly two men who were in cahoots with one another about their secret sexual life could gang up on a third man who either threatened them physically and/or threatened their military careers through exposure of that secret. Either way, it is a situation of self-protection, and a psychology that would congeal with the psychology of a man who would help protect another gay man in prison and then support him in a life of constructed of deceits to protect that secret. I'm not saying that this makes Alex Cobb a gay hero, but it certainly seems to be more explanatory than a "violent homophobe who has a classic gay panic" and then chooses to love another man for life in secret. I would think the violent homophobe or the man who experienced a gay panic would have chosen to live a life more like the 18-year-old from the original case.

A Response to Harrison

Daniel Hurewitz

Kelby Harrison's comments point to one of my questions for Jackson Florentine that remained unasked, namely, "Could you *really* not know who I am?" Certainly in this day of Google and Facebook, finding out the basic details of people's lives is becoming increasingly easy. But even more, as she notes, I have written and published and taught about LGBT history for several years now: I have explicitly put my thinking about sexuality into the public domain. And so she is right, finding out about me and my interest in the LGBT past is no great challenge.

When I spoke with Jackson Florentine, he said that he *had* googled me—which I thought, for sure would have resolved any mystery about my interests in his father and also relieved me of the burden of having to come out. But instead, what he said his googling led him to imagine was that I was interested in how a fellow from Mississippi ended up in a trial on the West coast and how those multi-state politics played out. I certainly did not understand his thinking, but I also, as in so many other things, did not try to correct him.

What Harrison's comments underscore is the possibility that Jackson knows that there is a secret—and a secret which he could know more fully—but which he is deliberately avoiding examining. As she suggests, "Some part of him knows there is a greater truth here that can unravel the fabric of his psychological assumptions of how his family is pieced together which may reveal some truths about his own life and relationships that he doesn't want to fully face" (see Harrison, this volume). And as she also make clear, he did not opt *not* to communicate with me. While he strikes me as a gregarious fellow who enjoys social interactions—and has spent some part of his life performing—it is also true that if I represented a threat that he really did not want to investigate, he need not have written me back or spoken to me on the phone.

In truth, after I discovered Florentine's son and began to imagine that the convicted men in my case probably had more sexually complex lives than I had previously thought, I began to look for other children. And one that I found had just the response that you are suggesting. He did not write back to me and, once I found his phone number, he did not return my calls. When I made one last-ditch call to his home, he actually answered the phone but then quite curtly stated that he had some inkling of the case I was researching and saw no benefit in discussing it with me. Why would he want to sully the memory of his father and his children's grandfather? And with just such a sense of protecting his father's legacy, he hung up.

Jackson, by contrast, stayed connected to me, stayed willing to hear what I might say. But he did not force my hand and I felt unable to force his. Even though I had a different, and ultimately, moving and compelling portrait of his father to offer him, I could not make him hear it.

In my deference to him, Harrison implies, I deferred to his homophobia, to the "gravely immoral" scourge of familial homophobia. While there is much that is true about me in that accusation, what I cannot say is that Jackson Florentine is homophobic. Even when we spoke on the phone, I did not engage him in any dialog about homosexuality. He said to me, at the end of our conversation, that there was nothing "that I wouldn't want to know." That even if his father "was some terrible person," he, Jackson, was ready to forgive him, given what a wonderful father he had been. it is quite possible that accepting his father's homosexuality would not be a devastating challenge for Jackson Florentine, that he would indeed embrace his father's complicated history. But as we spoke that day, I could not bring myself to test that theory.

I value very much Harrison's re-reading of Alex Cobb. In her re-writing, his claims of self-defense emerge as potentially true, and that in turn makes him appear as a more honorable character than I have cast him thus far.

In a similar vein, I can also imagine re-stating my articulation of Cobb and Florentine as "gay" men. That is, in truth, how I have related to them—as gay men trapped in a world that forced them into prison and then into marriages that, in all likelihood, they did not want. You have suggested that Florentine likely found "affection" in his marriage, and I am confident that is true. What I also wonder, however, is if it is possible to imagine Florentine choosing that marriage—choosing it with real desire and passion—just as much as he chose his relationship with Cobb. Which is to say, is it possible to envision Florentine having a more robust sexuality than simply one defined as either gay or straight? Perhaps he wanted—and had—sexual and romantic relationships with both his wife and Cobb. Given the evidence so far, it is hard for me to know. But what's also clear is that Florentine made different decisions and choices about his sexual life than Erickson, the hairdresser did. Erickson, after his release from prison, opted fully for "the San Francisco lifestyle," and as far as I know, neither married nor had children: he lived a gay-identified life.

Jackson and Cobb, confronted with similar circumstances, made different choices. They did not choose a gay-identified life. No doubt that was a hard choice for Erickson to make, but it was a possibility that Jackson and Cobb did not pursue. Is it not possible, though, that their choices could also be valorized as something more than "secret gays" or "gays with shame"—or, to use the language of Harrison's own argument, as gay men who were passing as straight. Rather than imagining that Florentine "would have preferred the resolve of a split life by living openly with Alex Cobb," as you put it, I wonder if we can imagine that Florentine and Cobb felt like they had it all: a female wife and lover, a home, children, and a male lover. For them, perhaps, that was an ideal package. In a way, rather than opting for Erickson's gay life, they opted for something much more queer. And while they no doubt would have shunned that term, perhaps that is appropriate for them. Or, at the very least, it is significant to note how much they did and did not construct their domestic lives around a singular notion of appropriate sexual activity. Their homosexual activity did not define the shape of their lives: it was a piece, but not *the* piece that explained them.

A Response to Hurewitz

Kelby Harrison

Is passing a victim-less crime? I have been the "victim" of my previous lovers' passing. I have been the "victim" of the subtle—yet ferocious—judgment of closeted individuals with professional power over me. My soul has been a "victim" of my own passing—not always, not in the little moments: at a register, or on a plane—but in the bigger moments, in a new learning environment, religious environment, or women's sports team. Which means I have suffered real emotional, financial and practical harms because of passing. But, I still dream of traveling to places where my female embodiment would make me feel vulnerable and to travel passing as a man. I dream of a world in which I do not have to ever come out again, but just remain perpetually seen as queer. Just because we can understand the cultural and social pressures that make passing an easy or even the only option does not mean that we should ignore the price we all pay for this loss of authentic voice and presence in the world.

Some definitions to clean up: I do not understand transgendered folks as passing in the way I have discussed in my argument; except for when they pass as cissexual. Gender passing in history—like in war, or in jazz—also seems to me to be a different kind of phenomenon: more pleasurable, rarer, and harder.

Yes, in my argument, I do not construct an ethics for the average queer person who passes often in ordinary life. Even though I am concerned about the Ted Haggards and Eddie Longs of the world—those condemnations are so easy to declare; I am more concerned with the vast majority of us queer folks who have accumulated ordinary positions of power and trust in our lives, and the necessary betrayals and social violence attached to our passing. But this is not a matter of condemnation vs. forgiveness. Instead, this is a matter of naming for the sake of accountability, sketching the fuller and very complicated ethical picture, and beginning to show the way towards greater queer fidelity and political community.

A note on forgiveness. I was recently at a talk in which the stunning theologian Monica Coleman spoke on forgiveness. Her words moved my spirit. And without engaging the complex ethical question of forgiveness in scholarly depth, her words gave my ethical intuition air through which to breathe. We do not forgive for the sake of the other person; we forgive for ourselves. Forgiveness is a *self*-ish act, it is about our own well-being. Do I forgive all those who have passed, will pass, will harm me in their passing, will harm my queer brothers and sisters? Yes, because I want to sleep at night, and I cannot spend my days practicing Karate to get all the anger out in a healthy way. But, forgiveness does not necessarily lead to reconciliation, nor should it. One should always figure out how to forgive, but if the relationship is not psychically or emotionally safe, one should not re-enter the relationship. Has the queer community reconciled with Ricky Martin? Ellen Degeneres? Jodie Foster? Yes. These people are lovely and we are reconciled. And in the case of Jodie Foster, very lovely. Should we continue to hold them *accountable* for the grace of the closet through which they rose to fame? Yes. Should we maybe ask more of them in terms of their contributions to our community now given the way they gained access to their resources? Yes. Should we repeat those stories as we compare them to the relative ease with which, for example, Lady Gaga has been able to be openly bisexual? Yes. Should we use these stories to ask for more acceptance and inclusion of our young folk for the sake of protecting their authenticity without requiring the sacrifice of their jobs? Yes. This is not a matter of forgiveness; it is a matter of storytelling, remembering our history, and holding individuals accountable.

I do not think the queer community should reconcile with Ted Haggard, or with Eddie Long until they evidence they are safe. But there remains a significant additional problem with this type of passer. Haggard and Long were caught! What do we do when they have not been caught, but are still causing damage? In a sense all of the individuals you have mentioned in your comments may only have one failing in common—they were not very good at passing, because we all know that they passed.

I appreciate your observation that the analogies fail between race, ethnicity and sexuality. We need our own phenomenological accounts of queer embodiment under oppression—lyrical and intellectual. We cannot ignore the lineage and relationships between subaltern identities and the way we pay prices across a continuum that are similar. I also think that the phenomenon of passing across identities is just as ethically interesting, especially when we start to think about the ethical requirements of identity, as when we think about the ethical responsibilities within sexual identities. In your heroic description of Jews who would pass in Nazi Germany in the early years of its regime, to accomplish ordinary life tasks, I must immediately rebut that their ability to hide their authentic selves may be impressive, but they had homes of Jewish kin to support and renew their authentic identities and religious commitments. Passing queer folk so rarely ever return to a space outside of heteronormativity without working very hard at cultivating those spaces. Let us continue to work together to name these differences—especially across our intergenerational lines.

In all this talk about passing, forgiveness, and condemnation, I want to close by making it perfectly clear that I understand Hurewitz's decision not to disclose the queerness in his research project that we have been discussing in this volume. There is nothing in that for me to condemn or forgive, there are only decision and interpretations I can challenge or re-interpret—and hopefully perhaps strengthen him in his commendable and inspiring out-ness and social commitments to our community in his scholarship.

References

Bartky, S.L. 1990. *Femininity and Domination: Studies in the Phenomenology of Oppression*. New York: Routledge.

Bordo, S. 1989. The body and the reproduction of femininity, in *Gender, Body, Knowledge*, edited by A. Jaggar and S. Bordo. New Brunswick: Rutgers University Press, 13-33.

Butler, J. 1990. *Gender Trouble*. New York: Routledge.

Card, C. 1999. Groping through gray zones, in *On Feminist Ethics and Politics*, edited by C. Card. Lawrence, KS: University Press of Kansas, 3-26.

Cudd, A. 2006. *Analyzing Oppression*. Oxford: Oxford University Press.

Deveaux, M. 1994. Feminism and empowerment: A critical reading of Foucault. Feminist Studies, 20(2), 223-47.

Fanon, F. 1967. *Black Skin, White Masks*. New York: Grove Press.

Foucault, M. 1985. *The History of Sexuality*, translated by R. Hurley. New York: Vintage Books.

Kitzinger, C.1994. Problematizing pleasure: Radical feminist deconstructions of sexuality and power, in *Power/Gender*, edited by L. Radtke. Newbury Park: Sage, 194-209.

Mackinnon, C. 1982. Feminism, Marxism, method and the state: An agenda for theory, *Signs*, 7(3), 515-44.

Mackinnon, C. 1983. Feminism, Marxism, method and the state: Toward feminist jurisprudence, *Signs*, 8(4), 635-58.

Mackinnon, C. 1988. Desire and power: A feminist perspective, in *Marxism and the Interpretation of Culture*, edited by C. Nelson. Urbana, IL: University of Illinois Press, 105-16.

Mackinnon, C. 1989. *Toward a Feminist Theory of the State*. Cambridge, MA: Harvard University Press.

Malcolm, J. 1990. *The Journalist and the Murderer*. New York: Knopf.

Rupp, L.J. 2002. *A Desired Past: A Short History of Same-Sex Love in America*. Chicago, IL: University of Chicago Press.

Todorov, T. 1996. *Facing the Extreme*. New York: Henry Holt & Company.

Chapter 4

Cross-Generational Risks of Ascribing and Employing "Queer," "Gay and Lesbian" or even "Straight"

Janna Jackson Kellinger and Rob Cover

Introduction

Janna Jackson Kellinger and Rob Cover discuss different tactics, risks, and available scripts of coming out as queer, lesbian and gay, or passing as straight. Both note a generational gap in preference for using "queer," and disagree with each other on the value of using scripted binaries of sexuality. Kellinger celebrates the liberative acts of teachers coming out as lesbian or gay, exploring nuance of self-ascription. Cover questions the binary of coming-out vs. passing in light of the value the literature on LGBTQ suicide has placed on an either/or choice between the two. He argues for using methods of queer theory to rupture the binary of sexual identity disclosure.

Unmasking Identities Revisited

Janna Jackson Kellinger

In 2007, I published a book titled *Unmasking Identities: An Exploration of the Lives of Gay and Lesbian Teachers* describing findings from a qualitative study conducted with nine participants who self-identified as gay and lesbian teachers. At the time, I did not give much thought to the title until, during a book talk to a group of undergraduate and graduate students, one of the audience members asked why I used "gay and lesbian" in the title instead of "queer" and another one piped up saying he was wondering the same thing. I was familiar enough with the literature to understand that using "gay and lesbian" implied that identities are fixed and stable, not shifting and fluid as queer theory argues and to conjure up an answer that was at least satisfactory on the surface—as a researcher, I was presenting participants' emic perspectives since all but one explicitly preferred the phrase "gay and lesbian" over "queer."

I was confident in this response as I had not only asked my participants what terms they preferred, but also what they thought of the term queer. Writing about their responses in a subsequent article which argued that, while nearly all identified as "gay and lesbian" teachers, their teaching practices reflected queer pedagogy, I reflected on their responses:

> Most participants in this study made clear they did not consider themselves queer. The primary reason for disliking the term was because of its association with childhood insults ...

> Interestingly, the two youngest participants did not state this as a concern for them. Another participant pointed out a probable reason: "Maybe that's why they embrace *queer,* because *queer* wasn't a putdown when they were growing up" (Tony). This lends support to Morris' (2005) statement that "queer ... signals a generational divide" (10). By and large, most participants had difficulty getting past *queer* as an insult. (Jackson 2009: 55-6)

Participants did acknowledge political dimensions of the term queer, but this was part of why they rejected the word: "I'm not going to do a political reclaiming the word thing. I don't mind people doing that. People say 'the queer community,' that does not sound to me empowering. It sounds like you're trying to reclaim a word deliberately. In other words, that sounds a little hollow to me" (Duncan). Instead, most participants chose "gay" because of its supposed "neutrality": "*Queer* is a negative word. *Gay* has no negative connotations" (Glen) and ease of use: "I use *gay* because it's easier to say" (Glen). Almost across the board, participants in this study rejected the word "queer."

However, claiming a "gay" identity does have its risks. Defining sexual orientation is problematic as everyone comes to his or her own understandings. Positing sexual orientation as a dichotomy "disguises widely varying individual experiences." Marilyn Cochran-Smith points out the dangers of dichotomizing:

> Many dichotomies are based on the mistaken assumption that the only alternative to a particular idea, concept, or position is its opposite or its absence. Although dichotomies are often rhetorically affective, they are rarely useful for sorting out complex issues. Instead they tend to reduce important differences to mere caricatures while obscuring equally important similarities and nuances. (2003: 275)

Not only do categories obscure differences, they also ascribe boundaries.As Bohan and Russell explain, "the very notion that one can or should define identity in terms of sexual or affectional preferences causes people indeed to understand themselves in that way" (1999: 18). Scholars argue language structures existence.

Depicting identities as fixed can also serve to re-inscribe "compulsory heterosexuality": "this may, in turn, lead heterosexual people to feel safer in their own identity; as long as the categories are distinct and the identity stable across time, they need not be concerned that their own identity might somehow transform into a non-heterosexual one" (Bohan and Russell 1999: 23). Glorianne Leck further describes the advantages of breaking free from binary thinking:

> As a society, we have set up heterosexuality and homosexuality as the two primary categories available for our understandings of sexual orientation. Thinking in such binaries appears to have limited our understanding of how identity, and, in particular, sexual identity, derives its complexities from within diverse social and cultural settings. Moving ourselves out of the limitations of working exclusively with binary frameworks will permit us to move out of our monocultural assumptions. (2000: 324)

Leck points out another risk of fixing one's identity, that of ignoring other possible constructions. Halperin deconstructs the notion that homosexuality is a fixed category of identity by making comparisons across time and cultures:

> Does the "paederast," the classical Greek adult, married male who periodically enjoys sexually penetrating a male adolescent share *the same sexuality* with the "berdache," the Native American (Indian) adult male who from childhood has taken on many aspects of a woman and is regularly penetrated by the adult male to whom he has been married in a public and socially sanctioned ceremony? Does the latter share *the same sexuality* with the New Guinea tribesman and warrior who from the ages of eight to fifteen has been orally inseminated on a daily basis by older youths and who, after years of orally inseminating his juniors, will be married to an adult woman and have children of his own? Does any of these three persons share *the same sexuality* with the modern homosexual? (1989: 46)

Sedgwick concurs, pointing out the arbitrariness of defining oneself by the gender to which one is attracted:

> Of the very many dimensions along which the genital activity of one person can be differentiated from that of another ... precisely one, the gender of object choice, emerged from the turn of the century, and has remained, as *the* dimension denoted by the now ubiquitous category of "sexual orientation". (1990: 8)

Almaguer used a modern comparison of cultures to demonstrate this arbitrariness by explaining that the European American sexual system "rests on the sexual object choice one makes—i.e. the biological sex of the person toward whom sexual activity is directed" whereas "the Mexican/Latin-American sexual system ... confers meaning to homosexual practices according to sexual aim—i.e., the act one wants to perform with another person (of either biological sex)" (1991: 77). These theorists destabilized the homosexual/heterosexual binary by showing that homosexuality is neither universal nor uniform across time and cultures.

Nevertheless, several participants in this study described being gay as a core part of themselves: "I look back and go, 'Well, I was a lesbian all my life.'"

(Summer). Interestingly, they did the same with being a teacher: "I always thought that I was naturally born to be a teacher and knew that that was going to happen. So I don't say that as a career statement like, 'I have a job as a teacher.' I think of it more as an identity, as a part of my being is to be a teacher" (Duncan). Duncan also described becoming a teacher as coming into his "natural self." Although Deborah Britzman claims assertions of being born into teaching and of being a "natural teacher" are cultural myths, nonetheless, these participants presented coming into teaching as part of their core selves (1990: 188). This suggests that the need to view one's current self as a discovery of a true self may be present in aspects outside of sexual identity.

In the article about gay teachers teaching queerly, I also wrote about the one participant who used the term "queer" to define herself. Leigh, the youngest of all the participants, had the most nuanced and accepting view of the term *queer*, defining it as "a flexible way of looking at sexuality":

> In the queer world…there's more kind of room for personal identification and it feels more inclusive. Maybe you're not lesbian, you're not gay. Maybe you're sort of like a straight girl or whatever but you, like, really like queer people or you're into that culture or you're, like, bisexual. There's more flexibility.

Leigh also had the most fluid definition of her own sexuality. As opposed to the other participants, who clearly placed themselves as gay or lesbian, Leigh *code-switched*, a term often used to mean alternating language use, but here used to mean identifying differently depending on the social context:

> It depends on the social dynamics in the group. Like, if I were in a group of straight people, I would identify as a lesbian. But then in a group of queer people, then there's a little bit more room for variation. The lines aren't as clearly drawn sometimes, at least with the people I associate with, like, trans friends, and I have super dykey friends, and then there are sort of femmy friends. In that sort of social situation, I'm much more comfortable with the nuances involved. But like at work, for instance, I definitely don't identify as much with my straight colleagues, you know? And I feel like I can be set apart because of my sexual identity.

Leigh went on to state that she uses the term *lesbian* to, as she said, "dumb it down" for straight people because she does not want to have to explain her usage of any other terms (Jackson 2007: 58).

Certainly, other research attests to younger generations embracing more fluid notions of gender and sexual identities, as Driver found in her online research a plethora of self-definitions: "In the middle of fem and butch," "A tom boy with a princess stuck inside of me," "andro," "fem-androgynous," "in-between," "boi," and 'birl' (2007: 41-2). Experiences in my own life also attest to an increase in playing with language as more than one male friend has been referred to as a "lesbian" in my younger social circles.

Reflecting on this notion of fixed versus fluid identities in terms of this particular research project brings up questions about how these perspectives on identities affect the coming out process. The notion of a core identity suggests that participants would either be in or out of the closet with a one-time revelation of their "true self" whereas a "queer" identity would suggest that participants might use their own shifting identities to challenge students' notions of identity. Reviewing the data, however, reveals that "fixed versus fluid" does not capture the complexities of self-definitions nor does it prescribe how participants share their identities with others.

Unmasking Identities argued for a more nuanced understanding of the closet by citing other scholars who did the same (2007: 9). For example, Epstein and Johnson discuss how teachers assess the risks and possible effects of being open about their sexual orientation based on a variety of situational factors numerous times during a workday (1994: 199) and Pat Griffin describes coming out as a continuum ranging from "passing" (explicit lying) to "covering" (lying by omission) to being in a "glass closet" (displaying symbols that indicate gayness) to being "out" (talking openly about being gay) (1992: 176-9). Despite my intentions, however, many participants described themselves as either being in or out of the closet.

Several factors could play into this either/or dichotomy. It could be because of the context of teaching. All participants described being out as being out to their students and, as students are apt to talk to other students: "[once] you let it out, you can't ever bring it back in ... you kind of just go off the cliff and you can't go back" (Carolyn). It could be because of the monumental shift out participants experienced: "When I came out, something else emerged ... Something inflated. Something got bigger. The fog lifted somewhere in there" (Duncan) or the shift from being teacher-centered to being student-centered they experienced prior to disclosing their "gay" identity which involved "getting over wanting everyone to like you" (Carolyn). This shift led some participants to describe their teaching in stages: "A lot of people think about their first year of teaching and then their next couple of years and then their veteran years. And I, it's funny, because I combine that first year and a half as my pre-coming out ... [which] seems a whole different part of my teaching career" (Glen). Certainly, there is no denying that being honest with students about how one regards oneself changes the dynamic in the classroom and participants provided plenty of concrete evidence that attested to this.

However, what I want to focus on and play with in this chapter is the idea that part of this "in or out" depiction may also reside in a need to narrate one's life as a coherent story:

> This metaphor of discovery makes sense of what is otherwise often experienced
> as a terribly confusing and painful sense of ill fit in the world ... The provision
> of a label for oneself and one's feelings brings closure to the identity confusion

that almost surely follows upon the awareness of feelings that are condemned by society. As a part of the process of coming to terms with this identity, the essentialist understanding of identity as permanent also provides a basis for a new self-narrative, for rereading the past as having contained the seeds of this identity, perhaps throughout one's lifetime. This reconstruction of identity as always having been gay or lesbian or bisexual lends a sense of continuity to one's personal history and a sense of integrity to one's current life. (Bohan and Russell 1999: 22)

Using labels to describe oneself and/or one's stage in life has advantages and disadvantages: "We are subjected to social categories in the sense that we are reduced by them (subjected to them) and we are subjected by, or made intelligible through, those categories (made into a subject)" (Evans 2002: 22). Just as individuals use labels to categorize and understand their own lives, labels can be used to explain life experiences to others in ways to make social and political advances: "Identity politics emerges out of the struggles of oppressed or exploited groups to have a standpoint on which to critique dominant structures, a position that gives purpose and meaning to struggle" (Hooks 1994: 88). However, these labels can also obscure the variety and flexibility of individual experiences. Thus, categories can be used as temporary scaffolding—both by individuals and by the collective—to deepen understanding which then can be challenged, questioned, and even abandoned in order to lead to further understanding.

In the case of the participants in this particular study, self-perception was used as a means of self-preservation: This was done in many different ways to reinforce the closet: from believing that being open about one's sexuality would inevitably lead to rejection and/or backlash to believing that people would only see them as gay. Some participants feared that this would then prevent students from learning in their classrooms: "if he knew I was the gay teacher he would immediately shut me off and want nothing to do with my classroom" (Patrick). Stories in the news, such as the straight teacher fired for teaching a novel with a gay main character, helped strengthen these beliefs.

These fears led all participants to initially hide their gayness upon entering the classroom.

Reality, however, countered participants' imaginations:

Reflecting back on closeted years, participants described these fears as stemming from their own minds. Carolyn realized "a lot of the discomfort around being out was my own fear of what might happen." Similarly, Duncan attributed his fear to internal machinations: "I would invent fear. I would invent a negative expectation." Duncan explained, though, he did not fantasize these fears. They were based in reality: "I created fears based on things I knew to be true. They just weren't true for me". (Jackson, 2007: 69-70)

Even though some participants claimed "invented fears" held them back, there were real consequences to their actions. However, how participants described these incidents is very telling:

> Ironically, some of these participants who reported a lack of backlash actually did recount individual negative incidents. For example, both Duncan and Summer had parents pull students from their classes. Summer had a student who made a death threat and her car window was smashed. Instead of allowing these incidents to scare them back into the closet or out of teaching, these participants downplayed the seriousness of the backlash. For example, Duncan verbally dismissed his principal's negative reaction: "My principal telling me that coming out to my students was inappropriate. It wasn't professional. I wasn't teaching when I did that. And so those were blips to me. And now they're not even blips. They're little rocks or something." Participants may have reported a lack of backlash yet described negative incidents because participants viewed these incidents as isolated, and therefore not as collective backlash. Perhaps the benefits of being out far outweighed individual negative reactions. Perhaps they were "willing to accept whatever bad things might happen," as Carolyn stated. Whatever the reason, it is clear that none of these openly gay participants regretted their decisions to come out at school. (2007: 69-70)

This lack of significance attached to these negative repercussions could be the decaying of importance over time or could stem from a need to focus on the positive outcomes of coming out. In homophobic atmospheres, the act of "coming out" is an irreversible decision that comes with an accompanying need to justify it.

Although most participants did describe coming out—to themselves ("it was like a bolt of lightning" [Lauren]) and at school ("you are my last closet" [Duncan])—as a one-shot deal, many acknowledged that there were other "layer[s]" of being out. Initially after coming out participants still monitored their actions as they felt the need to counter stereotypes:

> When I first came out it was so important that I be the poster child and not the stereotypical poster child. And so it was so important that when there was a faculty softball game, that I was good. It was so important that I won the faculty free throw competition [because] I was gay. That it was really important to me still to not perpetuate the stereotypes. (Glen)

However, participants soon realized that a better way to challenge stereotypes was to present all of themselves: "I [am] ... not just the gay teacher who lived in the outback and jumps out of airplanes but I can also be the one who likes Broadway show tunes and has dinner parties" (Glen).

In addition to how they presented themselves, how others described them also added an additional layer to their being out:

> It wasn't just me drinking my coffee. My partner was drinking the coffee, too.

> Then this other kid goes, "Was your partner addicted?" All of a sudden they were having this whole conversation about my partner and it was just totally normal. It was just so wonderful. And it was not like people were worried about saying partner or asking me about my partner. It was just like asking Mr. Bridle about his wife. And you have these kinds of experiences and you realize … there are probably a vast majority that are ok with it, especially at this juncture.

Although participants considered coming out to students the definitive act of coming out, they described it as an ongoing process.

As described in an article about "naturally queer" moments in classroom teaching, participants did use their identities to challenge assumptions made by their students, as exemplified in this one example:

> During an activity when students created symbols to represent themselves, Summer asked them what symbol they thought she would include. When students guessed that she would use a pink triangle to symbolize her lesbian identity, she challenged their thinking by saying that she would use the female symbol, because being female is more important to her. By making students' assumptions explicit, these participants were able to create spaces in their classrooms where queerness could naturally flow as part of the classroom conversation instead of being forced. (Jackson 2010: 44)

Participants did not view themselves just as "gay or lesbian" teachers, nor did they view that identity as primary, instead they played with their identities to present themselves in certain ways and to challenge others' representations.

Despite using language that describes their identities as core and being either in or out of the closet, a closer look suggests that these might be short-hand ways of describing themselves and their actions, but that participants held much more nuanced understandings of their lives, the stories they tell themselves, and the stories told about them. All of this, however, is filtered through my words and my choices of their words. In order to fit the proscribed length of this chapter, I have chosen exemplars to serve as evidence for my points, often claiming that "most participants" or "some participants" believed or did certain things while only using a selected quote from one or two leaving it up to the reader to trust (or question) my assertions. All of this leads back to my initial dilemma—who has the right to claim an identity? Would I be putting words into the mouths of participants in this study if I called them "queer" teachers? Or, by putting their own words into their mouths, am I erasing their more complex understandings of themselves?

Identity and Passing Critical Essays: Queer Youth, Risk and the Passing/ Coming Out Dichotomy

Rob Cover

A cultural injunction that queer youth self-declare their sexual non-normativity, or "come out," is widespread in popular culture, media, film, self-help books and queer community rhetoric. Often, this narrative structure depicts "passing" or "remaining closeted" as an obstacle to be overcome, with self-declaration a positive outcome and a resolution. Such structuration of passing and coming out is also a significant assumption in much research on queer youth suicide. In sociological and psychiatric/psychology literature on queer youth suicide, both passing (or closetedness) and coming out (or self-declaration of non-normative sexuality to significant others) have been depicted through discourses of risk and resilience. Coming out is understood as an act of de-victimization and an opportunity to build resilience while passing is, frequently but not universally, presented as a risk factor for suicidality, an added pressure on queer youth, and a stressor leading to suicide ideation. What literature on queer youth suicide lacks, however, is a queer theoretical framework through which to problematize the underlying assumptions around coming out and passing that include notions of identity, disclosure, honesty, risk and vulnerability (Cover 2005: 76-98).

I begin by presenting an overview of the competing ways in which coming out and passing have been represented in queer youth suicide research through discourses of risk. This will be followed by an argument for re-considering the ways in which passing is figured in terms of queer youth suicide by deploying queer theory as a means of problematizing passing beyond the binaries and dichotomies of private/public, inner/outer and closeted/outness.

Queer Youth Suicide and the Risk Discourse of Passing/Out

The idea of "coming out" or revealing one's non-normative sexuality is, in contemporary western culture, an expectation from every lesbian, gay man, or bisexual. Coming out is part of a narrative of queer self-hood governed by social practices that have become widely incorporated into the mythos around non-heterosexual experience (Saxey 2008: 2, 41). The conventions of coming out emerge in the recent history of queer sexual cultures and were originally motivated conjointly by the political and the personal. The rise of the Gay Liberation movement during the early 1970s in the United States, United Kingdom and Europe, saw the coming out story become a communicative form operating within a political and communitarian framework. In his *Homosexual Oppression and Liberation*, Dennis Altman suggests that to come out meant defying the most basic and deep-seated norms of a society that sees itself as based exclusively on the heterosexual family structure (1971: 27). He also described it as essential for those practicing non-heteronormative sexualities to come out as "gay" in order to facilitate the development of a sense of community (ibid.: 141), for the sake not only of the political benefits of numbers, but for the personal gains made by being a recognizable part of a community. As the rhetoric once suggested, "out of the closets, into the streets" (ibid.: 237). Although the Gay Liberation movement and its related discourses of anti-establishment, radical activism and opposition to heteronormative institutions and models lost dominance within queer culture from the mid-1980s adoption of a lesbian/gay civil rights political model that refrained from seeking to critique or undo heterosexuality, the unquestioned individual and political compulsion to "come out" has remained within queer discourse as a particular formation for coherent selfhood, social participation and belonging.

Academic, policy and public discussion on queer youth suicide has had a multiplicitous relationship with the ideas of both coming out and of passing, arguing at times both for and against passing; likewise both for and against pressures to come out. Coming out has been a major element in much research and writing on queer-specific suicide, with frequent discussion of either the benefits of coming out or the debilitating risks understood to be related to longer-term "passing" or "closetedness." It has often been assumed in such work that the distinction between passing and coming out is a discrete one (rather than the reality of blurredness and the need to repeat the coming out process to many others throughout the course of life). At the same time, and often following earlier queer writing that promotes outness, coming out is usually presented as wholly positive, with an implicit indication that passing is a failure. Influential in promoting this view is the foundational work that is Paul Gibson's chapter on "Gay Male and Lesbian Youth Suicide" in the 1989 United States *Report of the Secretary's Task Force on Youth Suicide*. Gibson's thirty-two page chapter drew together scarce previous research to provide an account for investigators, social workers and policy-makers. He usefully re-located sexuality-related youth suicide in a culturalist framework and shifted the articulation of risk from one which pathologized homosexuality to an approach acknowledging that causal factors are constituted at least in part through cultural formations, forms of sociality and politico-cultural arrangements. It is Gibson's foundational work that is the source of the frequently cited statistics on queer youth suicide. Drawing on previous research, he stated that "gay youth are 2 to 3 times more likely to attempt suicide than other young people" and "may comprise up to 30 percent of completed suicides annually" (Gibson 1989: 110).

In Gibson's account, closetedness, passing or a failure to come out or declare one's sexuality openly to peers and families was depicted as a stressor that increased suicide risk:

> If closed about who they are, they may be able to 'pass' as 'straight' in their communities while facing a tremendous internal struggle to understand and accept themselves. Many gay youth choose to maintain a façade and hide their true feelings and identity, leading a double life, rather than confront situations too painful for them. They live in constant fear of being found out and recognized as gay. (1989: 112)

For Gibson, passing or hiding one's identity can subject a younger person to homophobic attitudes and remarks by unknowing family members and peers, leading to emotional problems, withdrawal from sociality, chronic depression and despair (ibid.: 113). Gibson described the identity development process of queer youth through a linear pattern of milestones and crises: beginning with a pre-pubertal self-awareness of difference from heterosexual norms, followed by an awareness of attraction to persons of the same sex, awareness of not fitting the "social script" of heterosexuality, a period of crisis through self-denial or internalized homophobia, and finally coming out through public declarations that may carry risks and hardships, although it was implied that identity stability, overcoming of despair and thereby overcoming suicide risk is achieved through taking this final step (ibid.: 115-22, 138). Although coming out was depicted here as involving its own risks, coming out is presented as the solution and resolution to that risk, as the eventual final step in overcoming the majority of obstacles facing queer youth as seen at the time Gibson was writing. The compulsion to come out and the early research which indicated that it has both political and personal benefits is derived from the idea that to name oneself as lesbian/gay publicly or openly produces the stabilization of selfhood through acts of self-disclosure and self-labeling (Savin-Williams 1996: 153-82) often within a framework of overcoming of silence and shame (Rofes 1983: 28) and an act of sociality through the attempt to articulate similitude and thus membership of a queer community.

The benefits of coming out have, however, been debated to some degree in subsequent queer youth suicide literature. For one set of writers who have expanded on Gibson's initial claims, passing, remaining closeted or failing to disclose one's non-heterosexuality is seen to be damaging, dangerous and exacerbates suicide risks. For example, McAndrew and Warne argue that "'passing' can be detrimental to mental well-being" whereby an inability to integrate a sexual self with broader life compromises mental health, leads to inner conflict, internalization of homophobia and a desire to "destroy that part of themselves" (2010: 92-101). Thus "passing" is posited here as a risk, one leading not only to (self-) isolation but also to an instability of mental health and well-being. Likewise, other writers have found that there is a risk of low self-esteem, anxiety and depression in being isolated through not being able to discuss sexuality with one's family, school, peers and friends, effectively hiding in "multiple spheres of life" (Mishna et al. 2009). In some studies, coming out has been linked with positive self-esteem among queer youth, resulting in the sort of resilience and self-efficacy that operate as protective factors (Crisp and McCave 2007).

The emphasis on coming out draws at least partly on a North American identity discourse that posits integrity, honesty and openness, at times regardless of the risks that might be involved or claims to privacy (Cover 2000). Contemporary political cultures of governance are willing to give a non-heterosexual person equal opportunity, but only as long as that person is (a) open about their sexuality if questioned, and (b) makes that sexuality invisible if so required (Bersani 1995: 67). This is a double-bind that, within the same logic of suicide research, leads to an ambivalent articulation as to how and where to find that middle-ground between out and passing, between honesty and invisibility, the negotiation of which is a social requirement specific to queer persons. This is part of an obligatory culture of confession (Foucault 2004: 169) in which the compulsion towards confession constitutes sexual subjectivity through claims to truth and honesty. The notion of coming out has at times been depicted as a positive milestone, often a proxy for more complex understandings of identify formation or what has sometimes been referred to as "gay-related development" (Friedman et al. 2008). Where a declaration of non-heterosexuality as a milestone effectively "works" for older adolescents and adults, this has often been translated as a positive event for *any* adolescent, thereby ignoring the fact that for younger teenagers and youth in particular circumstances or environments the push for coming out does not necessarily have a positive effect. Certainly maintaining closetedness into adulthood has been shown to be an unhealthy strategy adding to ongoing, permanent stressors as the performance of passing becomes more complex (Hegna and WichstrØm 2007), although among the relatively young the heightened risk of losing friends, being harassed or bullied is of much greater concern (Mishna et al. 2009: 1607). The uncritical assumption that closetedness is a risk and coming out a solution in much suicide research has tended to lack age-specificity. Some recent work on youth suicide and isolation has pointed out that articulating non-heterosexual identity or behaviors at too early an age rather than delaying it "to a safer time" may indeed be a significant factor in creating the social context in which suicide becomes thinkable (Zhao et al. 2010) as an escape from intolerable emotional pain (Shneidman 1985: 36).

However, there is a counter-argument that while coming out might be highly beneficial for many youth—and studies of broad queer youth populations have generally shown this—the fact of being "out" can be an added risk factor, leading to either new or different forms of isolation, hopelessness or harassment or subsidiary risks such as family rejection and homelessness (Davis et al. 2009). In fact, this counter-argument was made very early on in the history of writings on queer suicide. Although he discussed some of the benefits of coming out, Rofes did point to the ways in which the idea of coming out had been mythically produced as a cure-all. Undoubtedly motivated by having witnessed the suicides of many adult gay men *after* publicly declaring a gay sexuality in line with the political motivation to do so in the early 1980s, and writing for a targeted queer community audience, he found that the community push for coming out uncritically held too many expectations while disregarding the risks. As he put it:

> Perhaps no myth is so dangerous to lesbians and gay men as the myth that claims that the act of 'coming out' as a gay person provides a person with a margin of insurance against self-hatred or self-destructiveness. This myth leads many lesbians and gay men to believe that, once able to be open about their homosexuality, their personal problems and anxieties will all fall by the wayside. Coming out is looked on as a miracle cure, a salvation from all shortcomings and malaise. (Rofes: 1983: 49)

"Passing" as a coping strategy undertaken by queer youth has been investigated in older sociological studies of non-normative sexuality (Edwards 1996). Warren referred to the necessity of character management and social presentation of one's self as a necessary coping strategy for marginalized youth and depicted this, in contrast to the idea that passing is dishonest, as "avoidance without hiding" (1974: 94); that is, as a slightly more complex concept than can fit neatly in a paradigmatic in/out dichotomy. Troiden likewise referred to it as "blending," suggesting that people in "coping" situations "blend act in gender-appropriate ways and neither announce nor deny their homosexual identities to non-homosexual others" (Troiden 1988: 56). As a strategy for coping with situations in which one would otherwise be *more vulnerable* if non-normative sexuality was revealed, there is certainly nothing unethical or dishonest about passing, nor is there a clear indication that remaining in this semi-closeted state is necessarily a greater risk factor than being otherwise open about non-normative sexual identity, desires or behaviors.

What is problematic, then, in some suicide research is the unquestioned assumption that coming out is a necessary activity for resilience, that remaining closeted is an unnecessary stressor for suicide, or that for some younger persons obscuring a non-normative sexual identity, behaviors or experiences is not only necessary but might be beneficial. In other words, there is a need for the notion of coming out to be understood as beneficial *variably*, and for intervention, counseling and advice to ensure that there is a suitable counter to the social pressure that comes most often from media and queer community to out oneself. The compulsion to come out rather than to pass has been further problematized by some recent research which has indicated that coming out in the very early teen years is associated with significantly greater risk of suicidal behaviors (Suicide Prevention Resource Centre 2008: 20, Schrimshaw et al. 2008), thought to be the result of having fewer coping strategies for dealing with stigma (Remafedi et al. 1991). Some writers have indicated that this may be related to "pinning down your identity at a time when you are not certain of what you are," (Hegna 2007: 591) which is of course reinforced by the articulation of sexual identity to those who then go on to maintain surveillance over the veracity of that identity statement. Others have found that early identification and declaration of non-heterosexuality have led to increased experience of violence and harassment, thus increasing the risk of suicidal behaviors (Friedman 2008: 892). Finally, there is also some evidence that the younger the adolescent at the time of identification and coming out, the less likely that person is to have access to supportive peers, thereby increasing the risk of suicide in the face of explicit or implicit harassment (Rutter and Soucar 2002). The considerable shift in age of declaring a non-normative sexuality, with increasing evidence of younger persons coming out in the earlier teens rather than the early twenties (Cloud 2005), therefore has some considerable implications for how the notion of coming out is addressed in queer youth suicide literature, prevention techniques and early intervention.

The ways in which the distinction between passing or non-disclosure and outness or self-declaration are framed in suicide literature draws, then, on a discourse of risk and risk mitigation. This is not surprising for suicidology, the primary aim of much research being to identify those at risk of suicidality before a suicide attempt or completion. In the discourse of risk management, risks are generally quantified whereby the chances of a negative event occurring are given numeric values, estimates or ratings (Wiegman and Gutteling 1995). Although the evaluation of risk occurs through claims to institutional expertise (Horlick-Jones 2003), all perception of risk is cultural constructed (Hope 2007). Where risk discourse becomes so ubiquitous both socially and within a field of research inquiry, it operates as a master narrative that thereby obscures the contingencies on which it rests and disavows alternative approaches (Schehr 2005). The implications of this for queer youth suicide research include the fact that determining passing as either a risk or a mitigation strategy results in the removal of agency from queer youth, ensuring that the act of passing (or, likewise, of coming out) remains *knowable* only through the extent to which it contributes or limits the assumed vulnerability or victimhood of queer youth.

Queer Theory and Beyond Risk

In suicide research, the categorization of available sexualities is almost always as heterosexual and homosexual (with bisexual and transgender identities typically added to the latter term as a coalitional LGBTQ or "queer"). What tends to be presumed in the vast majority of research is that these are the *only* ways in which sexuality *can* be categorized, and this is often the starting point for statistical data gathering and comparative research around different risk factors for heterosexual versus non-heterosexual youth (Walls et al. 2008). Since the early 1990s, queer theory has taken to task the self-evident, common logic of the "naturalness" of the binary opposition of heterosexuality and homosexuality and the idea that sexual and gender identities are innate, fixed and unproblematic. Eve Sedgwick critiqued the hetero/homo binary, pointing out that while it is the dominant means by which sexuality is categorized in contemporary western culture, there are alternative sexualities, desires and erotics that do not fit neatly in the same-sex attraction or opposite-sex attraction and, in some cases, may not be about the gender of the persons involved at all (Sedgwick 1990: 35). Drawing on Michel Foucault's *History of Sexuality*, Eve Kosofsky Sedgwick pointed to the ways in which the commonly-known categories of sexuality—"heterosexual" and "homosexual"—are presented through a binary that is historical, mythical and without "natural" or "essentialist" foundation. Sedgwick's analysis of the binary has been a significant cornerstone of queer theory, which has often sought to deploy poststructuralist and deconstructionist analyses to re-think sexuality along alternative lines.

By starting with the notion that sexual identities only emerge in the nineteenth century (there were always heterosexual and homosexual acts, but no identities or personages built on these acts, despite whatever preferences) when particular western medical and psychiatric discourses begin to dominate and describe sexuality through these two identity categories, queer theory opened a number of questions: (1) what other ways of categorizing or depicting sex, sexualities and sexual behaviors were there historically, before the dominance of contemporary discourses of sexuality; (2) what alternative ways of thinking about sexuality can be developed in the future; (3) who is excluded from the contemporary discourses of sexuality and the hetero- and homo- classifications; (4) in what ways do these categorizations constrain and/or regiment subjects in their sexual behavior, preference or identity? The very idea of heterosexual identity or homosexual identity is, rather, historical, discursively-produced but has come to appear natural and timeless. Other queer theorists have furthered this critique, indicating that other ways of thinking about or categorizing sexuality—including those which might be more sensible to a younger teenager than "gay" or "straight"—are suppressed and made silent by the monolithic nature of the hetero/homo binary (Hennessy 1994).

At the same time, the idea of a sexual *identity* as an inner core self which directs and projects desire and sexual behavior has been problematized (e.g. Butler 1990). Through the work of Judith Butler and others, queer theory has allowed us to de-naturalize the idea that sexual orientation or identity is innate, fixed and timeless for each individual and, further, that there might be better ways of thinking about sexuality and desire than through the notion of it emanating from an inner identity. None of that is to say that heterosexual and homosexual identities are not real or meaningful to the majority of sexual subjects today, only that (a) they are not natural or foundational but produced in contemporary culture through available discourses; (b) that there are other ways of categorizing sexuality that are also culturally-produced and might have a better "fit" for some vulnerable younger persons, although the discourses through which these alternatives are produces are often unavailable or marginal; (c) that heterosexuality and homosexuality as binary distinctions and as categories of sexual identity may not be meaningful to *all* youth.

Despite this 20-year-old critique, a broad range of research and writing on queer youth suicide have tended to leave the binary distinction of heterosexuality and queerness intact, as well as the expectation that youth who overcome risks in adolescence will or must stabilize an identity as either heterosexual or lesbian/gay/bisexual, which of course will not always be the case. What can be found in the majority of suicide research throughout the 1990s and the early 2000s, then, is the assumption of the innateness of (hetero/homo) sexual identity categorization which assumes a simple and uniform process of identity development, as well as a classification of risks for GLB youth that does not account for the broad diversity in how sexuality is thought and made meaningful or even expressed throughout different stages in adolescence. Much of this comes from the unproblematized and uncritical use of the notion of "sexual orientation," which assumes that while there may be differences in how one produces an identity, there is a natural drive or inclination to direct sexual desire towards either one gender or the other. By relying often on single-dimensional inquiries into sexual orientation that do not leave much possibility to account for differences between identity and sexual behavior. Additionally, some analyses of youth suicides have "read" cases through the common framework of normative hetero/homo sexualities, and determined that suicide can be the result of a refusal to come-to terms with *really* being lesbian or gay in a positive framework (McDaniel et al. 2001, Battin 1995: 12, Macdonald and Cooper 1998, Dorais 2004: 24, King et al. 2008), which effectively dismisses the possibility that the persons involved in those cases perceived sexuality in alternative ways.

Turning a queer theory lens upon the ways in which suicide literature has articulated a passing/outness distinction requires us, then, to reconsider the risk discourse through which this has been produced. Once sexual identity is understood as contingent, variable, fluid and constituted in the discursive arrangements through which one articulates inner/outer and public/private dichotomies and through which one *becomes* or is re-constituted as a sexual being, the linearity of the secrecy—passing—disclosure formation becomes one which needs to be understood only through constructedness, scripting and contingency. Rather than categorization through a risk discourse, what needs to be considered are the ways in which this scripting of the process and the pressures either to remain closeted and pass or to come out and declare a non-normative sexuality openly produces new forms of vulnerability. What, then, for the young person compelled to produce his or her sexual identity "in accord" with the cultural formations that make queer sexuality coherent, which includes outness? What then, for the young person whose only option in the face of perceived or potential discrimination or the violence of exclusion or, indeed, physical violence, is to pass, and thereby be constituted through an "inner" queerness and an "outer" persona (Straayer 1996: 34); a private performativity diametrically opposed to a public theatrics?

One possible solution in attempting to avoid the vulnerabilization of queer youth through this dichotomy and the risk discourse is to find ways in which queer theory itself can be pragmatically deployed in order to produce the notion of passing otherwise. That is, to blur the boundaries in precisely the way in early writers such as Edwards, Warren, and Troiden attempted to un-couple passing or closetedness from "dishonesty" or claims of a lack of "integrity." This is to work together the similarities between the notion of passing as "avoidance without hiding" and Butler's critique of the ways in which an inner/outer binary distinction constitutes and stabilizes the coherent, Enlightenment subject. It is to ask, as Butler does: "From what strategic position in public discourse and for what reasons has the trope of interiority and the disjunctive binary of inner/out taken hold?" (Butler 1990: 134). By increasing public awareness of the constructed and contingent formation of inner/outer, private/public and passing/outness, alongside the very contingency of sexual identity categories of hetero/homo, it is possible to foster as a means of reducing vulnerability a more complex relationship with the ways in which passing and disclosure are understood as necessary components of intelligible subjectivity.

Comments on Cover's "Identity and Passing Critical Essays: Queer Youth, Risk and the Passing/Coming Out Dichotomy"

Janna Jackson Kellinger

Rob Cover's chapter allowed me to step out of myself and my own experiences to reflect on how my own understanding of my self is shaped by the cultural narratives that surround me. He makes a strong and theoretically well-supported argument that complicates assumed binaries around passing and coming out, particularly in terms of literature about suicide, and points out that harm can accompany these false binaries. I would like to extend his arguments by supplying some examples of the "real harm to real people"[1] that can happen while complicating his complications even more.

Cover deconstructs the notion that there are only two options for gay people, passing or coming out, and argues there is no clear cut "in" or "out" of the closet, but rather that people negotiate their identities depending on the situation. This is a lived reality for teachers: "There are decisions to be made on a continuous, day-to-day basis—often several times a day. Decisions like these involve a careful scrutiny of each context. Each such decision is accompanied by a risk and a wide range of possible effects" (Epstein and Johnson 1994: 199). Something that often gets lost in discussions about coming out versus passing, however, is that how identity is presented, received, and circulated is not always completely within the control of the bearer of that identity. As teachers in this study point out, students talk so once a queer identity is disclosed—whether by the bearer of that identity or by others, there is no more contextual negotiation around coming out, except, perhaps, in how a teacher responds to any reactions.

When I taught high school in Georgia, I knew more than one teacher whose identity disclosure fell into the hands of others—one of whom was explicitly told she was being fired for being gay. Even when being outed does not lead to being fired directly, indirect means can be used to end employment, such as the special education teacher whose administrators stopped acting on any discipline referrals he sent to the office so word spread quickly that students could get away with anything in his class allowing administrators to fire him for lack of class management. Real risks and consequences accompany being out and being outed.

For students, since they do not have as much control over their lives as adults, being out carries even more risks, as Cover states: "for younger teenagers and youth in particular circumstances or environments that push for coming out do not necessarily have a positive effect." For example, when I was a high school teacher, a smart young woman in my class was verbally and physically assaulted by her father for being a lesbian, resulting in her moving out and subsequently dropping

---

1   This quote is from Jon Stewart when remarking on Michelle Bachman's husband practicing ex-gay ministry.

out of high school to work to afford her own apartment—drastically altering her life chances.

The digital age and the anonymity that accompanies it increases the likelihood of being outed and the ease of dissemination can make coming out and being outed much more public. The consequences of this can be devastating. Just recently, a college student committed suicide after his roommate and a friend surreptitiously videotaped his sexual encounters with another male and made this video public via the internet. Although the internet does allow youth to play with their identities as mentioned earlier, it allows others to play with their identities as well.

In addition to dismantling the false binary of being in or out of the closet, Cover also argues that how these two options are depicted, passing as "a failure" and "coming out as wholly positive," can do harm. I would like to play with this a bit by also arguing that reversing these depictions, passing as safe and coming out as dangerous, can do harm as well.

Even in instances when passing appears to be safe, it can do harm by not challenging people's assumptions. For example, I lost a teachable moment one time when I accidentally passed.: After interviewing a participant in a location I thought was private enough not to be overheard, a customer in the restaurant asked me, "So how *do* gay teachers teach?" It was only after the convoluted conversation that I realized she assumed I was straight. I wish I could relive that conversation in order to set her straight by confronting her assumptions by outing myself.

Although this example of harm is on a small scale, multiplying this one example by the number of lost opportunities over the lifetimes of queer people around the globe can contribute to massive ignorance. Not coming out has its risks too—not only does it mean that we do not give people the opportunity to confront their own prejudices, but it can result in continued or an increase in discrimination.

The recent paradigm shift in Massachusetts is a striking example of the power of telling our own stories, and speaks to the potential for coming out to increase safety. When the Massachusetts state legislature first voted on same-sex marriage in 2004, barely 25 percent of the state legislators supported same-sex marriage. Three years later when the final vote was taken that secured same-sex marriage in Massachusetts, over 75 percent of the state legislators supported same-sex marriage. In an era when "flip-flopping" is seen as a fatal political move, the reason cited repeatedly by legislators who changed their vote was the power of constituents' stories (Wangsness and Estes 2007). This was not easy. I remember going to the state house to lobby back in 2004. Although I considered myself an out and proud lesbian, the group of gay constituents who went to talk to legislators—a group that included an openly lesbian comic—experienced what I can only term "collective internalized homophobia." We stammered and stumbled, we were not used to the language of "same-sex marriage" at the time, and we had been trained by years of social messages to avoid making heterosexual people uncomfortable (despite the "discomfort" queer people have experienced at the hands of heterosexuals). This is in sharp contrast to the collective shrug by the people of Massachusetts four years later when the law that prohibited out-of-state couples from getting married in

Massachusetts if their marriage was not allowed in their home state was repealed as no one showed up to demonstrate on either side (Moskowitz 2008).

In contrast to people telling their stories in Massachusetts was the passage of Proposition 8 in California—an amendment to their state constitution that prohibits same-sex marriage, a right that had already been conferred on thousands of same-sex couples in California. Some claim that these civil rights/rites were taken away due, at least in part, to the failure of the campaign against Prop. 8 to "come out" as the campaign against Prop. 8 talked about civil rights in general instead of tying those civil rights to gay people. By thinking that passing was safe, this campaign turned back civil rights that were already gained. In contrast, Harvey Milk's successful campaign against an initiative proposed to prevent gay people from being teachers, a campaign that occurred over 30 years before the Prop. 8 debacle, was clear and direct that this was about gay people with its slogan "Come out, Come out, Wherever You are"—very different from No on 8's slogan of "unfair and wrong." While Cover dismantles the false assumptions that "passing is a failure" and "coming out [is] wholly positive," these two large scale examples demonstrate that "passing as safe" and "coming out as dangerous" are false and dangerous assumptions as well.

Instead, as Cover points out, there is no one size fits all. Passing is not always safe or risky, but neither is coming out, nor are any of the variations in between guaranteed to be safe or risky. In addition, the safety and risks are in the eyes of the beholder. Cover states that "all perception of risk is culturally constructed"—I would like to add that these perceptions are individually constructed as well. For example, participants in the study discussed in my chapter speak to their own "invented fears" about being out. In addition, these participants individually constructed their perception of others' reactions to their being out, for example, by viewing negative backlash as "blips to me. And now they're not even blips. They're little rocks or something" (Duncan).

Cover uses the phrase "culture of confession" to describe North American identity discourse, but this only occurs if people individually and collectively construe sexual orientation as something to be confessed. When gayness is discussed openly, it no longer becomes a confession. However, as pointed out earlier in this chapter, no one can control how something is received by others. As I am sure others have experienced, I have certainly had more than one straight person immediately confess something to me after finding out my sexual orientation.

Underlying all of these discussions about passing versus coming out is the assumption that people presume heterosexuality unless stated otherwise. This is not always the case. Again, this comes down to how people perceive others. While perceptions may be everything and no one can control another person's perceptions, when life's complexities are covered over in false binaries, perceptions are based on false realities. Queer people sharing their own perceptions with others—after determining it is either safe or worth the risk—has the power to change the perceptions of others, which, in turn, has the potential to make it more safe for others to come out as well.

Comments on Janna Jackson Kellinger's "*Unmasking Identities* Revisited"

Rob Cover

Kellinger's chapter presents a wonderful overview of her work that explores the questions of sexual identity and coming out among teachers. The chapter critiques some of the more common assumptions about the use of terms, the validity and value of coming out and the veracity of the hetero/homo binary, showing in many ways that in the act of coming out and describing one's sexuality, people make particular and sometimes self-conscious shortcuts in order not to have to explain sexuality in too much detail. It is demonstrated here in particular that those who express or feel a more fluid or nuanced sense of sexuality often feel the need to articulate sexual self-hood through language that filters self-presentation and outness in terms of identities as essentialist, core and innate and in terms of being either in or out of the closet, without more complex in-betweens or alternatives.

One of the elements that struck me most in reading this is the fact that in several ways this chapter demonstrates how language use and terminology choices in the process of speaking "outwardly" of sexuality are performative acts related to the cultural demand that we produce and articulate ourselves as coherent, intelligible, integral and recognizable, and very often in ways which foreclose on the possibility of being seen, read and understood as complex, multiply-constituted and always-contingent subjects (Butler 1993: 116). Within queer theory and cultural studies, Judith Butler projects one of the most useful post-structuralist discussions of identity as constructed in—and sometimes constrained by—language, culture and discourse. Butler demonstrates that identities are constituted through performances, which occur "in accord" with pre-existing culturally-given categories, processes, rituals and expectations of identity. For example, a queer male performs homosexuality through acts, desires, attractions, behaviors and tastes that are recognizably "homosexual" are made recognizable through culturally-shared understandings of sexuality and the category of homosexual. By implication, the expression, declaration of articulation of a sexuality, sexual desires or a sexual identity that does not conform to culturally-assigned categories, discourses and understandings is unrecognizable and thereby excludes the subject from social participation and belonging. In performing an identity—which is never a conscious or voluntary act—one cites and repeats the category and the information given culturally that makes that category intelligible—much like a script. Such performances are repetitive and come to stabilize over time, retroactively producing the illusion that the performances manifest from a fixed, inner identity core (Butler 1990: 143). That is, our actions and performances do not stem from an inner essence but constitute it. Following Nietzsche, she points out that there is no "doer behind the deed," that is, no static sexual subject (being) revealed through sexual behavior or desire (doing). Rather, we perform our sexual identities *over time* in accord with discursive expectations and cultural demands for coherence, intelligibility and recognizability. Identity is the compulsion to reiterate "a norm or set of norms" which "conceals or dissimulates the conventions of which it is a repetition" (Butler 1993: 12). The expression of same-sex desire constitutes the lesbian/gay subject much as the articulation of opposite-sex desire forms the heterosexual subject. For Butler, identity—and sexual identity—is thus manufactured in the languages, concepts and ideas available to a culture at a specific point in time, meaning the division of sexuality into heterosexual and homosexual identities is not only something relatively new, but may not be the only or best way in which to think about sexual desire, orientations, preferences or tastes. That is, all identities are constituted within ambiguities, incoherences and inconsistencies, but for the sake of coherence we are required to disavow, suppress or re-inscribe in order to perform as an intelligible and coherent self (Butler 1997: 27).

What Kellinger's research indicates is the fact that the process of coming out involves not just the disclosure of a concept of sexual orientation, but the explanation of non-normativity: "the act of 'coming out' is an irreversible decision that comes with an accompanying need to justify it." While the ways in which teachers (and others) make those explanatory justifications of non-normative sexuality is undoubtedly diverse, the justification is framed and produced in the cultural demand to perform and articulate sexuality through coherence and intelligibility. While listeners, students, parents, and others who "hear" the story in the act of disclosure may react negatively to the knowledge that one's teachers, peer or responsible person is non-heterosexual, in a culture in which identity coherence is the bottom-line and occurs through the persistent reproduction of the hetero/ homo binary and surveillance built on that dichotomy, the idea of non-intelligible, fluid, unclear, incoherent and unrecognizable sexualities is far more significantly problematic for many listeners and witnesses than just being lesbian/gay.

This includes the ritual process of disclosure or coming out which, as Esther Saxey has demonstrated, is selective and potentially constraining. Disclosing a non-heterosexual sexuality is, then,

> a process of selecting significant events, and arranging and interpreting them.
> That process will always be affected by the culture and politics that surround
> the author, including the coming out stories that already exist. (Saxey 2008: 3)

That process of selection as part of an "explanation" of the non-normative sexual self is governed by conventions and discourse, and underlying that governance is the demand for coherence and intelligibility to be made, performatively, through explanation—a demand that is (perhaps tacitly) represented by the desire of the listener to "know."

So what does the demand for coherence do for the performance of sexual self-hood in the act of disclosure and the subsequent on-going stabilization of that knowledge of sexual identity? For Butler—and, by extension, for queer theory—the performative self is produced as an effect not just of language, discourse and cultural significations but of *regulation* and *regulatory ideals*. Regulatory ideals are truth regimes, which establish norms, exclusions, categories and identities (Butler

2005: 30). Through processes of subjection and regulation, subjects are produced and required to perform, behave and desire by maintaining and exploiting the cultural demand for "continuity, visibility, and place" (Butler 1993: 29). That is, it requires the subject to respond and "fit" within regulatory norms in order to fulfill the condition of existence through performing as a "recognizable social being" (ibid.: 27). In the case of sexuality, it is what Butler refers to as the heterosexual matrix or the cultural expectation of a mutual relationship between gender, sex and desire that operates as "a norm and a fiction that disguises itself as a developmental law regulating the sexual field that it purports to describe" (Butler 1990: 136). The demand that non-heteronormative desire and behavior be encapsulated into the latter term of the hetero/homo binary as an identity that is intelligible and recognizable to others and to society more broadly is the *truth regime* which regulates sexuality, sexual behavior and desire into a coherent identity—an identity which works for some but which, for others, may be an unliveable, inarticulable form of self-hood. Importantly—and from a Foucauldian perspective—regulation is not repression acting on a natural "field of pleasure and desire" (Butler 1993: 58); rather, it is part of a cultural, discursive and knowledge—based apparatus which constitutes subjects under the rubric of regulation and formation. Thus, it is not to say that the regulation of sexuality into recognizable heterosexual and homosexual subjects represses some kind of natural, broad or fluid sexual desires or that we can throw off the shackles of regulation of sexuality in favor of the pre-Nineteenth Century greater pleasures and behaviors that did not transform into categories or attributes of individual subjects (Butler 1999). Rather, regulation is the current *condition* of all identity, including sexual identities as they are articulated through contemporary acts and conventions of disclosure in coming out.

However, for some the experience of becoming sexual and thus being "regulated" will be different from others. For those who will—for whatever reason—not "fit" or be able to perform coherently within the dominant (hetero/homo) sexual regime, there is the consequential risk that imperils

> the very possibility of being recognized by others, since to question the norms of recognition that govern what I might be, to ask what they leave out, what they might be compelled to accommodate, is, in relation to the present regime, to risk unrecognizability as a subject or at least to become an occasion for posing the questions of who one is (or can be) and whether or not one is recognizable. (Butler 2005: 23)

In other words, to risk not being a coherent and recognizable sexual subject by questioning, critiquing or resisting the violence of social regulation or over-regulation is to risk access to subjectivity, social participation and belonging, to risk exclusion from intelligibility and self-hood.

Ultimately, in formulating the articulation of sexual self-hood in coming out, teachers (and others) are regulated. As Kellinger puts it, the "stories we tell ourselves largely determine the actions we take or don't take." In other words, to explain non-normativity in a particular way plays a constitutive role in the on-going performativity of selfhood. It narrows the possibilities of self, it produces the self through speaking, disclosure and explanation and it does so in a way which regulates in order not just that one's explanation be recognizable, but that one's sexual self-hood be recognizable. Where does this regulation and regimentation through the demand for coherence, intelligibility and recognizability lead? To one of the first points made in the chapter: the critique of a number of commonly held assumptions of empowerment and agency around the ways in which disclosure is articulated. Defining sexual orientation, as Kellinger notes, "is problematic as everyone comes to his or her own understandings. Positing sexual orientation as a dichotomy 'disguises widely varying individual experiences.' ... Not only do categories obscure differences, they also ascribe boundaries." In reading these arguments from a queer theory perspective, then, it is possible to see how the act of disclosure or coming out is one in which the hetero/homo binary—however unfeasible or insensible to the subject—is restored through regimentation and regulation. While agency is a questionable value at any time, the sense of *having agency* is important for subjectivity and selfhood to be liveable in contemporary culture. Where coming out occurs through a framework in which regulatory ideals are restored through the need to provide and present an adequate explanation of one's sexuality, then, the sense of agency is lost in the face of the difficulty of giving a lengthy, broad and complex argument about how one's sexuality works, is understood and is emotively felt.

In several ways, then, this opens further the possibility of critiquing the validity of the closeted/out dichotomy, which is often culturally perceived as parallel to oppression/liberation or trapped/free or self-limiting/opened-possibilities. As coming out and the concomitant stories involved operate through the framework of regulation, coming out may not be quite so liberating, freeing or opening of possibilities, as the articulation of self-hood and its regulation is not one marked by agency but by the constraints of discourse. Implied here, therefore, is the idea that passing, or operating outside of the clear-cut binary of disclosure or non-disclosed, might act towards the undoing of the requirement or demand for explanation that regiments and regulates the sexual self into a constrained category of sexual identity coherence.

Response to Cover

Janna Jackson Kellinger

Rob Cover's response articulates the complexity of identity development. However, data from this study of teachers contradicts some of his statements. For example, he states: "Where coming out occurs through a framework in which regulatory ideals are restored through the need to provide and present an adequate explanation of one's sexuality, then, the sense of agency is lost in the face of the difficulty of giving a lengthy, broad and complex argument about how one's sexuality works, is understood and is emotively felt." Although it makes sense that squeezing something as complex as sexual identity into a single word or two would cause a loss of a sense of agency, this is not true for everyone. Many participants described the liberation they felt when they finally had a term that helped clarify their own feelings. Perhaps most striking is the incident relayed by Lauren, one of the older participants:

> I mean no clue, none, zero, other than something was very wrong. … But then this older guy in his thirties had been trying to get me to go out with him for months and months and months. So I said, "Oh, what the hell." I liked him. He was polite. I just didn't want to go out with him. So I went out with him and it was just a disaster. We had a good time except that being thirty something and my being a slightly older student than the others, he was expecting that we were going to have sex. So we got as far as getting to bed and it was very clear that I wasn't interested. And he asked me point blank, "Well, have you ever considered that you might be a lesbian?" And I said, "What do you mean?" And he explained what it was. And I said, "Huh. You know, that might be the case." And he said, "You mean that doesn't upset you?" And I said, "No, it sounds like a good idea." It's weird. It was pretty weird, actually. Then he says, "Well, you know. I guess that takes care of that." And we just stopped, and that was it. That was certainly our last date.

Clearly in this case, the explanatory power of a term increased Lauren's sense of agency. But for many, just as coming out to others is described in both our chapters and responses as not being a one-shot deal, coming out to oneself is not either:

> By the time I was in fourth grade, I knew that I was gay. Probably seventh grade was when I could look in the mirror and say it out loud. Ninth grade is probably when I stopped crying myself to sleep every night, praying to a God I didn't know whether or not existed that I'd wake up and be changed. But I didn't really come out to people until college. (Glen)

In this case, Glen describes being able to say the word as an important step in his coming out process. In a heteronormative society, these terms that are used in attempt to circumscribe aspects of ourselves that are as messy and fluid as sexuality and emotion can have both a liberatory and a limiting function. Liberatory when the term helps explain something that is incomprehensible in the face of a culture that does not even hold out these types of feelings as an option; limiting when one's own understanding of oneself has grown beyond a particular term—as demonstrated by Leigh, a participant quoted in my original chapter who explains that she presents herself differently depending on what she thinks her audience will be able to comprehend.

Leigh describes a very conscious means of altering her identity performance depending on her audience, just as all the teachers in this study did—not just when attempting to pass at school, but even after initially coming out as they were careful not to perpetuate stereotypes. Even when participants described themselves as being "authentic," they were very articulate about the ways in which they performed that authenticity, such as Duncan when describing joking in class that if he were a lesbian, he would be in love with Minerva:

> As natural as it was, it was calculated when I said if I was [a lesbian, I would be] in love with Minerva. I knew exactly what it was doing even though it was an absolutely spontaneous and natural joke. I knew what it represented. I knew it represented to some a risk. It represented to somebody else maybe a political statement.

Even though most likely the vast majority of the time people are not aware of the ways in which they perform identity, contrary to Rob Cover's statement that "performing an identity ... is never a conscious or voluntary act," the teachers in this study are at times hyper aware of their identity performances and how those performances may or may not be perceived and received by others. This could be due to the public nature of teaching, but I suspect that increased identity awareness is necessary when crafting an identity that is outside the identity options presented by society.

Although the terms used to describe our identity performances can be limiting, they can also be building blocks towards more complex understandings of ourselves by re-mixing them as described above: "Certainly, other research attests to younger generations embracing more fluid notions of gender and sexual identities, as Driver found in her online research a plethora of self-definitions: 'In the middle of fem and butch', 'A tom boy with a princess stuck inside of me', 'andro', 'fem-andrognynous', 'in-between', 'boi', 'birl.'" These mash-ups suggest a conscious construction of identity. Perhaps it is these increased awarenesses of one's own identity performances that contribute to a stronger sense of agency, and this stronger sense of agency that allows people to complicate their own identity performances.

Reply to Kellinger

Rob Cover

I thank Janna Kellinger for her response to the chapter, and particularly for the ways in which she draws on the theoretical and deconstructionist work around inside/outside, closetedness and passing by pointing to a number of real-life examples drawn from her own work in the context of school teachers and the lived reality of passing and coming out. An interesting option raised by Kellinger in her response is to reverse one of the possible cultural arguments around passing—that passing is often perceived as "failure" and "coming out as wholly positive," by indicating instead that the reverse can *also* be true. While I agree that this usefully complexifies the common perceptions of closetedness and outness, I would also like to expand on this by arguing that there is a social and *ethical responsibility* to break down the binary system of passing/outness altogether. This is on the basis that such a regimentary system does violence to queer subjects, regardless of which term in the binary is deemed positive. One way of tackling this is to look at how queer sexuality is "framed" in such a way that a broad population in sociality and relationality can suspend its ethics around acceptability and normality in order to make judgments on the "right and proper" ways in which to be a queer person— that is, to set prohibitive norms around outness *or* closetedness, as we have seen in "Don't Ask, Don't Tell" (DADT) policies that operate either formally or, more tacitly, in the informal arena of youth environments.

Some of Butler's more recent work (e.g. 2004, 2005, 2009) explores the possibilities of an ethics of non-violence that can be fostered through recognition of the vulnerability of others. Butler develops a way of conceiving of the human subject as predicated on a primary vulnerability to and dependence on others, meaning that all our identities are built on our relationality with others. This is marked by the fact we are vulnerable to the violence of others and yet always from the beginning our lives are dependent on others for physical support. This ethics is not a simple injunction to behave in a particular way. Rather, it produces a quandary, a requirement persistently to question ones' actions and a situation that produces the subject anew in the encounter with the others. What the encounter with the other describes is a "struggle over the claim of nonviolence without any judgment about how the struggle finally ends" (Butler 2005: 187). In other words, it does not resolve the ethical problem it raises, but opens the *possibility* for subjects to recognize the vulnerability of others through understanding it in terms of their own vulnerability and thereby initiating a struggle one must undertake with one's own violence (ibid.: 181). In suggesting that the social imposition of *either* compulsory closetedness *or* compulsory outness is a repetitive and ongoing act of violence, there is a call for an ethical intervention—not to operate as an injunction but as a means by which those who claim to be offended either by outness or closetedness can engage with queer persons differently—in a manner less injurious.

In *Frames of War*, Butler further develops her ethics of vulnerability and recognition of the other by questioning some of the power regimes that operate to make some subjects appear human and others as less-than-human. Butler here takes to task the earlier ethical work, shifting from the question of recognition, which is too problematically characterized as an act or practice or scene between subject, towards the idea of "recognizability" which characterizes instead the "general conditions that prepare or shape a subject for recognition" (Butler 2009: 5). This allows us to ask, then, what it is that prevents a general populace from viewing queer persons as worthy of determining *for themselves* the extent, timing or conditions of "confession" (if it should in fact be characterized as such) or, indeed, the right to ambivalence, fluidity or blurredness.

Through opening ethics onto the field of recognizability, Butler presents a number of ways in which we can understand what *prevents* that ethical relationship of responsibility (2009: 50). First among these is her return to the question of norms and normativity. Norms, she points out "allocate recognition differentially" (ibid.: 6), due to the fact that all subjects are constituted through norms which produce but also "shift the terms through which subjects are recognized" (ibid.: 3-4). Butler asks, significantly, what are the schemas of intelligibility that condition and produce norms of recognizability (ibid.: 6-7), according some lives as worthy of a non-violent response and others as not. She indicates that norms are enacted and conditioned through visual and narrative frames (ibid.: 75), meaning that the discourses that govern which lives will be regarded as *human enough* to be recognized as worthy of an ethical and non-violent response operate through the ways in which various persons, subjectivities and lives are framed (ibid.: 77-8). Norms are given culturally (ibid.: 141), but it is through the methods by which subjects are framed that norms take hold of subjects and present precarity and responsibility differentially across different lives (ibid.: 23-4). Queer persons may be *figured* as vulnerable by some when closeted or when outed—but frequently *not vulnerable* in the way that demands an ethical response, a withdrawal of the violence of the demand for clarity, for passing or outness. Framing queer sexuality through the imposition of either a closet or a demand for honesty produces a normativity whereby any queer person who is ambivalent in his or her passing, who is semi-out, or who refuses the hail of either remaining hidden or being fully out is not only figured as not worthy, but becomes a figure of suspicion.

While I do not want to suggest that there is an inherent right of agency, by working outside of the frame and accepting in a non-violent way (that is, without demand) that queer persons might determine their outness or passing in their own, complex, myriad forms is a step towards an ethical manner in which to deal with questions of sexuality. The end result of such an ethics—idealistic as it may seem—is that no one is necessarily straight or queer, because no one is necessarily known to be passing or not.

References

Almaguer, T. 1991. Chicano men: A cartography of homosexual behavior and identity. *Differences: A Journal of Feminist Cultural Studies*, 3(2), 75-100.

Altman, D. 1971. *Homosexual Oppression and Liberation.* New York: New York University Press.

Battin, M.P. 1995. *Ethical Issues in Suicide.* Englewood Cliffs, NJ: Prentice Hall.

Bersani, L. 1995. *Homos.* Cambridge, MA: Harvard University Press.

Bohan, J. and Russell, G. 1999. Conceptual Frameworks in *Conversations about Psychology and Sexual Orientation*, edited by J. Bohan and G. Russell. New York: New York University Press, 11-30.

Britzman, D. 1999. Cultural myths in the making of a teacher: Biography and social structure in teacher education. *The Complex World of Teaching: Perspectives from Theory and Practice*, edited by E. Mintz and J.T. Yun. Cambridge, MA: Harvard Educational Review, 179-92.

Butler, J. 1990. *Gender Trouble: Feminism and the Subversion of Identity.* London: Routledge.

Butler, J. 1993. *Bodies That Matter: On the Discursive Limits of 'Sex'.* London: Routledge.

Butler, J. 1997. *The Psychic Life of Power: Theories in Subjection.* Stanford, CA: Stanford University Press.

Butler, J. 2004. *Precarious Life.* London: Verso.

Butler, J. 2005a. *Giving an Account of Oneself.* New York: Fordham University Press.

Butler, J. 2005b. Revisiting bodies and pleasures. *Theory, Culture & Society,* 16(2), 11-20.

Butler, J. 2009. *Frames of War: When is Life Grievable?* London: Verso.

Cloud, J. 2005. The battle over gay teens. *Time Magazine* [Online, October 2]. Available at: http://www.time.com/time/magazine/article/0,9171,1112856,00. html [Accessed: November 10, 2010].

Cover, R. 2000. First contact: Queer theory, sexual identity, and mainstream film. *International Journal of Gender and Sexuality,* 5(1), 71-89.

Cover, R. 2005. Queer subjects of suicide: Cultural studies, sexuality and youth suicide research/policy in New Zealand. *New Zealand Sociology,* 20(1), 76-98.

Crisp, C. and McCave, E.L. 2007. Gay affirmative practice: A model for social work practice with gay, lesbian, and bisexual youth. *Child Adolescent Social Work Journal,* 24(4), 403-21.

Davis, T., Saltzburg, S., and Locke, C.R. 2009. Supporting the emotional and psychological wellbeing of sexual minority youth: Youth ideas for action. *Children and Youth Services Review,* 31(9), 1030-41.

Dorais, M. and Lajeunesse, S.L. 2004. *Dead Boys Can't Dance: Sexual Orientation, Masculinity, and Suicide*, translated by P. Tremblay. Montreal: McGill-Queen's University Press.

Driver, S. 2007. *Queer Girls and Popular Culture: Reading, Resisting, and Creating Media.* New York: Peter Lang.

Edwards, W.J. 1996. A sociological analysis of an invisible minority group: Male adolescent homosexuals. *Youth & Society,* 27(3), 334-55.

Epstein, D. and Johnson, R. 1994. On the straight and the narrow: The heterosexual presumption, homophobias and schools, in *Challenging Lesbian and Gay Inequalities in Education*, edited by D. Epstein. Buckingham: Open University Press, 197-230.

Evans, K. 2002. *Negotiating the Self: Identity, Sexuality, and Emotion in Learning to Teach*. New York: Routledge Farmer.

Foucault, M. 1990. *The History of Sexuality: An Introduction*, translated by R. Hurley. London: Penguin.

Foucault, M. 2004. *Abnormal: Lectures at the Collège de France 1974-1975*, edited by V. Marchetti and A. Salmoni, translated by G. Burchell. New York: Picador.

Friedman, M.S., Marshal, M.P., Stall, R., Cheong, J.W., and Wright, E.R. 2008. Gay-related development, early abuse and adult health outcomes among gay males. *AIDS and Behavior*, 12(6), 891-902.

Gibson, P. 1989. Gay male and lesbian youth suicide. *Report of the Secretary's Task Force on Youth Suicide, Vol 3: Prevention and Interventions in Youth Suicide*. Washington D.C.: U.S. Department of Health and Human Services; Alcohol, Drug Abuse and Mental Health Administration.

Griffin, P. 1992. From hiding to coming out: Empowering lesbian and gay educators. *Coming Out of the Classroom Closet*, edited by K. Harbeck. New York: Harrington Park Press, 167-96.

Halperin, D. 2007. *One Hundred Years of Homosexuality*. New York: Routledge.

Hegna, K. 2007. Coming out, coming into what? Identification and risks in the 'coming out' of a Norwegian late adolescent gay man. *Sexualities*, 10(5), 582-602.

Hegna, K. and Wichstrøm, L. 2007. Suicide attempts among Norwegian gay, lesbian and bisexual youths: General and specific risk factors. *Acta Sociologica*, 50(1), 21-37.

Hennessy, R. 1994. Queer theory, left politics. *Rethinking Marxism*, 7(3), 85-111.

Hooks, B. 1994. *Teaching to Transgress: Education as the Practice of Freedom*. New York: Routledge.

Hope, A. 2007. Risk taking, boundary performance and intentional school Internet misuse. *Discourse: Studies in the Cultural Politics of Education*, 28(1), 87-99.

Horlick-Jones, T. 2003. Commentary: Managing risk and contingency: Interaction and accounting behavior. *Health, Risk & Society*, 5(2), 221-8.

Jackson, J. 2007. *Unmasking Identities: An Exploration of the Lives of Gay and Lesbian Teachers*. Lanham, MD: Lexington Books.

Jackson, J. 2009. How do you spell homosexual? Naturally queer moments in K-12 classrooms. *International Journal of Critical Pedagogy*, 3(1), 36-51.

Jackson, J. 2009. Teacher by day, lesbian by night: Queer(y)ing identities and teaching. *Sexuality Research and Social Policy*, 6(2), 52-70.

King, M., Semlyen, J., Tai, S.S., Killaspy, H., Osborn, D., Popelyuk, D., and Nazareth, I. 2008. A systematic review of mental disorder, suicide, and deliberate self-harm in lesbian, gay and bisexual people. *BMC Psychiatry*, 8(1), 70-86.

Leck, G. 2000. Heterosexual or homosexual? Reconsidering binary narratives on sexual identities in urban schools. *Education and Urban Society*, 32(3), 324-48.

Macdonald, R. and Cooper, T. 1998. Young gay men and suicide: A report of a study exploring the reasons which young men give for suicide ideation. *Youth Studies Australia*, 17(4), 2-27.

McAndrew, S. and Warne, T. 2010. Coming out to talk about suicide: Gay men and suicidality. *International Journal of Mental Health Nursing*, 19(2), 92-101.

McDaniel, J.S., Purcell, D., and D'Augelli, A.R. 2001. The relationship between sexual orientation and risk for suicide: Research findings and future directions for research and prevention. *Suicide & Life-Threatening Behavior*, 31(1), 84-105.

Mishna, F., Newman, P.A., Daley, A., and Solomon, S. 2009. Bullying of lesbian and gay youth: A qualitative investigation. *The British Journal of Social Work*, 39(8), 1598-614.

Moskowitz, E. 2008. A curb on gay marriage will fall. *Boston Globe*, 30 July, A.1.

Remafedi, G., Farrow, J.A., and Deisher, R.W. 1991. Risk factors for attempted suicide in gay and bisexual youth. *Pediatrics*, 87(6), 869-75.

Rofes, E.E. 1983. *"I Thought People Like That Killed Themselves": Lesbians, Gay Men and Suicide.* San Francisco, CA: Grey Fox Press.

Rosario, M., Schrimshaw, E.W., and Hunter, J. 2008. Predicting different patterns of sexual identity development over time among lesbian, gay, and bisexual youths: A cluster analytic approach. *American Journal of Community Psychology*, 42(3, 4), 266-82.

Rutter, P.A. and Soucar, E. 2002. Youth suicide risk and sexual orientation. *Adolescence*, 37(146), 289-99.

Savin-Williams, R.C. 1996. Self-labeling and disclosure among gay, lesbian and bisexual youths, in *Lesbians and Gays in Couples and Families: A Handbook for Therapists*, edited by J. Laird and R.J. Green. San Francisco: Jossey-Bass, 153-82.

Saxey, E. 2008. *Homoplot: The Coming-Out Story and Gay, Lesbian and Bisexual Identity.* New York: Peter Lang.

Schehr, R.C. 2005. Conventional risk discourse and the proliferation of fear. *Criminal Justice Policy Review*, 16(1), 38-58.

Sedgwick, E.K. 1990. *The Epistemology of the Closet.* Berkeley, CA: University of California Press.

Shneidman, E. 1985. *Definition of Suicide.* New York: John Wiley & Sons.

Straayer, C.1996. *Deviant Eyes, Deviant Bodies: Sexual Re-Orientation in Film and Video.* New York: Columbia University Press.

Suicide Prevention Resource Centre, 2008. *Suicide Risk and Prevention for Lesbian, Gay, Bisexual, and Transgender Youth.* Newton: Education Development Center, Inc.

Troiden, R.R. 1988. *Gay and Lesbian Identity: A Sociological Analysis.* Dix Hills: General Hall.

Walls, N.E., Freedenthal, S. and Wisneski, H. 2008. Suicidal ideation and attempts among sexual minority youths receiving social services. *Social Work*, 53(1), 21-9.

Wangsness, L. and Estes, A. Personal stories changed minds. *Boston Globe*, 15 June, A.1.

Warren, C.A.B. 1974. *Identity and Community in the Gay World.* New York: Wiley.

Wiegman, O. and Guttleing, J.M. 1995. Risk appraisal and risk communication: Some empirical data from the Netherlands reviewed. *Basic and Applied Social Psychology*, 16(1, 2), 227-49.

Zhao, Y., Montaro, R., Kgarua, K., and Thombs, B.D. 2010. Suicidal ideation and attempt among adolescents reporting "unsure" sexual identity or heterosexual identity plus same-sex attraction or behavior: Forgotten groups? *Journal of the American Academy of Child & Adolescent Psychiatry*, 49(2), 104-12.

Chapter 5

At the Intersection of Racial and Sexual Passing and African-American Celebrity

Willie Tolliver and C. Riley Snorton

Introduction

Willie Tolliver and C. Riley Snorton take on the complex issues of racial and sexual passing. Tolliver develops new ways of thinking about the intersection by examining Asian and African-American passing and sexuality in Paris during the age of the Harlem Renaissance. Among other issues arising from the intersection of race and sexuality, Snorton focuses on Oprah Winfrey's celebrity exploitation of the "down low" and what that entails for African-American male sexuality. The dialogue following Tolliver's and Snorton's development of their main themes delves into a different understanding of how the intersection works, as well as clarifying its key concepts.

Looking for Lattimore: The Passing Male as Sexual Chameleon in Monique Truong's *The Book of Salt*

Willie Tolliver

Monique Truong's *The Book of Salt* concerns the experiences of Binh, a Vietnamese expatriate in 1930s Paris, who finds work as the cook for Gertrude Stein and Alice B. Toklas. The narrative shifts between his memories of Saigon and his observations of the fabled household. Basing this character on references to two Vietnamese male cooks in *The Alice B. Toklas Cookbook*, Truong interweaves historical recreation and fictional speculation to explore the dynamics of colonialism, displacement, nostalgia, sexuality and desire. One narrative layer traces the relationship Binh forms with a particular habitué of Stein's Saturday afternoon teas: Marcus Lattimore, an iridologist, who happens to be an American from the South who is passing for white. Binh works for the two American women, or my Mesdames as he names them, every day except Sunday when he goes to Lattimore's garret for an extra day's work and for sex. Binh calls Lattimore "Sweet Sunday Man" and addresses parts of his narrative directly to him.

Lattimore as a character is a compelling invention because his presence brings into play a number of political and racial issues. The intimacy of the two men recognizes the possibilities of coalitions between marginalized groups across racial lines. David Eng notes this alliance:

> This is a queer diaspora in which the gentlemen from the American South and the Vietnamese servant-cook, despite their disparate class positions, can both appear, a racialized space and time they can collectively inhabit and share. (2008: 1489)

Yet there are ruptures within this shared queer diaspora. The histories of African-American enslavement and Asian subjugation are unequal in their relation to the center of power. Lattimore, through his biraciality, through his partial whiteness, enjoys class and social privilege that Binh as a displaced Vietnamese laborer cannot hope to attain. Binh is limited by his visual difference while Lattimore benefits from his racial ambiguity. Binh is aware of their marginalizations' inequity and of Lattimore's advantages when Binh recalls one of their exchanges:

> I hide my body in the back rooms of every house that I have ever been in. You hide away inside your own. Yours is a near replica of your father's, and you are grateful for what it allows you to do, unmolested, for where it allows you to go, undetected. This you tell yourself is the definition of freedom. (Truong 2003: 151)

In an earlier conversation, Binh recounts what Sweet Sunday Man has told him about his mother:

> But you are not like her, you say, touching the tips of my eyelashes. The blood is your key, not your lock. A southern man without his father's surname is a man freed, you tell me, dispensing irony like a hard, uncrushed peppercorn. A man with a healthy income from his mother is also a freed man, you add, with a laugh that falls to the ground, exhausted and sad. Your mother's money has paved your way to this city. It first sent you to the north of your America for college. It knew that there the texture of your hair, the midnight underneath the gauze of your skin, were more readily lost to untrained eyes. (Truong 2003: 112)

What Binh indicates here are the deep historical sources of his lover's position: the white slave-owning father who will not claim him, the not so tragic mulatta mother who gains a fortune through her concubinage, the one drop of black blood that defines both his mother and himself, the educational and geographic mobility that passing affords, and the final leap of luck and imagination that lands him in Paris. While his trajectory describes an escape from his past, his relationship with Binh ironically returns him to it. When he asks Miss Toklas if he might secure the services of Binh on his day off, she agrees and informs Binh that Lattimore is "an American, but one who could still afford to pay a premium" (Truong 2003:

38). This transaction replicates the practice within the slave system of loaning out slaves for their labor. Despite his black blood, Lattimore assumes the position of his white, slave-owning ancestors, and, through the functioning of a democratic capitalism, a position of equal status with Toklas.

Lattimore deepens his complicity in American imperialist power when he finally betrays Binh. Impressed by Stein's literary reputation, Lattimore persuades Binh to steal one of Stein's unpublished manuscripts. This has been Lattimore's covert objective all along. When he acquires the notebook, he disappears from Binh's life and from the text. The market exchange basis of their relationship becomes clear to Binh. He ruminates:

> Sweet Sunday Man … I knew that I could offer you something no other man could. With my eyes opened, sensitive to these Mesdames of mine, my value to you I thought would surely increase, double and sustain itself. Value, I have heard, is how it all begins. From there, it can deepen into worth, flow into affection, and artery its way toward the muscles of the heart. (Truong 2003: 150-1)

Where Binh expected love, he finds that he has been a means to an end. As Y-Dang Troeung notes, "Truong uses the discourse of economics to register Binh's feelings of betrayal [and] the reduction of Binh to a commodity of pure use value" (2010: 118). Sweet Sunday Man is revealed as a consummate agent of American power, practicality, and greed.

Lattimore's ambiguity has its limits because his performance of whiteness cannot completely overcome the mark of race. He is not able to deceive the Emperor of Vietnam who has summoned him for an iridological reading and who immediately perceives Lattimore's racial identity (Troung 2003: 116). Stein and Toklas have their suspicions and ask Binh directly if Lattimore is a Negro. When he is loaned to the American, Binh is charged with the task of looking for proof of his race. In their racist action, the Mesdames seek to strip the passing Negro of his equal American status, to put him in his place, and to affirm their white supremacy and power (Eng 2008: 1488). They are frustrated in their efforts because, in an act of love and solidarity, Binh never tells.

When the two women make this request, it seems almost as though they expect Binh to find the evidences of Lattimore's racial identity by having intimate access to his body. This expectation is not so unreasonable because so many of the novel's political, racial, and cultural meanings with all their contradictions and ambivalences are written on his body. The most powerful meaning perhaps is what that body means to Binh (Truong 2003: 151-2). With clearheaded shrewdness, Binh captures Lattimore's complexities. He notes his lover's fundamental flaws, his alienation from himself, his living an unsustainable life, his deceit, and his inauthenticity. Given these insights, Binh should have from the beginning been able to predict his betrayal. He also describes his lover's ability to change, his body constantly transforming to match his circumstances. He acknowledges how difficult it is to capture such an evasive object of desire and ultimately how little he knows of him. For instance, Binh's passion for The Sweet Sunday Man is clear, but whether that feeling is reciprocated remains a mystery. He may be willing to share his body, but it cannot be determined if for him sex is an act of opportunism or the expression of identity and need. He truly does hide within his body, both racially and in terms of his sexuality.

Contrary to Binh's conclusion that Lattimore is a "dubious construction," this character is a fascinating and significant creation, virtually a template for the figure of the racially passing male. His meaning is not fully articulated satisfactorily through the perspectives of the critics who have focused on the novel. Eng sees Sweet Sunday Man as a victim of history in "the making of the political and aesthetic realm of Euro-American modernity" (Eng 2008: 1491). Troeung reads him as an example of the colonizing power who attempts to consume the stories of the colonized in the process of collaborative autobiography. It might also be profitable and revelatory to read this character through an African-American lens, against the cultural stereotypes about mulatto men as well as his historical and literary precedents. My other aim here is to explore the necessary connections between racial and sexual identity as figured in such a representation of gay multiracial masculinity.

To find historical traces of Sweet Sunday Man one need only look to the Harlem Renaissance's cast of characters, which were sustained by a network of gay, lesbian, and bisexual writers, artists, and musicians. Wallace Thurman chronicled Harlem bohemian life in the satiric roman a clef *Infants of the Spring* (1932) and anatomized the colorism of the times in *The Blacker the Berry* (1929). Published in the decadent and controversial single-issue magazine *Fire!!*, Bruce Nugent's story "Smoke, Lillies and Jade!" is the first explicitly gay-themed short story to be published by an African American. Like Sweet Sunday Man, Nugent was so light-skinned that he was able to pass without intention or effort, gaining housing in white hotels when he first moved to Harlem (Messerli 2010) Harold Jackman was not a major figure within the movement, but he was ubiquitous. Carl Van Vechten used him as the model for the protagonist of *Nigger Heaven* (1926), the novel that helped to define the Harlem Renaisssance. Jackman's one mark of distinction was his passion for rare books (Byrd 1993: 56). His bibliophilia may serve as a historical precedent for Lattimore's preoccupation with the manuscripts of Gertrude Stein.

In order to explain the presence of a figure like Lattimore in *The Book_of Salt*'s diegesis, Harlem would need to be displaced to Paris, which is exactly what happened. As Tyler Stovall notes, "So many [black writers] visited Paris that at times it seemed that the entire Harlem Renaissance had transferred its seat of operations overseas" (1996: 60). A homosexual biracial man passing as white in 1920s Paris would not have been an anomaly although there would have been no need for this strategy given the open and relatively non-racist nature of Paris and Parisians in the wake of modernism. On the other hand, racial mixing was not extensive among the American expatriate set at this time. A few black gay and bisexual men, however, were able to cross the social and racial line. Claude McKay, political activist and author of *Home to Harlem* (1929), at home in both high and low Parisian societies, straight and gay, did attend Gertrude Stein's teas (ibid.: 79). In Truong's novel, Paul Robeson makes an important appearance. Poet Countee Cullen, the greatest of the African-American Francophiles, enjoyed several artistically and socially productive sojourns in France. After marrying the daughter of W.E.B. Du Bois in 1928, he sailed off to Paris for an extended vacation—with Howard Jackman (Watson 1995: 81).

As a source for the character of Marcus Lattimore, Langston Hughes proves an interesting case. He, too, lived for a brief period in Paris during the 1920s, but, according to his autobiography *Big Sea*, his experience was different from that of his black compatriots. He did not move among the intellectual and artistic elite. Working as a dishwasher and doorman for the popular black nightclubs, he saw Paris from the bottom. Nonetheless, he fits Sweet Sunday Man's phenotype and psychosexual profile. Hughes was known for his beauty and his charisma, and was attractive to both men and women. Countee Cullen was frustrated in his pursuit of Hughes and passed him along to Locke (Watson 1995: 55). When Locke visited Paris in 1925, he took Hughes under his wing and introduced him to the cultural riches of the city. The two spent an idyllic spring in the city as flâneurs. At the end of the summer, Locke confessed his love in a letter. He, too, would get no response from Hughes and abandoned him in frustration. Just as Hughes offered no clear responses to his admirers, Lattimore gives no indication of genuinely reciprocating Binh's desire. In terms of his sexuality, Hughes was not only a chameleon, but a sphinx. Rampersad writes: "Amiable, fun-loving, Hughes was yet a sexual blank; his libido, under stimulation or pressure, seemed to vanish into a void" (Rampersad 1986: 289).

Sexuality is a constitutive component of prevailing cultural stereotypes of mulatto men. This is particularly true of the character type generated at the turn of the century by white racist writers such as Thomas Dixon, Jr., the author of *The Leopard's Spots* and *The Clansman*. Anxiety and fear over miscegenation motivated the construction of mulatto male characters as hypersexual with a propensity toward violence, particularly the rape of white women. George Frederickson explains that "many White Americans believed that mulattoes were a degenerate race because they had 'White blood' which made them ambitious and power hungry combined with 'Black blood' which made them animalistic and savage" (Frederickson 1971: 277). Black writers formulated an oppositional paradigm for the mixed race hero: a paragon of black pride and uplift. According to Naomi Zack, "when he was good the male mulatto embodied moral courage, altruism, moral purity, and the added masculine virtue of being a good provider" (Zack 1993: 130).

Sweet Sunday Man fits into neither of these characterizations, but does find description in other notions about biracial masculinity that circulate in literature and culture. Three defining traits would include: duplicity, intelligence, and sexual ambivalence. The double nature of the mulatto allows him to cross back and forth across the color line undetected. The very act of passing is a deception, a joke on the world. In doing so the passer becomes a trickster figure who functions to call into question and subvert the existing hierarchy of power. When Lattimore acquires the notebook of Gertrude Stein, he gets revenge on the literary establishment. While he plays a trick on Stein, it is at the expense of the duped and betrayed Binh for whom Lattimore is passing not only as white but as a lover as well.

The intelligence of mulatto males is attributed to their inherited whiteness, or "the mulatto hypothesis" (Russell et al. 1992: 5). This mental keenness is frequently illustrated in fictional characters through descriptions of their eyes. Dr. Frank Latimer in Frances Harper's *Iola Leroy* (1895) is the biracial hero who marries the novel's eponymous protagonist. Here is his introduction: "His complexion was blonde, his eyes bright and piercing" (Harper 1990: 425). Similarly in Pauline Hopkins's 1900 novel *Contending Forces*, the heroic male figure, Will Smith, "was tall and finely formed, with features almost perfectly chiseled, and a complexion the color of almond shell … His eyes were dark and piercing as an eagle's" (Hopkins 1988: 90). This descriptive convention is reflected in *The Book of Salt* when Binh meets Lattimore for the first time and experiences his penetrating gaze: "After years of the imposed invisibility of servitude, I am acutely aware when I am being watched, a sensitivity born from absence ... As I checked the teapots to see whether they needed to be replenished, I felt a slight pressure. It was the weight of your eyes resting on my lips" (Truong 2003: 37). Truong reworks the trope of the gaze of the mulatto male here to eroticize it and to move it into the space of same sex desire.

The intersection of biraciality and sexual transgression is a theme deeply embedded in African-American literature. Throughout black literary history the racially ambiguous character is associated with ambiguous sexual desire and identity. This phenomenon appears with such frequency that a new stereotype comes into being: the biracial bisexual. This type is articulated in different ways at different historical moments. During the Harlem Renaissance, Wallace Thurman extolled the figure of the sweetback or the sheik dandy as he appeared in fiction and on the street. A counterforce to the bourgeois heterosexual ideal of masculinity of the time period, the sweetback was an urban survivor who hustled women and who expressed his individuality through dandified fashion. He purposefully flouted the conventions of black manhood, and Wallace saw this persona as participating in the "queering of the black male body as part of a cosmopolitan aestheticism that crosses over racial and cultural borders" (Knadler 2002: 902). Furthermore:

> [the] sexually (and we might even add racially) ambivalent … .sheik … is both virile and 'femininely' seductive—both a gazer and dandified object of voyeuristic erotic pleasure. The sweetback assumed traits and roles traditionally segregated among the genders, and in most of Thurman's texts, this doubleness is replayed in the hustler's bisexuality. (ibid.: 920)

Given his adeptness at the hustle (albeit on a high literary level), his seduction of Binh as well as of the Mesdames with his sartorial flair, his versatile racial identity and sexuality, Sweet Sunday Man embodies the sheik's allure.

In antebellum fiction, the mulatto hero steps outside heterosexuality's confines by cross-dressing. One of the strategies used by slaves to escape to freedom was to dress in the clothing of the opposite sex. Mulatto boys and men are especially convincing when dressed in female clothing because of their perceived beauty. In an early scene in James Weldon Johnson's *The Autobiography of an Ex-Coloured Man*, the passing narrator recalls the pivotal moment in his life when learns that he is black. This passage could also be a page from Sweet Sunday Man's life. The offspring of a wealthy Southerner and a beautiful mulatta, the narrator has grown up in the North assuming that he was white. One day at school, his teacher asks all the white students to stand, and he is instructed to stay in his seat. Traumatized, he goes home to verify this news by looking at his reflection in a mirror, and this is what he sees:

> For an instant I was afraid to look, but when I did, I looked long and earnestly. I had often heard people say to my mother: "What a pretty boy you have!" I was accustomed to hear remarks about my beauty; but now, for the first time, I became conscious of it and recognized it. I noticed the ivory whiteness of my skin, the beauty of my mouth, the size and liquid darkness of my eyes, and how the long, black lashes that fringed and shaded them produced an effect that was strangely fascinating even to me. (Johnson 1990: 11)

This is a moment when he could come to terms with his racial identity. Instead, he is mesmerized by his own beauty. Even more problematic is that this beauty is perceived in terms of whiteness. The narrator is applying the logic of the prevailing notions about racial hierarchies: If beauty equals whiteness and I am beautiful, then I must be white.

Beneath this line of thinking are other cultural stereotypes about race and color. Within African-American communities, light skin is equated with beauty and dark skin with masculinity. Therefore, light-skinned women are seen as beautiful. This creates a problem for light-skinned black men, whose beauty aligns them with females and renders them less masculine. These men can resolve this crisis of racial and sexual identity in two ways: performing a hard masculinity or finding the positives in the color of their skin, such as greater opportunities for education and upward mobility (Russell et al. 1992: 66-7). Both the Ex-Coloured Man and Lattimore exercise the latter option.

Siobhan Somerville offers an interpretation of this primal scene with a focus on the narrator's incipient sexual identity. She identifies the erotic nature of the boy's response to his image in the mirror. He is transfixed by his own beauty, which is described in the same way that the beauty of mulatto women is inscribed in literature (Somerville 2000: 113). He has crossed a border from one gender to the other; he may even occupy both positions simultaneously. As Brian Philip Harper claims,[1] this moment is about the narrator's nascent sexual orientation and is not a crisis of racial identity. Harper makes the following point about the feminizing process: "This feminized orientation itself potentially constitutes the protagonist's personal tragedy, indicating a gender identity that is anything but properly masculine, and verging dangerously on a sexual identity that is anything but hetero" (Harper 1996: 110).

The result of such a psychosexual development is dramatized in the adult life of the unnamed narrator of *The Autobiography of an Ex-Colored Man*, whose original title was *The Chameleon* (Leiter 2010: 74). The parallels between the experiences of this narrator and Truong's Sweet Sunday Man are many. The premise of the novel is that the passing protagonist recounts his life without understanding its meaning. He discloses the joke he feels has perpetrated on the world by passing as white. The joke, however, is on him as he reveals more about himself than he intends. As Michael Hardin (2004) observes, "At the textual level *The Autobiography of an Ex-Coloured Man* is about passing as white, and the resultant challenge to stable notions about race; however, at the subtextual level, this novel also seems to be about passing as heterosexual." Throughout his accounts of his various experiences in the cigar factories of Florida, in the New York club world and his travels through the American South, the unnamed narrator is more attentive and drawn to men rather than to women. The most significant relationship he develops is with the unnamed millionaire who becomes his benefactor. The narrator is a musician, and the millionaire hires him to perform for his parties. He even "loans" him out to friends for special occasions. The replication of slave market exchange is clear. This relationship is also a reproduction of his mother's concubinage, for the homosexual nature of the bond is readable as is the imbalance of power. Cheryl Clarke asserts that the passages describing the narrator's playing of music at the demand of his patron to the point of exhaustion are metaphoric descriptions of their sex (1995: 90).

The relationship reaches a crisis in Paris where the narrator and the millionaire have enjoyed an idyllic season, much like Langston Hughes and Alain Locke as well as Lattimore and Binh. The Ex-Coloured Man who has thrived in Europe decides to return to the United States with the contrived mission of studying the black South's native music. His real motivation is that for him to remain with the millionaire would require an admission of his sexuality. Instead, following the pattern of his life, he escapes. His decision turns on the precise point of the intersection of his racial and sexual identities. He embraces one when he is unable to face the other.

The connection between racial ambiguity and sexual ambivalence is a constant in African-American literature. Cheryl Clark asserts, "This tradition of covert, subtextual discourse on transgressive sexuality has persisted in black narratives of

---

1   As quoted in Somerville.

all kinds" (Clark 1995: 96). The best explanation for the source of this connection comes from Somerville who looks to the history of sexology. She finds that at the turn of the twentieth century when sexual classifications were being formulated, American society was also undergoing a process of formulating its racial ideology. These two discourses were shaped by the same cultural assumptions and attitudes. Somerville suggests that "the structures and methodologies that drove dominant ideologies of race also fueled the pursuit of knowledge about the homosexual body" (Somerville 2000: 17). The result was that racial and sexual norms were defined against the Other. If whiteness and heterosexuality were the norms, then the non-white and non-heterosexual were the aberrations that affirmed those norms. Additionally, identities that fell between the binaries of black and white and homosexual and heterosexual existed in an intermediate space that was deemed dangerous and perverse, which justified the marginalization and persecution of individuals within that group. This process thus created a close association between the interracial and homosexual, both being equal or even merged in their distance from the purity of the racially unmixed and heterosexual norm. These ideas permeated scientific thinking and found their way into the culture in the forms of public policy and artistic representation. Because of this process and the naturalization of these racial and sexual ideologies, within the pages of an early modernist novel or a work produced by a member of the Harlem Renaissance, a mulatto male character who sleeps with men would not have been surprising.

Monique Truong constructs this one significant line of narrative within her novel upon layers of such scientific, cultural, and literary history. In the process she recognizes and subverts stereotypes about mulatto men, invents possibilities for new images, and explores new alignments of marginalities, such as those between blacks and Asians. She resurrects the figures of the past and weaves intricate webs of intertextuality. All of this has been wrought to make it possible for Binh on Sundays in Paris sometime in the 1930s to find his way into Lattimore's bed.

Negotiating the Glass Closet: Sexual Passing and the Queer Politics of Black Celebrity

C. Riley Snorton

On April 16, 2004 global media icon Oprah Winfrey introduced an episode, titled "A Secret Sex World: Living on the 'Down Low,'" which was arguably responsible for mainstreaming discourses about the "down low," a term typically used to describe black men who have sex with men and women and do not identify as gay or bisexual. On that day, she began her episode with an unusual announcement. "I'm an African-American woman," she said. At which her studio audience responded with laughter (presumably, because they did not feel such information needed to be declared). Perhaps realizing that her show opener did not elicit the intended effect, Winfrey explains that her producers had a similarly skeptical, perhaps even dismissive, reaction when she discussed her choice to open with a declaration of her identity. Winfrey states:

> When I told the producers I wanted to say that, they go like, '*Really* now?' But, I'm an African-American woman so when I picked up the paper the other day, and saw this headline, it really got my attention. The headline says, "AIDS is the leading cause of death for African Americans between the age of 25 and 44." That is startling! All my alarms went off. Not only are more Black people getting AIDS in record numbers … more women, listen to me now, more women, more college students and people over 50 are at greater risk than ever before. Today, you're gonna hear many reasons why AIDS is on the rise again. Here's a shocker! It's one of the big reasons why so many women are getting AIDS. Their husbands and their boyfriends are having secret sex with other men. (*Audience moans*) Okay, I'll let that sink in for a minute. (*Audience laughs*) Okay, so this lifestyle even has a name. It's called "Living on the Down Low". Okay, living on the down low. (Winfrey 2004)

Winfrey's uncharacteristic opening gestures toward the various kinds of affective responses people have to the news. Her identifications heighten her attentiveness to certain dimensions of the story, increasing her sensitivity to recent news reports about HIV/AIDS rates for black women, college students, and people over fifty. On the other hand, Winfrey's response also demonstrates a type of preferred performance to the "news" of the down low, more specifically, which, in her own words, is a "shocker!" Winfrey's distinctive mode of punctuating exposition with her own commentary: "That is startling!" "Here's a shocker!" is intended to translate these emotions to her audience and viewers at home. Indeed, we as her audience respond with equal measures of attentiveness even if we are not shaped by the same forms of identification or history. Journalist and media analyst Ellen Hume (2010) describes Winfrey as a host who acts as "fellow sufferer" with her viewer. And in her 2004 episode, perfectly pitched to reach black, middle class heterosexual women, Winfrey aims to expose her viewers to the suffering caused by secrecy. As a consequence of her sensationalistic tone, this episode encourages and even articulates ways to surveil one's potentially duplicitous lover.

But Winfrey's media persona also helps us understand how "down low" rhetoric can be usefully observed by peeking through the analytical frame of the glass closet, a term I have developed to understand public black sexualities as already figured as deviant, while simultaneously read as mysterious and untenable in mediated space. I suggest that the glass closet, as a metaphor and analytic, plays a critical part in the emergence of "down low" rhetoric, while it also demonstrates how the "down low" signifies a frequent relation between representations of blackness and queerness. Adhering glass to closet highlights and elaborates upon processes of racialization, and the supposed transparencies of racial difference, left out of queer theory's canonical treatments.[2] Marlon Ross, in his essay "Beyond the Closet as Raceless Paradigm," makes a related argument as he describes the various problems attendant to using the "closet" as structuring metaphor for epistemologies of sexuality. For Ross, the claustrophillic obsession with the closet as it appears in Foucault, Sedgwick, and other canonic works of (white) queer theory obscures and ignores the variations and discrepancies in the processes of identification within and among people of color and poor people. In broad strokes, Ross argues that (white) queer theory's "fixation on the closet function as the grounding principle for sexual experience, knowledge, and politics ... diminishes and disables the full engagement with potential insights from race theory and class analysis" (Ross 2005: 161). Moreover, the closet as it appears in (progress) narratives about gay subject-making serves to draw on an implicit colonialist sensibility that figures the "dark secrecy" of the closet with the pre-modern and primitive and the subsequent open consciousness of an "outside" of the closet with modernity and Civilization (ibid.: 162-3). To push Ross's interpretation a bit further, I offer that there is no cover for blackness just as there is no escape from the colonialist legacies of whiteness. The closet, as metaphor, then is a supple fantasy that seeks to construct a space of confined refuge but also a space (of freedom) beyond these constraints.

Moreover, I suggest that when rigorous attention is paid to race and sexuality—"the color line" and the "closet"—the structure of the glass closet emerges. Part, if not the primary objective, of the color line is the visualizing of difference and the concurrent production of mechanisms by which to delineate race as an obvious ontological fact. Therefore as Ross concludes, "crossing the closet threshold is ... not like crossing the color line" (2005: 161) because there is no obfuscation of what exists on the other side of the threshold. It is transparent rather than translucent. However, rather than viewing the closet as a potential "claustrophillic distraction," it may be more pertinent to think about why closets (rather than lines or veils) prevails as a metaphor to think through sexuality. One must also consider that the closet as a space of confinement is also a space of display. As such it is also ironically able to dramatize the very narrowing in, the claustrophobic feelings produced by the mechanisms of identity.

Robert Reid-Pharr argues that the "myth" of black sexual potency has, despite disavowal, been a strategy for resistance—a veritable tool in navigating the color line—for Black Americans. For Reid-Pharr, "This resistance turns, moreover, on our ability to cleverly rearticulate the very logic of an ancient and profound distinction between black and white that stands behind all of the ugly racism for which our proud nation is so famous" (2007: 32). Drawing on his provocative discussion of black sexuality and the implications of the metaphorical power of the "Negro"—as referent and signifier—for American political culture, this argument interrogates

---

2   Although Sedgwick and other queer theorists, most notably Diana Fuss and Judith Butler, have all offered a version of the always already transparent closet, each of their models attend to sexuality without consideration of other forms of identification, like race, class, or gender, that shape the closet's construction.

the public nature of black sexuality and the frequent pairing of blackness and queerness in the popular imagination—reading this relationship as an inflexion, as Roland Barthes (1957) suggests in *Mythologies*. The term, "inflexion," typically refers to a change in the form of a word, which in turn changes its grammatical function. Reading Barthes alongside Reid-Pharr then, we understand that myths about black sexuality cannot register as "lie" or relative truth, or confession—and thus giving one the opportunity to come clean. Rather they can only be understood as a variation of existing discourse: as an inflexion. Reading black sexuality and all of its public configurations as exceeding simple designations of "direct object" or "subject" demonstrates how black sexuality modifies American culture, writ large, and constellates and reconfigures other concepts, like celebrity, race, sexuality, and the increasing availability of "information" about our most notable public figures. Oprah Winfrey, as a multimedia entrepreneur and household name, is one such figure that merits an investigation along these lines. In what follows, I offer up an interpretation of Winfrey's public persona and personal scandals—making use of debased discourses, like rumor and gossip, as well as the official rhetorics of episodes from *The Oprah Winfrey Show*—to explore the myriad ways that black celebrity is queerly figured on the down low.

In an update to the first down low show, titled "Why She Sued Her Husband for $12 Million and Won," and aired on October 7, 2010, Winfrey demonstrates that not much has changed in her approach to the subject matter:

> Oprah Winfrey: Imagine finding out your soul mate, the man you share your life with, and your bed with, is sneaking out and having sex … with other men. Uh huh. I see your eyes. There are two words for this. It's called down low, as in living on the down low. It's a dirty little secret that we first talked about six years ago on our show. (Winfrey 2010)

Demonstrated in the visual editing of the opening segment, we see that Winfrey anticipates a particular reaction to the revelation of the down low, and her camera people quickly provide us with the visual proof of the intended effect of what Winfrey described as a "dirty little secret," still in need of exposition six years after her initial report. Winfrey's update episode is a roadmap with which to explore how down low rhetoric is critically shaped by institutional and vernacular discourse and includes one segment on the multi-million dollar settlement one woman, simply called "Bridget" on the show, received after suing her "down low" ex-husband and a series of extended conversation with some of her guests from the 2004 episode, most notably, the self-proclaimed expert J.L. King, motivational speaker and author of *The New York Times* Best-Seller, *On the Down Low: A Journey into the Lives of "Straight" Black Men Who Sleep With Men*.

In a series of clips from her original 2004 episode, Winfrey restates the contours of down low mythology, eagerly provided by co-conspirator King. In an exchange between the two, we see how one of the primary definitions of down low hinges on the concept of deception even to one's self.

J.L. King: Why do I have to label myself? Why do I have to put a label on myself to make you comfortable?

Oprah Winfrey: Ok, I don't want to be comfortable. I just want to know what it is.

J.L. King: In the black community, when you come out and say that you're gay and proud, then automatically people look at you differently. They treat you differently. All of a sudden, they're like I want you to meet my gay friend, J.L. Oh I want you to meet my gay brother, J.L. I want you to meet my gay father, J.L.

Oprah Winfrey: Ok, so that's the reason why it's called the down low.

J.L. King: Down low means that I don't want anybody to know. I want to do what I do. It's my business, and it's none of your business what I do. It's wrong. It's wrong.

Oprah Winfrey: Ok, would down low also mean denial? Ok. (Audience laughs, applauds)

J.L. King: Denial, yes, yes. (Winfrey 2010)

What begins as a heated exchange about the utility of sexual identity markers or labels, and the radical potentialities of resisting categorization very quickly becomes a meditation on how the "black community" necessitates the "down low." In this regard, King gives us several examples, in which the "black community" would affix "gay" to the various roles he embodies as a black man, which one might read as a community's unwillingness to allow black gay men the flexibility and freedom to claim an authentically black identity.[3] Literary critic Scott Herring reads this scene as an exchange that "goes nowhere," as a moment where "inarticulation" functions as "sexual disarticulation." "Winfrey's 'excavations' in Herring's interpretation, make King only more undetectable; the more she researches, the more he recedes" (Quoted in Lofton 2011: 111). However, King's strategy relies on deploying various narratives about the hyperbolic nature of black homophobia. Indeed part of down low's rhetorically seductive power lies in its ability to confirm and reconstitute popularly circulating narratives about its specifically racialized context of homophobia. In such a way, the down low serves as a popular tautology where pathologized black sexuality is derived from pathologized black culture writ large. We might recall similar rhetorical moves

---

3   For a more detailed analysis of the tensions produced between race, sexuality, and authenticity, consult E. Patrick Johnson's *Appropriating Blackness: Performance and the Politics of Authenticity.*

made in materials as diverse as the Moynihan Report and contemporary debates about the homophobia rampant in hip hop culture. This language is particularly acute when linked to HIV/AIDS discourse. As Cindy Patton has argued, AIDS is often attributed to "types of people" who get what they "deserve" (Quoted in Fine and Turner 2004: 165). Patton's point highlights a critical dimension of popular understandings of AIDS more generally, which is that most often AIDS bodies are stigmatized even before they are in fact infected.

A good illustration of this is found in the case of Nushawn Williams who was sentenced to a four-twelve year prison term for having unprotected sex with women while knowing he was HIV positive. Garnering widespread media attention, Williams was credited as the source of a micro-epidemic of HIV cases in the small, mostly white town of Jamestown, NY. While Williams was not described as "down low," he was, for a greater part of the late nineties, the black male face of sexual danger and duplicity. Thomas Shevory provides a productive reading of Williams' case in his book, *Notorious H.I.V.* Citing Stuart Hall's work on crime, Shevory explains, "The perception of and control over crime exist ... within an ongoing 'crisis of hegemony' that pervades the postwar capitalist state" (2004: 6). The demonization and potential criminalization of the "Down Low" (DL) helps to explain newsrooms' focus on the urban, under-class rather than the structural factors, which constitute the phenomenon. The down low figure often appears alongside other more "respectable" figures—the out gay man, the unknowing, virtuous wife, the heterosexual male friend or father figure. Often these figures are represented as responsible through their oppositional relationship to the DL character. Winfrey's update episode brings all of these caricatures to bear in a personal narrative of self-aggrandizement. As Kathryn Lofton explains, "Winfrey, the talk show preacher, is a 'story dramatizer' with her confessional prodding, with her attempts to 'heal' the guest and the greater society whose 'problem' he or she supposedly represents" (2011: 117).

Indeed it seems that Winfrey returns to the DL to prove that these men were gay all along, and as King segment shows, the performance of "coming out" serves as a redemptive act for the down low figure. Greeted by applause, King's declaration of accepting his status as a black gay proud man redefines, and incidentally coincides with his earlier theorization of the down low, that sexuality is not shaped by who you sleep with but who you are, i.e. where behavior does not equal identity. In their exchange, however, we understand very clearly what's at stake for Winfrey in down low narratives—namely that down low represents a problem because it seems in contradiction to Winfrey's media persona as a guru that helps people to be their best selves, which ultimately means, living a life that falls into the recognizable parameters of among other things, sexual identity. Toward the end of the episode, Winfrey cites Maya Angelou, stating, "when you know better, you do better." However, knowing better for Winfrey, unfortunately does not mean informing her viewers that the majority of medical researchers argue that "down low," as they have been able to study and define, has been vastly exaggerated as a source of increased rates of HIV, a fact she does include on her website under "7 Myths about HIV/AIDS." "Knowing better" for Oprah is about choice and order—about rejecting the kinds of vestibular grays—and here, I am referring to Hortense Spillers' work on cultural vestibularity and the work black bodies do to produce and trouble particular binaristic senses of culture. It is these vestibular grays that trouble Winfrey and the members of her audience.

Yet there is an explicit irony here as well: Winfrey, a celebrity dogged by her own persistent rumors about same-sexual desire and practice (namely that she has been in a secret long term relationship with best friend and *O* Magazine Editor-At-Large, Gayle King) must also convincingly perform a disconnect from her lived reality, offering up a series of identity markers that lead her to a response of shock rather than empathy. On December 9, 2010, Winfrey received a rather pointed set of questions about her own sexual practices, albeit not for the first time, on Barbara Walter's Special: Oprah the Next Chapter. Intensified by her emotional outpouring, Winfrey describes the importance of her relationship with King. King is mother, sister and friend, a true kinfolk/skinfolk:

> Barbara Walters: A lot of women have close friends. Very few have friends as close as yours. Describe that friendship to me.
>
> Oprah Winfrey: Mmm hmm, wooo. Ok, uh … .she is the mother I never had. She is the sister … everybody would want. She is the friend that everybody deserves. I don't know a better person … .I don't know a better person.
>
> Barbara Walters: Why is it making you cry?
>
> Oprah Winfrey: (deep sobbing breath) Shoot, I wasn't going to cry here, but it's making me cry because I keep thinking about how much I've never told her that. Tissue, please. Now, I need tissue. I never told her that.
>
> Barbara Walters: So, when, to me, those dumb rumors come up, that you are gay. What do you say?
>
> Oprah Winfrey: mm hmm, well I have said, uh..we are not gay enough times. I'm not lesbian. I'm not even kinda lesbian. And the reason why it irritates me is because it means somebody must think I'm lying. That's number one. Number two: why would you want to hide it? That is not the way I run my life. (Walters 2010)

Winfrey's candid response not only marks the seasoned rejoinder of a public figure for whom these rumors will not quell but also highlights how such speculations require a double concealment in order for them to be credible. Winfrey has often been questioned about why she did not marry Stedman Graham and conform to heteronormative ideals of womanhood. However, if we follow these rumors' logics—casting Graham as Winfrey's "beard"—then we must not only believe that she is queer but also on some level, homophobic. Homophobic, not in the sense of committing a violent act against members of the LGBT community, but paradoxically in the display of a form self-repudiation that motivates her to remain "closeted." Hence what irritates Winfrey about the "dumb rumors" are the very logics that animate her discussions about the down low. I would argue that we could view Winfrey's coverage as a performative and rhetorical tactic, which we could call ignorant. I offer "ignorance" here as an alternative mode for thinking about how the co-constitutive processes of race and sexualization interact. As we know, ignorance carries various connotations. The word, "ignorance," is derived from the Latin word *ignorans*, which carries two meanings: to be unknowing or to ignore knowledge of some specific issue, idea, or thing.

Contemporarily, if we were to call someone ignorant, we would presumably mean that the person in question is uninformed about a particular matter. However, the double valence of the term—both as the unknowing and ignoring of information—gestures toward the rhetorical and performative potentialities of the concept. That is to say that what we might call, feigned ignorance, which relies on willfully ignoring certain realities, a powerful tool to negotiate prohibition and taboo, as we see here in the clear disjunctures between Winfrey's sensationalistic account on the Oprah Winfrey Show and her affect inflected response to rumors about her same-sexual desires.

Ignorance, however, also has several meanings, which circulate very specifically in black vernacular speech, including, lacking "typical" regards for decorum, the state of being flagrantly politically incorrect, or acting shamelessly. In this sense, to be ignorant also carries a definite affective charge—and those to whom it is attributed are both chastised and applauded for their flagrant disregard of social laws and codes. This notion of ignorance also intersects with the generic forms of melodrama and comedy, often connoting a playful but potent subversion of societal norms. Ignorance, as I make use of it, diverts us away from the turn to shame in contemporary queer theory as an analytic to describe these issues.[4] To analytically deploy ignorance—both in its theoretical and performative possibilities—requires considering a space where blackness and queerness can and do combine in such a way that they suspend (rather than reinforce) social prohibitions. And here I'm thinking about one of the fundamental principles of social code, where exception is necessary to create order. This momentary, mystical space of subversion and suspension is one way to understand the function of the glass closet through which we see that Winfrey is confined by the very rhetorical strategies she uses to constrain others. Focusing on the invisibility of glass in structuring the glass closet also becomes a useful analytical keyhole by which we may understand what makes Winfrey's report compelling to various

---

4   In my forthcoming monograph on the same subject matter, I focus particularly on Kathryn Bond Stockton's *Beautiful Bottom, Beautiful Shame: Where 'Black' Meets 'Queer'* and Sedgwick's *Touching Feeling: Affect, Pedagogy, Performativity* as theorizations of the relationship between "black" and "queer" under the analytic rubric of shame.

audiences, as her rhetorical strategies attempt to deploy the glass closet as shelter from speculation about her own sexuality. Stabilized by biopower, the glass closet is sutured together by institutional and social modes of regulation. As such the glass closet relies on the literalization of scopic-enabled modes of supervision, or what we might call a kind of popular panopticism. The bodies, trapped inside, whether J.L. King, Winfrey or the litany of black public figures who are routinely questioned about their secretive and potentially duplicitous sexual practices, are determined (perhaps even overly determined) by a panoptical public imaginary.

In other words, we should think of biopolitics as invisibly (like glass) defining the parameters of acceptable social performance, regulating how we act and what we say. On the other hand, there are these nearly imperceptible cracks—like the unsanctioned and devalued discourses of rumor and gossip—that allow us to glimpse the contours of the glass structure. Down low rhetoric brings the glass closet into stark relief, for it is the hum of down low discourses, whispered on the low down, that bring into view the workings of a biopolitical regimen that includes a constellation of more celestial bodies, including, among others, mass media, the federal justice system, and the Centers for Disease Control and Prevention.

Winfrey, then, encourages us to think precisely about how race, class, gender, and sexuality, both popularly and epistemologically, are structured by the space of the glass closet; this contradictory space marked by concealment and display. Apprehending the glass closet in our analyses of representations of black sexuality allows us to conceptualize the "down low" as a rhetorical refrain in an existing concerto of representations of black sexual duplicity. In this way, the glass closet demonstrates how the black body is always already sexually passing. Narratives like the "down low" and the ubiquity of so-called queer images of black celebrities suggest that destabilizing and disavowing black heteronormativity is perhaps a condition of the mass mediation of racialized bodies and performance. Or put another way, since heteronormativity is not afforded to blackness, it should be of no surprise that black celebrities are always failing to pass as heterosexual. And yet the glass closet is also a reflection of the way panoptical modes of viewing, like the gossip blogs, the paparazzi industry, and the popular tabloid press, shape popular reading practices of public racialized bodies.

John Erni, in his elegant reading of Michael Jackson's child abuse sex scandals, defines "queer sexuality" as a "practice of discursive excess that twists normal notions of gender and sexuality" and the "queer body" as "an adventure in surplus representations" (1998: 158-80, 160-1). While Erni attributes these excesses to queer mediation, the element of racialized celebrity is something that he does not explicitly thematize in his essay. But what Erni describes as "queer figurations in the media" are also already racialized figurations as well. Erni posits that these queer figurations have the potential "to positively re-invent, re-figure, and re-define ideas and events" (ibid.: 175). However, these figurations are similarly structured by forces of categorization—an outgrowth of a biopolitical "will to know," which structures our panoptical public imagination and supports the growing industry of celebrity gossip media. What we think we know about a black public figure almost always outweighs whatever claims a celebrity might make. As such, and what a figure like Winfrey emblematizes, is that the figuring of black bodies publicly is analogous to entering a "zone of socially licensed excess ... without guarantee" (ibid.). This is the relationship between mass mediation and the glass closet; it is also the relationship between black and queer.

Comments on Snorton's "Negotiating the Glass Closet"

Willie Tolliver

In his argument, C. Riley Snorton offers significant insights into the ways in which race complicates the constructions of celebrity and sexuality. His thesis is that the figure of the closet as conceptualized by white queer theorists is inadequate to account for differences in race and class. His redefinition posits the closet as a glass structure through which the sexuality of black celebrity is perceived as non-normative and through which that sexuality is on view because of blackness's permanent visibility. In this way queerness and blackness become necessarily connected in popular culture. In common usage the closet functions as a private space for queer identity's creation, and the glass closet allows unofficial, unacknowledged disclosure of sexual identity for white celebrities. In his discussion of the glass closet in a popular gay monthly, Michael Musto (2007) describes the situations of various actors, actresses, and media personalities whose homosexuality is commonly known, but whose positions are protected by the invisible enclosure of their silence. It is telling that most of the people described are white, which supports Snorton's claim that the glass closet operates differently and has a different meaning for people of color.

Snorton argues that highly visible black bodies as sexualized spectacle are subject to extraordinary scrutiny, which is intensified when those bodies may possibly inhabit a queer identity. This surveillance makes it impossible for the black gay celebrity to find a haven in the closet. The racialized and sexualized gaze is so insistent that it renders the walls of the closet transparent. In such a case the individual is enclosed but is seen nonetheless, which allows both the individual and the spectator to invest in the fiction of the closet. Snorton also suggests that black objects of this gaze, rather than hiding, can find within the glass closet through the opportunities for subversive display the possibility of a liberating space.

Snorton focuses on Oprah Winfrey's treatment of the Down Low phenomenon as an example of the functioning of the glass closet, and his analysis is fascinating and suggestive. In his discussion he scores a number of critical points which amount to a cogent critique of Oprah's image and her role as a cultural savior and authority. He articulates her complicity in the production of the exploitative gaze that transfixes the Down Low identity, her enforcement of traditional values, and the hypocrisy of her own negotiation of the glass closet.

In her presentation of the Down Low syndrome on her talk show, Winfrey sensationalizes, exoticizes, and demonizes this sexual identity through her spectatorial gaze which is informed with vestigial homophobia. She certainly plays upon the unacknowledged homophobia of her audience in order to create her rhetorical effect. Also inherent in her narrative is a criticism of the Down Low, claiming that this identity is based on a contradiction or a delusion. Men Who Have Sex with men is synonymous with gayness, according to her, and the black men who cannot claim this are in denial. When Oprah persuades J.L. King to come out and renounce his Down Low identity, she enforces the societal sexual binary and maintains the line between homosexuality and heterosexuality, a line that the Down Low effectively blurs. In achieving King's conversion, Winfrey in her liberal zeal, ironically employs a tacit homophobia to affirm a preferred and acceptable gay identity. In eliding the Down Low, Winfrey also achieves an erasure of a truly queer identity that does the social and cultural work of creating a new liberating space for black male sexual identification.

This instance of sexual policing is indicative of Winfrey's larger objective of affirming and advancing mainstream values. Certainly this is how she deals with race. Sherryl Wilson writes, "what is offered on her show is a safe and therefore acceptable version of blackness, that normative codes are upheld in the celebration of this exemplar of the American project—life, liberty and the pursuit of happiness for all" (Wilson 2003: 173). This containment of race is extended into the realm of sexuality. Epstein and Steinberg assert that:

> [A]lthough the *Oprah Winfrey Show*, regularly addresses issues of gender and sexuality, it does so without an analysis of gender politics and compulsory heterosexuality … At the heart of these problematics, is a presumption and, indeed, a pursuit of normalized heterosexuality … heterosexuality is construed as the ultimate object of desire. (Epstein and Steinberg 1997: 34-5)

An understanding of Winfrey's basic sexual ideological position renders quite clear the meaning of her utterance at the beginning of the show that Snorton describes. When she claims her identity as an African-American woman, she is claiming her privilege as a heterosexual woman who has the power to other homosexual black men for her purposes. Her affirmation of heterosexuality is a constituent element of her celebrity identity.

Yet, there are fissures in that identity. Winfrey's hypocrisy resides in the fact that in forcing King from a Down Low to a black gay identity, she denies him the liminal space that she herself claims.

Oprah's deft manipulation of the glass closet discloses the bivalent nature of Oprah's star persona. Snorton's critique of Winfrey points to this central mechanism of her celebrity: a conflation of the public and the private self. Harris and Watson note this in explaining her ability to use herself, her body, and her personal traumas to connect in an intimate way with her audiences. They write, "The parasocial relationship viewers imagine with Winfrey is no doubt assisted by her seeming willingness to collapse the boundaries between the public and the private (Harris and Watson 2007: 6). Interestingly, this elision is integral to the nature of television communication and its personalities. P. David Marshall writes, "Whereas the film celebrity plays with aura through the construction of distance, the television celebrity is configured around conceptions of familiarity" (Marshall 1997: 119). He elaborates:

> [T]the television star who emerges as host and interpreter of the culture for the audience is treated as someone everyone has the right to know fully … the television talk-show host, though constructing a public persona, is also constructed as clearly presenting him- or herself. The gap between the fictional or mythical and the real life of the celebrity is narrowed. (ibid.: 131)

Marshall concludes, "The real life of the host, if the host is constructed, like Oprah, as authentic and sincere, is never elided from the stage performance. This unity of being goes beyond a homology between the person and the celebrity" (ibid.: 148). The glass closet is predicated upon an elision of the private and the public identity. It is an apt metaphor for Oprah's condition because as the particular kind of celebrity that is defined by this conflation, she already and in fact has always inhabited it.

Snorton's invocation of the glass closet is useful not only in understanding the fundamental dimensions of Winfrey's celebrity but also in reading two other current public narratives, those of CNN anchor Don Lemon and the disgraced celebrity minister Bishop Eddie Long.

The African-American church is well known for its homophobia and for its construction of its own glass closet. Horace Griffin asserts:

> Lesbians and gay men both experience a history of ridicule, hostility, pain, suffering and death … Black gay men in the church have been the target of this derision and live with the reality of scriptures, perspectives, and actions being directed against them and their love relationships. (Griffin 2006: 111)

The result of this pressure on homosexual church members is an enforced silence:

> Lesbians and gays in most black churches are subjected to being silent about their partners, vague or deceptive about marriage interests, or dishonest about their relationships for fear of repercussion. Gay relationships are not recognized publicly along with those of heterosexuals, and in order to pastor or serve in the black church, gays and lesbians must learn to stay in their place and shut up about 'it.' (ibid.: 111- 12)

The black church's mechanism of this enforcement is a heavy and intense surveillance of the private lives of its ministers and members, rendering those private lives public with the expectation of conformity to a compulsory heterosexuality. Yet, within this practice, despite its general and official condemnation, the church tolerates its homosexual members who are known and seen. The price is that they must construct their own walls of glass by not privileging their individual sexual identity over group solidarity. This is a bargain many gay men accept in exchange for the rewards of community. The author and scholar, bell hooks, writes of one acquaintance who finds personal freedom within these constraints:

> One black gay male I spoke with felt that it was important for him to live in a supportive black community, where his sexual preferences were known but not acted out in an overt public way, than live in a gay subculture where this aspect of his identity could be openly expressed. (hooks 2000: 68)

The glass closet is a powerful force in the black church. One's sexual nature is seen and recognized, but a performance of sexual convention is expected. Griffin explains:

> Passing as heterosexual in black churches is not only common, *it is expected* … Even in churches where it is "known" that the pastor is gay, black church Christians are content to remain in the church if the pastor is willing to present himself as heterosexual with a wife and children. (Griffin 2006: 145-6)

This seems to be the case with Bishop Eddie Long of Atlanta. He is the charismatic minister of New Birth Missionary Baptist Church, one of the nation's foremost mega-churches with a membership in excess of 25,000 (Leslie 2010). Atlanta's black elite from the worlds of sports and entertainment worships each Sunday in his $50 million cathedral (Haines 2010). The pastor has a high profile in the worlds of television, international charity, and politics. In 2006 his church was the site of Coretta Scott King's funeral, which was attended by four presidents of the United States. In the fall of 2010 a lawsuit was filed against him by four young men who accused him of sexual improprieties. He exacted sexual relationships from them in exchange for sharing the perquisites of his celebrity such as expensive cars and foreign travel in private planes.

The irony of the case is that Long has been a vocal opponent of gay marriage, and his ministry includes gay conversion therapy. When the scandal broke, Long's congregation was inclined to stand by him. Commentator Wayne Besen (2010) takes Long's followers to task: "his flock, in my view, deserve to be fooled and fleeced. Time and again, these now 'stunned' parishioners ignored the pertinent facts of Long's sketchy life to buy into the fabulous fiction he peddled each Sunday." This primary fiction is his performance of compulsory heterosexuality. At the same time that his sexuality and his duplicity have been uncovered, Long finds a space within his situation for defiance. In his first sermon after the revelations, he stated, "I have never in my life portrayed myself as a perfect man. But I am not the man that's being portrayed on the television"

(Long 2010). These sentences are remarkable for their balance of ambiguity; he is both making a veiled admission of his guilt at the same that he shields himself from blame. It is one of the most stunning negotiations of the glass closet in recent memory.

In the aftermath of the Bishop Long scandal, CNN broadcast a show featuring interviews with members of Long's congregation. During the course of the discussion and in response to an opinion that the young men should not believed, CNN anchor Don Lemon made the surprising disclosure that their stories were indeed credible because they were consistent with his own experience with pedophilic sexual abuse. The viewership's reaction to his confession was overwhelmingly positive. Weeks later, in anticipation of the publication of *Transparent*, a memoir of his career and earlier life, Lemon revealed to *The New York Times* that he is gay (Carter 2011). He details his motives for coming out, and they are closely related to his sense of vocation:

> As a journalist, I'm a huge believer in transparency. I don't like communication with a hidden agenda, and I don't like people who conceal things to make themselves look better ... In the interest of transparency, it also seems fair for viewers to know something about the people from whom they get their information. (Lemon 2011: x-xi)

Therefore, he feels compelled to disclose the nature of his private life, his sexual identity, in order to be a better conduit of information to the public.

What is the relationship between the glass closet and Lemon's transparency? There is no denial here, no penetrating surveillance, no requirement of compulsory heterosexuality, no subversive sense of liberation. Is he any more visible because he is black gay celebrity? Lemon's act takes him to a place beyond the Down Low and beyond the glass closet. He writes of all the other open secrets in his life, such as the identity of his father, and he claims that he has only been harmed by them. By never constructing those walls and by offering full disclosure, he removes the secrecy from the open secret, and all that remains is openness.

Comments on Tolliver's "Looking for Lattimore"

C. Riley Snorton

My colleague, Willie Tolliver, directs his critical attention to the relationship between protagonist, Binh and his Sweet Sunday Man, Marcus Lattimore, as it unfurls in Monique Truong's *The Book of Salt*. In his compelling analysis, which provides necessary political and historical references to ground Truong's work of historical fiction, Tolliver speculates about new possibilities for reading sexual and racial alliance across an uneven field, marked by the material conditions of colonialism and slavery, as well as Binh and Lattimore's attendant performative tactics of in/visibility and disidentification. Aptly describing Lattimore as a trickster figure, Tolliver offers up a number of roughly contemporaneous historical figures from the era of the Harlem Renaissance and before to untangle the various plots inscribed on the Sweet Sunday Man's narrative body. The political and representational alignment of multiraciality and bisexuality, resulting from shared marginalization, situates Lattimore in a rhetorical matrix that connects him to figures like the unnamed protagonist in James Weldon Johnson's *Autobiography of an Ex-Colored Man* and myriad historical figures, including Langston Hughes, Bruce Nugent, and Alain Locke. Reflecting on the expressed relationship between Binh and Lattimore, which too might be described as an uneven field of sexual desire, Tolliver makes a persuasive argument about Lattimore's multiple acts of passing—racially and sexually—arguing that the Sweet Sunday Man may indeed be hiding "within his body" (see Tolliver, this volume). This short argument, a rejoinder of sorts, takes up this idea as a provocation to think through the broader implications of hiding in the body and its consequences for our understandings of passing and processes of identification.

To hide in one's body, to use one's body as shelter, to allow it to be read or to direct its audience's readings theoretically reframes the f/utility of passing. That is to say, it begs the question, to whom is one passing and why? Can one "pass" as one's self? And if so, what is that self—is it accessible through the body or is it a more illusive entity that lurks below the body's surface? Lattimore's profession as an iridologist parallels and heightens the dynamics of racial and sexual passing and their relationships to the body. Generally regarded as pseudoscience in contemporary scholarship, iridology instructs its practitioners to examine the characteristics of the iris in order to determine the health of the body's internal systems and organs. Rather than regarding the eye as a window into the soul, iridologists view the eye as an entry point to the internal workings of the body, to gain entrance to those things hidden by skin, synapse, and bone. The eyes' orientation in the face and the parallel relationship between theories of visuality and scripts of personhood are similarly discussed in Marlon Ross's essay, "Pleasuring Identity, or the Delicious Politics of Belonging," in which he explains:

> The face, as the front door of the head, has, not surprisingly, been the most intensely scrutinized body part—whether by gentle scientists cautiously manipulating calipers in the ethnological laboratory or by brutal bigots brandishing guns in the lynching mob. Eyes, nose, ears, forehead, mouth, lips, eyebrows, nostrils, teeth, tongue, all have been calibrated and recalibrated with both the most delicate instruments and the clumsiest weapons of the cartoon, the camera, and the naked eye of the white supremacist. (Ross 2000: 828)

Here Ross illustrates how the eye is often both the object and method of analysis. In both instances, the eye might act as a portal to white supremacist modes of thinking. Indeed, famous iridologist, Dr. Henry Lindlahr, considered the founder of "scientific naturopathy" in the United States, explicitly linked iridology and eugenics in his treatise, published in 1919, *Iridiagnosis and Other Diagnostic Methods* (2004). For Lindlahr, eye color, as determined by racial heredity, is divisible into two primary groups: brown and blue. And while both are considered "normal," the Aryan race was graced with the preferred, "outstanding racial characteristics" of "tall stature, egg-shaped skull, fair skin, yellow hair and azure blue iris" (Lindlahr 2004: Chapter IV). Unsurprisingly then, the eyes and the face are regarded as an indication of both categorical difference as well as individuality, punctuating the desire "to turn sameness into manageable difference," (Eng 2008: 1488) even the difference that marks off one body—one face—or pair of eyes—as a unique invention. In this regard hiding in the body might be seen as a strategy that resists both impulses—where the corporeal husk neither defines the individual nor the force of human categorization.

While hiding does not foreclose the possibility of being found, as is the case when Lattimore is "discovered" by the Emperor of Vietnam to be non-white, it does introduce a space of interiority that has the possibility to remake this scene. The Emperor of Vietnam says upon meeting Lattimore, "I can smell the bleach in your hair, the touch of lye. I'm not a bigot, Doctor Lattimore, but I'm no fool" (Truong 2003: 116). That the Vietnamese emperor is tipped off by smell—as oppose to sight—is of import in thinking through passing as a manipulation of the visual field. However, when taking Lattimore's interiority into account, we might recall the adage "who's fooling who?" as an apt retort. Indeed while the reader is acutely aware of Binh's inner most thoughts, a practice of articulation, which we might call embodied consciousness, Lattimore is a more "dubious construction," a disembodied figure, whose presence is marked by absence, and whose later narrative absence providing an eerily haunting presence, in which readers are left to speculate about many of Lattimore's intentions. Thus, Lattimore hides in his body, in terms of race and sexuality, just as he hides in the nation of France, in his class position as a member of the medical profession, and in the text itself. And yet, these practices are analogous to inhabiting a glass closet—to hiding in plain sight, concealed and yet exposed in Truong's narrative.

Yet, we must also understand that the glass closet is also a quintessentially ignorant move. It is a space of not knowing—wilfully or "innocently"[5]—as well as a site of disregard for the protocols established by a "politics of respectability," an idea explained by Evelyn Higginbotham as an adoption by of white, middle class norms, which serve to regulate performances of race, gender and sexuality.[6] However, the glass closet is not a site of suppression but a suspension of these swirling

---

5   And by "innocently," here, we might think of this as without forethought.

6   E. Francis White elaborates on Higginbotham's analysis when she argues, "black people have developed African-American nationalism as an oppositional discourse to counter [racism]. Ironically, though not surprisingly, this nationalism, too, draws on the ideology of respectability to develop a cohesive political movement" (2001: 122).

ideologies of racial respectability, class propriety, and "proper" sexual conduct. In its suspension, those who inhabit the glass closet deploy a form of ignorance conversant with Robert Reid-Pharr's notion of "funniness" (Reid-Pharr 2007: 46).[7] Reid-Pharr argues in his chapter on Richard Wright, another contemporaneous figure to the people discussed in Tolliver's argument, that part of the intriguing ingenuity of such a performance is its ability to deftly manipulate publicity such that it ultimately establishes "him neither as potential 'sexual minority,' ripe for the queering, nor even as a suspect Black American ... precisely because it is built upon a sort of awkward, childlike Black American civility" (ibid.). Ignorance implies an innocence as well—precisely because we expect adults to understand and internalize various taboos. This suspension of prohibitions, facilitated by a technology of ignorance, creates the conditions for behaving shamelessly. It is the moment when, as Georges Bataille argues, we are no longer conscious of the taboo we observe because we have fully submitted to it (1987: 37-40).

While ignorance, as I make use of it, carries the possibility of resistance, even as it is certainly not a wholly liberatory act, hiding in the body seems to be more of a tactic of interpretation—an interpretive frame, which brings the notion of the "self" into view. As John L. Jackson and Martha S. Jones explain, "There is no way to be(come) a human subject without recourse to the practices/readings intrinsic to most understandings of passing—that is, except by passing through passing itself (2005: 11). Or as I have said elsewhere in regards to the practice of passing and transgender identity, "Through the experiences of psychic dissonance, affirmation, disavowal, and recognition, we engage in the process of passing off our daily experiences of embodiment as identifications—creating 'fragile fictions' of personhood" (Snorton 2009: 87). In this way, passing is the substance of identification.

Turning to Gertrude Stein, another key figure in Truong's *The Book of Salt*, it may behoove us to look again at arguably her most famous and most misunderstand line. First published in a 1913 poem, entitled "Sacred Emily," and later appearing in Stein's other writings: "A rose is a rose is a rose." The sentence is often mistaken as an example of a tautological construction, taken to mean that things are simply the way they are, "a rose is a rose ..." However, the phrase might also signify upon the relationship between images and emotions in language, where the rose (which is a rose ... which is a rose) is each time "new," and thus reflecting the shifting representations of a rose, as it changes depending on the speaker, the context, and the time. Then let us consider if we substitute a rose with a body, to allow the body to take new shape each time, and therefore to pass all the time, and to shelter us from those things which threaten that which we hold dear—to hide us from exposure.

---

7   Reid-Pharr, in his discussion of Richard Wright, suggests that funniness could be described as one of the major "technologies of publicity to American intellectuals who produced their work in the years defined by World War II and its aftermath" (2007: 46).

A Response to Snorton

Willie Tolliver

C. Riley Snorton's reconsideration of the concept of the glass closet generates a number of resonances with the area of my argument concerning black gay identity during the period of transatlantic modernism, particularly the Harlem Renaissance. The scholarship on that cultural moment reveals that its genius was driven by the energy of its creative black gay men. Their sexuality has been discussed by contemporary commentators, and that sexuality was also common knowledge at the time. Nevertheless, the cultural establishment exerted a regulatory power on its queer brothers. Gay male literary figures such as Countee Cullen and Wallace Thurman entered into covering heterosexual marriages even though their same sex desires and behaviors were generally known.

Christa Schwarz writes, "It seems true that indiscretions on the part of male Renaissance artists were usually overlooked by the guardians of Harlem's morality if general standards of decency were adhered to—their homosexual inclinations were generally treated as 'open secrets'" (2003: 23). The Open Secret of the Harlem Renaissance was a precursor of the Down Low.

Snorton's reading of the glass closet allows for a provocative defense of Down Low identity. Rather than a hiding place, it becomes a free and protected space for black men to inhabit a queer identity without claiming it and to feign ignorance while flaunting their transgressiveness. From the perspective of the gaze that penetrates the glass closet, the identities thus contained become one. Racial and sexual marginalities are conflated. Such a formulation answers the question about the necessary connection between racial and sexual ambiguity in the construction of passing narratives. This perceptual resolution explains how in the workings of the literary imagination, from James Weldon Johnson to Monique Truong, the one drop of blood that renders a character black also makes them queer.

Snorton's analysis also uncovers aspects of the nature of passing itself. If the act of passing involves simultaneous concealment and disclosure that can have a liberatory benefit for the passing identity, what then is the experience of the witness who sees through the walls of the glass closet? Snorton's concept recognizes the power of this gaze. If the passer is both hiding and seen, he or she needs the pressure of surveillance. The act of passing within the glass closet becomes collaborative, which may also describe passing in general. It must be remembered that passing is a form of border crossing which requires a gatekeeper who regulates and permits the passage from one territory to another. Usually passing is accomplished with the complete and undetected assumption of a desired identity, in which case the gatekeeper is duped. With the glass closet, the passing performance is always imperfect. The impersonation of normativity is always detected, and the deception is given sanction by the gatekeeper.

This economy of queer passing, which valorizes the observer, is corroborated by theories of racial passing. Kroeger states that "we can know people are passing when people effectively present themselves as other than who they understand themselves to be ... and when other people actually see or experience the identity that the passer is projecting" (2003: 12-13). The pass is not complete until it is validated by the observing audience. Dawkins supports this claim when she observes: "The audience constructs or deconstructs the pass" (2009: 31). Dawkins goes on to cite Robinson's conception of the dramatic theatre of passing, which is based upon a triangular configuration consisting of the passer, the second persona or the dupe, and the third persona or the in-group clairvoyant (Robinson 1993: 17-18). The dupe is the observer who is taken in by the deception and who belongs to the system into which the passer wishes to gain entry. The in-group observer sees through the impersonation but allows the pass through not telling. The latter posture prevailed as racial passing was practiced in the American past. Those who disappeared into the white world were given permission by friends and family who knew their true identities but maintained their silence out of racial solidarity. These gatekeepers understood the material advantages their passing brethren stood to gain. This position is pointedly articulated in an exchange between the characters Irene and Brian Redfield in Nella Larsen's *Passing*: "'It's funny about "passing." We disapprove of it and at the same time condone it. It excites our contempt and yet we admire it. We shy away from it with an odd kind of revulsion, but we protect it.' 'Instinct of the race to survive and expand'" (1986: 185-6).

The complicity of the black observers of passing is carried out today in the contemporary cases of black congregations and their closeted ministers. Gay ministers construct their glass closets and people them with the requisite wives and children as a spectacle for their congregations, who know the open secret. The church members act as regulators who allow these men to pass as one of them. At this point, the intersection of queer and racial passing becomes complicated. In-group clairvoyants share an identity with the observed passer. In this instance, the congregation and minister are joined by their blackness. However, how does the minister's queerness redound upon his observers? Is this not also a part of the shared group identity? Where does the willingness to overlook queerness begin to converge with an investment in that identity, or at least a deep understanding or connection with it? Dawkins observes a mistake that is made by the observers and gatekeepers of passing: "Second and third persona audiences believe they can see acts of passing without being seen themselves" (2009: 32). They are in some way defined by what they do not acknowledge. The implicated and complicit observer further supports Snorton's conflation of blackness and queerness within the glass closet.

The glass closet does complicate the triangular formation of passing in one more interesting way. If the observer sees the deception and permits it, then who is duped? There appears to be no second persona in the mechanics of the glass closet. Snorton's idea about the "ignorance" of the passer might offer an explanation. The gatekeeper's knowingness is equaled by the passer's heightened self-consciousness. Snorton's idea about the passer's "ignorance" of his or her situation does not preclude this knowledge. The act of passing within the glass closet requires a deliberate suppression of self-awareness. This willed, disingenuous obliviousness of conventionality has another dimension. The passer may possess an "ignorance" that goes beyond his or her intention. Snorton's discussion of how Lattimore's subterfuge is seen through and how this revelation indicates his own self-deception and exposure reveals another aspect of passing. In James Weldon Johnson's *Autobiography of an Ex-Coloured Man*, the passing protagonist tears down the walls of his closet to reveal the joke he has played on the world. What he does not realize is that he is not able to shed the remaining glass walls through which the reader can see his internalized racism as well as the homophobia that informs his ambiguous sexuality. The final joke is on him. Similarly, in Nella Larsen's *Passing*, Irene Redfield lives within her own glass closet and unintentionally reveals to the reader her own ambivalences about blackness and her fraught same-sex desires. In both cases, the connections between queerness and blackness are clearly seen and necessary.

Snorton's conception of the glass closet proves to be a useful critical tool which, when applied to literary texts as well as current narratives in popular culture, can help us survey the contradictions and complexities of intersectional identity and to understand and appreciate the slippages between hiding and exposure.

A Response to Tolliver

C. Riley Snorton

My colleague, Willie Tolliver, raises profound questions about the glass closet and its relationship to open secrecy that I address in a different venue (Snorton 2012). Figures like Bishop Eddie Long and Don Lemon two public personas who brilliantly stage the dynamics of the glass closet—undergird my reading of black sexual syncretism and the irrevocable blending of race and sexuality, mind and body, capitalism and religious expression. The frequent pairing of the down low and the black church in popular culture is not simply another titillating, if banal, coupling of the secular and the sacred. Nor is it analytically sufficient to think of the DL and the black church as two opposing poles of black sexual morality.

Locating the down low in the black church exposes many of the church's contradictory, paradoxical, and just plain unclear teachings and practices on the subject of sexuality (see Snorton, this volume) Often analogized to the now defunct "Don't Ask, Don't Tell" (DADT) military service policy, queer members of the black church are often described as practicing a form of sexual passing, which functions similarly to understandings of down low in popular mythology. In each narrative, they practice a form of self-regulation that requires, in some cases, a conspicuous silence that their fellow parishioners (or unsuspecting girlfriends) cannot hear. This formulation of tolerance resonates with the often-expressed maxim, "Love the Sinner, Hate the Sin," which as Janet R. Jakobsen and Ann Pellegrini have explained is an inadequate construction for dealing with sexual politics. They write, "The line between whom we are supposed to love (the sinner) and what we are supposed to hate (the sin) is impossibly moveable and contradictory" (Jakobsen and Pellegrini 2004: 45). As such, the black church facilitates the down low's rhetorical hold in popular culture, confirming for some what they already regard about homosexuality: it is a sin that requires repentance and a disease, which requires treatment or cure.

The frequency with which homophobia and its inverse—homophilia— haunt and animate both black church and down low rhetoric underscores the relationships between these signs and a broader mediated discourse, which figures black masculinity, leadership, and the heteronormative family as crises of representation. Part of what makes the down low so terrifyingly captivating as a cultural narrative is the idea that these men cannot control their sexual yearnings, regardless of their educational status, economic standing, or spiritual convictions. Thus Long and Winfrey share at least several commonalities worth our attention. The characterization of both figures as sexually duplicitous, I would argue, goes hand-in-hand with their shared status as renowned black *spiritual* leaders, whether in the Protestant or New Age tradition. Religious leaders have often been ripe for ridicule and satire in folklore and popular culture, frequently likened to the pimp in black vernacular expression.

In addition, Long and Winfrey's representations of redemptive suffering also elucidate how theories of identification can provide a critical lens through which to explore their public personas. Long's theosophy of "kingdom business" reflects a masculinist ideology, which encourages his parishioners (and particularly his female congregants) to follow three principles: respect, submission, and obeyance to God, their pastor, and their husband even if their male leaders are not being led scripturally. "A man can be out of divine order in relation to his family (i.e., breaking divine commands, like the prohibition of adultery), but it remains the God-ordained call for women to submit to their husbands" (Walton 2009: 150). Indeed, Walton explains that Long sees women's adherence to the three principles in these circumstances as a form of redemptive suffering. On the other hand, as I have mentioned earlier, Winfrey is known for bringing suffering into the homes of millions of viewers, setting the stage for a recurring redemption narrative where anyone and everyone can live their best life. As John L. Jackson, Jr. explains race, as a concept, has often served as "a powerful and necessary frame for thinking 'the body in pain,' both individual bodies and the collective body politic" (2005: 393-402, 395-6). Thus while both figures are interested in representing their mastery over suffering, they are both circumscribed by a discourse of sexual duplicity that suggests these performances are somehow disingenuous. Thus, and as with the down low more generally, the point is not whether Bishop Eddie Long or Oprah Winfrey are gay but how their racial performances inflect public speculation about their putative queer appetites.

In this regard, when Tolliver raises the case of Don Lemon, articulating a very important point as it relates to the concept of the glass closet. Expressing his conclusion as a question: if the glass closet helps to describe the queering of blackness, then what happens when queer blackness is in its frame? By way of response, I offer up two related points and a final example. Part of what I am suggesting is that queerness and blackness is for all intents and purposes a semiotic redundancy. That is to say that these two signs are inextricably linked. But also, and perhaps more importantly, the glass closet is not about sexual orientation but rather a presumption about sexual practice and a "deviant sexuality," which the public both feels it has the right to know and knows already. Indeed, that seems to be what underlies Michael Musto's musings when he speculates about white celebrities for the Village Voice. Thus, we might say that Lemon, Long and Winfrey are all "trapped" in the glass closet, confined by the popular naturalization of a voyeuristic will-to-know that sutures together sex and black bodies in public. As Hortense Spillers explains, "From the point of view of the dominant mythology, it seems that sexual experience among black people (or sex between black and any other) is so boundlessly imagined that it loses meaning and becomes, quite simply, a medium in which the individual is suspended" (2003: 164). In short, mythologies magnify the apparent transparencies of black sexuality inasmuch as it re-presents blackness alongside and through images of explicit violence and sexuality. In this way, the glass closet acts as a unique vehicle with which to explore the popular imaginings of black sexuality, presenting a version of individual suspension that carries resistant possibilities even as it is also deeply problematic.

References

Barthes, R. 1957. *Mythologies.* London: Vintage.

Bataille, G. 2005. *Eroticism: Death and Sensuality.* San Francisco, CA: City Lights Books.

Besen, W. 2010. Bishop Bling and the gay fling: Rev. Eddie Long's downfall. *The Huffington Post* [Online], October 2. Available at: http://www.huffingtonpost.com/wayne-besen/bishop-bling-and-the-gay-_b_742709.html [accessed: August 14, 2011].

Byrd, R. editor. 1993. *Generations in Black and White: Photographs by Carl Van Vechten.* Athens: University of Georgia Press.

Carter, B. 2011. Gay CNN anchor sees risk in book. *The New York Times* [Online], May 15. Available at:http://www.nytimes.com/2011/05/16/business/media/16anchor.html [accessed: August 20, 2011].

Clarke, C. 1995. Race, homosocial desire, and "Mammon" in autobiography of an ex-coloured man, in *Professions of Desire: Lesbian and Gay Studies in Literature,* edited by G.E. Haggerty and B. Zimmerman. New York: Modern Language Association of America, 84-97.

Dawkins, M.A. 2009. Impurely Raced Purely Erased: Toward a Rhetorical Theory of (Bi)Racial Passing. Ph.D. dissertation, University of Southern California.

Eng, D.L. 2008. The end(s) of Race. *PMLA*, 123(5), 1479-89.

Epstein, D. and Steinberg, D.L. 1997. Love's labors: Playing it straight on the Oprah Winfrey Show, in *Border Controls: Policing the Boundaries of Heterosexuality*, edited by D.L. Steinberg et al. London: Cassell, 32-65.

Erni, J.N. 1998. Queer figurations in the media: Critical reflections on the Michael Jackson sex scandal. *Critical Studies in Mass Communication*, 15(2), 158-80.

Fine, G.A. and Turner, P.A. 2001. *Whispers on the Color Line: Rumor and Race in America*. Berkeley, CA: University of California Press.

Fredrickson, G.M. 1971. *The Black Image in the White Mind: The Debate on Afro-Americana Character and Destiny 1817-1914*. New York: Harper & Row.

Griffin, H.L. 2006. *Their Own Receive Them Not: African American Lesbians and Gays in Black Churches*. Cleveland, OH: Pilgrim Press.

Haines, E. 2010. Ga. Megachurch pastor's flock standing by him. *Atlanta Journal Constitution* [Online], September 27. Available at: http://www.ajc.com/new/nation-world/ga-megachurch-pastors-flock-633300.html [accessed: August 14, 2011].

Hardin, M.H. 2004. Ralph Ellison's invisible man: Invisibility, Race, and homoeroticism from Frederick Douglass to E. Lynn Harris. *Southern Literary Journal* [Online], 37(1). Available at: http://wf2dnvr6.webreat.org/H9suO1966/url=http://proquest.umi.com/pqdweb?vinst=PRO [accessed: September 12, 2010].

Harper, F. 1990. Iola Leroy, 1895, in *Three Classic African-American Novels*, edited by H.L. Gates Jr. New York: Vintage, 225-463.

Harper, P.B. 1996. *Are We Not Men? Masculine Anxiety and the Problem of African-American Identity*. New York: Oxford University Press.

Harris, J. and Elwood W. 2007. Introduction: Oprah Winfrey as subject and spectacle, in *The Oprah Phenomenon*, edited by J. Harris and E. Watson. Lexington, KY: University Press of Kentucky, 1-31.

Hooks, B. 2000. Homophobia in black communities in *The Greatest Taboo: Homosexuality in Black Communities*, edited by D. Constantine-Simms. Los Angeles, CA: Alyson Press, 67-73.

Hopkins, P. 1988. *Contending Forces, 1900*. New York: Oxford University Press.

Jackson, Jr., John, L., and Jones, M.S. 2005. Passed performances: An introduction. *Women and Performance: A Journal of Feminist Theory*, 15(1), 9-17.

Jakobsen, J.R. and Pellegrini, A. 2004. *Love the Sin: Sexual Regulation and the Limits of Religious Tolerance*. Boston, MA: Beacon Press.

John Jr., L.J. 2005. A little Black magic, *The South Atlantic Quarterly*, 104(3), 393-402.

Johnson, J.W. 1990. *The Autobiography of an Ex-Colored Man, 1912*. New York: Penguin Books.

Jonathan, L.W. 2009. *Watch This! The Ethics and Aesthetics of Black Televangelism*. New York: New York University Press.

Knadler, S. 2002. Sweetback style: Wallace Thurman and a Queer Harlem renaissance. *Modern Fiction Studies*, 48(4), 899-936.

Kroeger, B. 2003. *Passing: When People Can't Be Who They Are.* New York: Public Affairs.

Larsen, N. 1986. *Passing, 1929.* New Brunswick: Rutgers University Press.

Leiter, A. 2010. *In the Shadow of the Black Beast: African American Masculinity in the Harlem and Southern Renaissances.* Baton Rouge, LA: Louisiana State University Press.

Lemon, D. 2011. *Transparent.* Las Vegas, NV: Farrah Gray Publishing.

Leslie, K. 2010. Bishop Eddie Long- pastor prominent on the National, World stage. *Atlanta Journal-Constitution* [Online], September 23. Available at: http://www.ajc.com/news/bishop-eddie-long-pastor- 619404?printArticle=y [accessed: August 14, 2011].

Lindlahr, H. 2004. *Iridiagnosis and Other Diagnostic Methods.* Whitefish: Kessinger Publishing.

Lofton, K. 2011. *Oprah: The Gospel of an Icon.* Berkeley, CA: University of California Press.

Long, E. 2010. Transcript of 8 a.m. sermon. *The Atlanta Journal-Constitution* [Online], September 26. Available at: http://ajc.com/news/dekalb/bishop-eddie-long-transcript-634624.html?printArticle=y [accessed: August 14, 2011].

Marshall, P.D. 1997. *Celebrity and Power: Fame in Contemporary Culture.* Minneapolis, MN: University of Minnesota Press.

Messerli, D. 2010. Between heaven and hell. *American Cultural Treasures* [Online], January 27. Available at: http://americanculturaltreasures.blogspot.com/2010/01/betwee-heaven-and-hell.html [accessed: June 24, 2011].

Musto, M. 2007. The glass closet. *Out* [Online]. Available at: http://www.out/detail.asp?page=3&id=22392 [accessed: August 19, 2011].

Rampersad, A. 1986. *The Life of Langston Hughes*, vol. 1. New York: Oxford University.

Reid-Pharr, R. 2007. *Once You Go Black: Choice, Desire, and the Black American Intellectual.* New York: New York University Press.

Robinson, A. 1993. *To Pass/In Drag: Strategies of Entrance and the Visible.* Ph.D. dissertation, University of Pennsylvania.

Ross, M. 2005. Beyond the closet as raceless paradigm, in *Black Queer Studies: A Critical Anthology*, edited by E.P. Johnson and M.G. Henderson. Durham, NC: Duke University Press, 161-89.

Ross, M.B. 2000. Commentary: Pleasuring identity, or the delicious politics of belonging. *New Literary History*, 31(4), 827-50.

Russell, K., Midge, W. and Hall, R. 1992. *The Color Complex: The Politics of Skin Color among African Americans.* New York: Anchor Books.

Schwarz, A.B.C. 2003. *Gay Voices of the Harlem Renaissance.* Bloomington, IN: University of Indiana Press.

Shevory, T. 2004. *Notorious H.I.V.: The Media Spectacle of Nushawn Williams.* Minneapolis, MN: University of Minnesota Press.

Snorton, C.R. 2009. A new hope: The psychic life of passing. *Hypatia: A Journal of Feminist Philosophy*, 24(3), 77-92.

Somerville, S. 2000. *Queering the Color Line: Race and the Invention of Homosexuality in American Culture*. Durham, NC: Duke University Press.

Spillers, H.J. 2003. *Black, White and In Color: Essays on American Literature and Culture*. Chicago, IL: University of Chicago Press.

Stovall, T. 1996. *Paris Noir: African Americans in the City of Light*. Boston, MA: Houghton Mifflin.

Troeung, Y-Dang. 2010. A gift or a theft depends on who is holding the pen: Postcolonial collaborative autobiography and Monique Truong's "The Book of Salt". *Modern Fiction Studies*, 56(1), 113-35.

Truong, M. 2003. *The Book of Salt*. Boston, MA: Houghton Mifflin.

Watson, S. 1930. *The Harlem Renaissance: Hub of African-American Culture, 1920-1930*. New York: Pantheon Books.

White, E.F. 2001. *Dark Continent of Our Bodies: Black Feminism and the Politics of Respectability*. Philadelphia, PA: Temple University Press.

Wilson, S. 2003. *Oprah, Celebrity and Formations of Self*. New York: Palgrave Macmillan.

Zack, N. 1993. *Race and Mixed Race*. Philadelphia, PA: Temple University Press.

Chapter 6

Margins within the Marginal: Bi-invisibility and Intersexual Passing

Samantha Brennan and Maren Behrensen

Introduction

Samantha Brennan and Maren Behrensen debate questions of visibility and queer identification of two marginal groups within LGBTQ communities: bisexuals and intersexuals. Working through questions of political recognition, fashion, and sexual citizenship Brennan explores the limits and possibilities of the communicative process of bisexual visibility. Behrensen develops arguments that established intersexuals as queer with qualification, yet separates intersex visibility from other types of queer visibility via the medical trauma of intervention on intersex bodies which simultaneously also adheres the history of queerness to contemporary concerns for intersex persons.

"Those Shoes Are Definitely Bicurious": More Thoughts on the Politics of Fashion[1]

Samantha Brennan

I am going to begin this chapter with a brief bit of autobiography. I feel like I have been coming out for my entire adult life. I came out first as a lesbian, predictably during my undergraduate student years, and then a few years later as a bisexual, when I discovered I still liked men after all but did not stop liking women. For a number of years I chose to regard this as essentially a private fact about myself. I told family and friends, but only close friends and immediate family, and certainly not workplace colleagues, unless they also happened to be close friends. Over time my thinking has changed and I now try to be out as a bisexual in the communities in which I move. But there have been limits to my success at being out and this chapter is in a part a chance to work through some of my thoughts about the limits and difficulties there are for women who choose to come out as bisexual,

---

1 For my first thoughts on these matters, see my essay "Fashion and Sexual Identity, or Why Recognition Matters," (2011). My argument here rehearses and expands some of the arguments found there. The title is taken from *30 Rock*.

especially for women who are both bisexual and femme. This essay then has a personal impetus but the arguments it explores are ethical and philosophical.

The Causes of Bisexual Invisibility

Sex advice columnist Dan Savage frequently argues that bisexuals have moral and political responsibilities to come out and to be forthcoming about our sexual orientation in a wide range of contexts (e.g. Savage 2010). His view seems to be that bisexual invisibility as a problem, insofar as it is a problem, can be laid at the door of individual bisexual men and women. I am not going to rehearse here the arguments about bisexual invisibility, assuming the problem and the issues it raises are familiar to most readers of this volume. I am going to focus instead on causes and solutions. The problem of bisexual invisibility stems from three different aspects of bisexual life, according to Savage.

First, it is a numbers game. If I'm a bisexual woman, and lesbians and bi-women make up—let's be very generous—15 percent of the population, then there is a much larger group of male partners available to me than there are female partners. Of course, the ratio gets worse if we have to subtract from the overall total the lesbians who will not enter relationships with bisexual women. Hence, odds are, I will end up with a male partner. That's not selling out, that's just the statistics of dating and partner selection. You might also add pressures to conform and the desire to please one's family to the list of factors that pushes bisexuals in the direction of opposite sex partners but we do not need to go there to see the problem. Other than thinking of ourselves as having a moral obligation to be polyamorous and find partners of both sexes (thus confirming another stereotype of bisexuals as hyper-sexual and always non-monogamous), there is little we can do about the numbers problem.[2] Of course, having an opposite sex partner need not stop me from identifying as bisexual and this is connected to the next part of the problem.

Second, I will tend to be seen as whatever sexual orientation best matches the partner I'm with. If most bisexuals end up with opposite sex partners, then most of us will be seen as straight. It is true that if I'm with a woman, I will be seen as a lesbian, but either way, my bisexuality disappears from view. Barring wearing a t-shirt that lists all of my past, or other, sexual partners and/or attractions down the back—like a rock concert tour t-shirt—and drawing peoples' attention that way, it is a challenge to assert one's identity as a bisexual. I do not possess such a t-shirt but I do have one that simply proclaims "bi" on the front, for times when I want to make it very clear. The linguistic challenge is especially tricky. I often correct people who say of me that I'm in a heterosexual marriage. Marriages do not have sexual orientations, I respond. If instead what you mean by "heterosexual marriage" is a marriage of two heterosexuals, then the claim is false. I think it's more correct to refer to my marriage as an opposite sex marriage, or a different

---

2   This would be a stronger version of the claim that Kayley Vernallis (1999) makes.

sex marriage, in contrast with same sex marriage. The same error occurs when two women marry—even if both women are bisexual, people will still tend to refer to them as in a lesbian marriage.[3]

Third, not all people with a sexual history which would be consistent with an ascription of a bisexual identity choose to claim that identity. A woman may be with a male partner for most of her adult life and then realize she is "really" a lesbian and come out as such. A man may occasionally have sex with other men in circumstances where that option is easy and available while still remaining firm in his conviction that he is really heterosexual. A history of bisexual behaviour is not sufficient to determine bisexual identity. (Of course, a history of bisexual experiences is not a necessary condition either. I might be bisexual in my attractions and not had success with men. Or, I might be young and sexually inexperienced.)

Here is yet another example, the movie *Brokeback Mountain*. Is *Brokeback Mountain* a movie about two bisexual men, two gay men, or a combination? I'm persuaded that we do not know what the sexual orientation of the characters was meant to be or even if it's the same for both men. *Brokeback Mountain* was most easily seen as a story about deep closets, conservative cowboy values, and sexual repression. While the lead male characters in the film engage in bisexual behaviour, we do not really know what their attitudes about sex with women are, or what motivates them to have relationships with women. Surely the answer is not just determined by behaviour but rather by what identity one claims.

Even for those of us who are certain of our bisexual identity, being bisexual does not mean that one is attracted to both sexes equally. Some may find that their sexual desires and emotional/romantic/affective desires pull in different directions. Others may be drawn to one sex a lot and the other, just a little. Given the variability it can make sense to round up as "gay" or round down as "straight" (to use Savage's terms) and it's not for others to insist, "no, you're really a bisexual." The demands of the Bisexuality Visibility Police must yield to an individual's right to claim his or her own sexual identity.

I will raise one final worry,[4] a fourth worry, about why bisexual invisibility happens, although it is also connected to the choices one makes about identity. For some, the notion of bisexuality assumes a gender binary and that everyone sits nicely on one side of the line. On this way of understanding bisexuality then, bisexuals recognize the existence of just two sexes and we are attracted to both of them. But for many people, this is not quite true to one's desires. You might think there are many genders and you're attracted to all of them and identify as "pansexual." There are also those who identify with some version of bisexuality-

---

3 Leslie Green argues in favor of sex neutral marriage: "A different-sex marriage need not be a marriage between heterosexuals, and a same-sex marriage need not be a marriage between homosexuals. This shows how little the law of marriage cares about the sexuality of parties to a marriage; it does not show that sex-restricted marriage laws do not discriminate on grounds of sexual orientation. They do" (2011: 1).

4 This worry is not one of Dan Savage's worries.

lite, usually as a way of reflecting their stronger preference for and/or history with the opposite sex. One can be "hetero-flexible" or "bi-curious." Others skip the whole debate and identify as "queer." The range of labels which are consistent with the ascription of bisexual identity is staggering. And so with a plethora of labels to choose from, and as a small group to begin with, again bisexuality tends to disappear.

So let us assume that bisexuality invisibility is a problem, and that the reasons given above are at least part of the story as to its origin, what then is the solution? Savage calls on bisexuals to come out, to positively identify as bisexual. Set aside Savage's tone—"Oh, stop whining, you've caused the problem, what with your silence and your rounding up and rounding down. Claim your bisexuality or shut up"—and look at the claim that bisexuals have an obligation to come out. Savage (2010) puts the point this way, "More out bisexuals would mean less of that bisexual invisibility that bisexuals are always complaining about. If more bisexuals were out, more straight people would know they actually know and love sexual minorities, which would lead to less anti-LGBT bigotry generally, which would be better for everyone."

I want to side with Savage on the prima facie obligation to be out but in this essay I also want to argue that bisexuals can only do what's possible—"ought implies can" being a long established principle in ethics[5]—and that being seen as bisexual can be difficult, especially for women, especially again for femme women.

Citizenship and Visibility as a Political Strategy

How easy it is it for bisexuals to be out? What's required of us in the name of visibility? Dan Savage is, of course, an advice columnist, not a political theorist, but his claim that what bisexuals need to do is become more visible is connected to work in queer theory about the politics of visibility as a strategy for advancing LGBT rights. In the essay on fashion and visibility, Brennan (2011), I looked at the political strategy of visibility in advancing the cause of gay, lesbian, and bisexual equality and argued that visibility as a strategy had its limits. This argument continues that discussion of the limits of visibility arguing that visibility, like fashion, is a communicative process and there are limits on what an individual can do on his or her own. Visibility requires recognition; being out as bisexual requires being seen as bisexual. But what's the connection between bisexual visibility, fashion, and sexual citizenship and rights of recognition? The story, I think, goes something like this.

In contrast to the abstract citizen of liberal political philosophy, the sexual citizen is offered as an alternative account of what it means to be a citizen. The sexual citizen moves in the public realm as a sexual being. According to *GLBTQ Encyclopaedia of Culture*, the sexual citizen "bridges the private and public, and

---

5   Tracing back to Immanuel Kant.

stresses the cultural and political sides of sexual expression. Sexual privacy cannot exist without open sexual cultures. Homosexuality might be consummated in the bedroom, but first partners must be found in the public space of streets, bars, and media such as newspapers and the internet." Cultural theorist Jeffrey Weeks writes: The "sexual citizen" is a recent phenomenon. Making "private claims to space, self-determination and pleasure, and public claims to rights, justice and recognition" (1998: abstract). According to Weeks, the sexual citizen is a hybrid being, who tells us a great deal about political and cultural transformation and new possibilities of the self and identity.

Political theorists writing about citizenship have identified two aspects of citizenship. The first is about legal rights to equality before the law, very familiar territory for liberal theorists, but the second is about the right to recognition, about being recognized as a fellow citizen. Queer theorists have tended to focus on the second aspect of citizenship believing that's where most obstacles to citizenship for sexual minorities can be found (Phelan 2001).

The idealized citizen of the liberal state, abstracted away from sex, race, class, ability, and sexual and gender orientation, renders those invisible who are only ever seen in their particularity. Here is an example: I'm told that when I identify myself as North American, people know right away that I'm Canadian. Denizens of the United States simply identify themselves as "American." Likewise, there is same sex marriage, but no one speaks of different sex, or opposite sex, marriage. The default option does not need naming. There are attempts to shift the burden and to introduce names for that which previously did not seem to need naming, so obvious was it. Those in the LGBT community will be familiar with cis-gender as the complementary term for transgender. To be cis-gendered is to have your birth sex match your body and your gender identity. Likewise, bisexual activists have attempted to introduce the term "monosexual" for those, gay or straight, whose sexual preferences extend to only one sex.[6]

Thus the political strategy of visibility had a certain necessity to it. According to Phelan, a group "that is consistently present only as the opposite or outside of the nation, that has no part in the national imagination except as threat, cannot participate in citizenship, no matter what rights its members have come to enjoy" (2001: 7). As a strategy visibility is connected to the quest for rights of recognition. One of the main rights claimed on behalf of the sexual citizen is the right of recognition. Queer theorists have argued that gay men, lesbians, and bisexuals do not merely want the same rights as the sexual majority. Rather a large part of what the queer community wants is to be recognized as having legitimate identity. That is, queer activists want to be recognized as queer citizens. Lisa Walker writes, "privileging visibility has become a tactic of late twentieth-century identity politics, in which participants often symbolize their demands for social justice by celebrating visible signifiers of difference that have historically targeted them for discrimination" (2001: 68).

---

6   See, for example, the tumblr, http://stfumonosexuals.tumblr.com/.

I think the notion of the sexual citizen gets some things right and other things wrong. While it is true that the notion of the abstract liberal citizen fails to be truly inclusive, building in as it does ideals of masculinity, ability, and heteronormativity, I do not think we need to so quickly abandon all hopes of a universal notion of citizenship. What we see at work here is the combination of failed abstraction and idealization. Abstraction would not be so worrisome were it not for its constant companion, idealization:

> Abstraction, taken straightforwardly, is a matter of bracketing, but not denying, predicates that are true of the matter under discussion … Idealization is another matter: it can easily lead to falsehood. An assumption, and derivatively a theory, idealizes when it ascribes predicates—often seen as enhanced, 'ideal' predicates—that are false of the case in hand, and so denies predicates that are true of that case. (O'Neill 1996: 40-1)

My other worry about the notion of the sexual citizen, as opposed to the abstract citizen of liberal political theory, is whether the notion is broad enough to include all persons. While it's true that we can each be seen in our particularities and that heterosexuality is a sexual preference too, I'm not so sure that the concept of the sexual citizen so easily suits children (not to deny children's sexuality entirely) or that it fits so well with those whose life path does not have a large role for sexuality (think here of priests and nuns, or of the asexual). There is both an optimism and an individualism that I find disturbing in visibility as a strategy: individualism in that we each have an obligation to be visible—even though that achievement is much easier for some than for others—and optimism in that it assumes that a world in a which there was greater visibility is a world in which sexual minorities would be more justly treated. I am not convinced that this is necessarily true. But let's set these doubts about sexual citizenship aside and look again at the strategy of visibility.

Who is Recognized and Who is Invisible?

Recognition as a sexual citizen, being seen as a group member, being able to speak as a member of a group, is often not a something an individual can do on his/her own. Recognition will depend on issues of power, appearance, and context. If "visibility" is a success term, an achievement, then visibility depends on recognition. The simplest example is one that I gave in my analysis of queer politics and fashion: one can be seen and identified as a queer femme in Toronto or San Francisco while in smaller towns and cities such an option does not exist. To dress in a feminine fashion is, in many spaces and places in the world to invite being misread as straight. The same difficulty applies if one wishes to be identified as bisexual. While there are times when the mysteriousness of sexuality might be desirable, when "is she or isn't she?" might be part of the allure in bisexual friendly spaces, suggests Hemmings,[7] there are other times when one simply wants to be seen for what one is. I've argued that fashion occurs at the boundary of the personal and the political, at the edge between private and public. Fashion achievements are a kind of successful communication which requires the right community. Fashion cannot be an individual enterprise. Consider an example from outside the context of sexual identity. I wear an orange belt to my Aikido classes signifying the grade level I've achieved. But I do not expect people who are not familiar with martial arts to know what an orange belt means. In terms of details, I would not expect anyone except a fellow practitioner of Yoshikan Aikido to know what exact skills were associated with that level of achievement. Likewise, in a world of ever changing and complex gender identities, there are limits to recognition based on community. This creates challenges in these days of internet communities where even in small towns one can gain access to particular gendered sub-cultures. You might try to come out as power femme, or a faggy boi, in small town Northern Canada but likely the best you'll be able to manage is gay or queer.

Consider another example which illustrates limits on visibility. "Flagging," the practice of wearing a coloured hanky to signify one's sexual preferences and preferred role only really works if there is a community who knows what the hanky-code means. In the absence of a leather community with shared understanding of what various colours and their placement mean regarding your sexual preferences, you are not really flagging. You're just wearing a hanky in your pocket. I am a member of a book group and we joked about flagging "book" at an upcoming community event with a paperback in the rear pocket of our jeans to indicate a preference for reading aloud or being read to. But our code would only work for other book club members. Other people would just wonder, if they noticed at all, why we were carrying books in such an odd location.

In a recent blog post Drew Cordes talks about flagging as a way of identifying as both queer and femme. Cordes does not feel that people have recognize exactly what her hanky indicates, though it's nice if they do, but they do have to recognize that she is flagging for the identity marker to succeed. Hankies are used mostly by members of the kink community to identify particular sexual practices and preferences but they have a history that goes back to early times in the queer community. Cordes writes that she flags for reasons that go beyond kink identification: as a way to recognize the struggles and sacrifices of those who came before, to connect to the culture, to keep the culture alive, and to ensure that she is identified as a member of the community. Cordes reminds us that being visible is easier for some than for others.

Lisa Walker deals with visibility from the perspective of lesbian identity and the problem of recognition for women who are lesbians but who are not seen as such. Walker argues that there are both benefits and costs to strategies of visibility. She focuses on the identity issues facing lesbians who identify as femme.

7　For a discussion of the playful aspects of identity judgments, see Hemmings 1997.

While Walker's work examines visibility from the perspective of the femme lesbian, there are other issues tied to recognition and visibility. Recognition is an important theme in queer culture and queer politics. Note that recognition has two aspects. First, there is recognition by the members of one's own group. This can matter even more in contexts in which public recognition is too dangerous and so systems of secret signals develop, such as wearing a single earring in a particular ear. I have written about the loss one experiences when that sense of recognition disappears. For me, that's most often occurred when travelling. In some countries I was shocked that I could not recognize lesbians as lesbians and yet in other places it seemed to me that no one was queer though I knew that could not be right. Second, there is recognition by a larger community and this can be more difficult to accomplish as it requires education on the part of a larger group.

Fashion is one way we recognize one another, but what do lesbians wear? Obviously this varies across times, places, and generations. It also varies from subculture to subculture. From sporty to femme, from butch to leather, from dandy to geeky, there is a wide range of styles one might associate with a lesbian aesthetic. The issues get tougher still if what one wants to identify is not a lesbian aesthetic but rather a bisexual aesthetic. It's worth noting that if a queer aesthetic works at all, then by necessity it does so by way of inclusion and exclusion. Think about your own judgments about sexual orientation. Some people get counted in and others out on the basis of such factors as handbag style, lipstick color, fingernail length and amount of hair styling product used. Hair length is especially tricky and important to get right both for those who want in and those who want out.[8]

Could there be such a thing as a bisexual haircut? Bi-blogger Amy Andre writes,

> How can someone wear their bisexuality on their sleeve, if people's assumptions about our sexuality are based on things like haircuts? Especially if those haircuts are also being assumed to only belong to monosexuals[?] … The only conclusion I could draw is: we need a bisexual haircut! I think the bi community needs to come together and decide on one hair-style, and that will be the bi hair style. Then, we need to be able to advertise the fact that that is the bi hair style, so that people can recognize us… . But what I'm talking about here is developing a signifier, an aesthetic, a queer/clear marker for bisexuality.

However, the problem of exclusion is that it may end up excluding those who we did not intend. Alison Rooke explores themes of exclusion and inclusion in the lives of working-class lesbian and bisexual women (both transsexual and nontranssexual):

> it is worth noting that the aestheticization of lesbian and gay identities and bodies into 'lifestyle' had become more apparent in the past 20 years. The lesbian body

---

8   For a discussion of "lesbian hair" and the media, see Russo 2007.

politic has significantly changed since the 1980s and 1990s. The lesbian feminist critique of 'patriarchy' was borne out through embodied practices. The lesbian feminist body was unruly, questioning the discourses of appropriate femininity by sprouting hair, changing shape, refusing constraining clothes, and so on. Lesbian feminist culture offered the opportunity to experiment and explore dominant conceptions of gender; it offered a space to rethink heteronormativity and for some the possibility to live, at least temporarily in space and time, outside of its bounds. (2007: 246-7)

But Rooke's subjects were unable to fit in to be recognized:

They fell short of a recognizable lesbian habitus in more embodied ways. They were not androgynous, gym toned, or tanned or were not displaying the appropriate haircuts. It was not merely that they did not wear the right labels. It was also the case that they did not possess the requisite cultural capital to know which brands should be worn even if they could afford them and how to wear them. (2007: 247)

So while the politics of recognition seems to call for visibility as a strategy, there are dangers in relying too heavily on visibility. Writes Walker:

Within the constraints of a particular identity that invests certain signifiers with political value, figures that do not present these signifiers are often neglected. Because subjects who can pass exceed the categories of visibility that establish identity, they tend to be understood as peripheral to the process of marginalization … The paradigm of visibility is totalizing when a signifier of difference becomes synonymous with the identity it signifies. In this situation, members of a given population who do not bear that signifier of difference, or who bear visible signs of another identity are rendered invisible and are marginalized within an already marginalized community. (2001: 68)

The political strategy of visibility has its dangers and those dangers extend beyond the LGBT movement. Ellen Samuels (2003) compares the problems faced by femme lesbians to the problems of those with invisible disabilities: "In the dominant cultural discourse, as well as in lesbian and disability subcultures, certain assumptions about the correlation between appearance and identity have resulted in an often exclusive focus on visibility as both the basis of community and the means of enacting social change. Discourses of coming out and passing are central to visibility politics, in which coming out is generally valorized while passing is seen as assimilationist. Thus vigilant resistance to external stereotypes of disability and lesbianism has not kept our subcultures from enacting dynamics of exclusion and surveillance over their members. Nor does a challenge to those dynamics necessarily imply a wish on my part to discard visibility politics or a rejection of the value and importance of visibility for marginalized communities.

This is a short argument ranging over a variety of themes, starting with the request for bisexual visibility and ending with thoughts about the ways in which visibility as a strategy may be problematic. I hope to have shown that there are some difficulties with privileging the strategy of visibility. I hope to have also shown that being "out" requires recognition and that this is not something one can easily do on one's own. Along the way I explored the politics of fashion and looked at fashion as one communicative approach to being out and showed that it does not work equally well for all sexual orientations or genders. It is not enough to insist that the problem lies with bisexuals and our failure to be visible. I would like to end with a quote by Clare Hemmings (1997), a question she poses about bisexual visibility: "As bisexuality becomes more visible, as bisexual identity becomes more solidified (if it does), will there be a way of being 'read as' bisexual?" I hope very much that Hemmings' hope is correct.

Passing Bodies: Are Intersexuals Queer?

Maren Behrensen

In this section I attempt to answer two related questions:

1. Is intersexuality a queer identity?
2. Compared to other queer identities, are passing and outing fundamentally different for intersexuals?

My answer to the first question is a qualified "yes," my answer to the second question will be a qualified "no." My argument proceeds as follows: I present two reasons to think that intersexuality is *not* a queer identity, and two reasons to think that passing and outing *are* fundamentally different for intersexuals. I then examine each of these four reasons and show that they are not compelling reasons.

Is Intersexuality A Queer Identity?

Any answer to this question has to offer or refer to a definition of queerness. The definition I adopt in this essay is "queer" as referring to sexual practices, behaviors, or appearances which challenge the norms of gender dichotomy, i.e., the assumption that there are sexual practices, behaviors, and appearances which are suitable only for males or for females, respectively. We may suggest that engaging in queer practices and appearances is a necessary condition for queerness, but not a sufficient one, since the queer person, in addition to engaging in queer practices and appearances, also has to *identify* as queer. Part of this essay will be devoted to dispelling this suggestion.

We may also suggest that intersexuals challenge the norms of sex dichotomy, but not the norms of gender dichotomy, and are thus not queer. For the purpose of this essay, I will take for granted that there are queer *identities*—that is to say that I will take for granted that queerness does not *merely* denote an anti-essentialist rejection of stable categories of sex, gender, and sexuality. If the latter were the case, then queer identities would seem to be by definition impossible.

LGBTQ-I

Suppose that identifying as queer was a necessary condition for having a queer identity. In this case, the question whether intersexuality is a queer identity could easily be answered by asking intersexuals whether they identify as queer. The answer to this question would probably be "no," or, more likely, silence. The number of organized intersexuals in the United States, Canada, Great Britain, Australia, Germany, and other European countries ranges in the hundreds.[9] These organized intersexuals represent only a fraction of all intersexed persons. Even according to conservative estimates of the frequency of intersex births—0.2 percent of all live births[10]—the number of all intersexuals in *each* of the aforementioned countries would exceed 5,000 persons.[11] Furthermore, organized intersexuals may not identify as queer, or they may only identify as queer insofar as they are

---

9   The reasons for the small number of organized intersexuals could be a) ignorance of the existence of support groups or b) ignorance of the intersex condition. It was part of the old treatment protocol to keep the condition secret from the patient, so that even adult patients were lied to about the nature of their condition. For instance, adult patients with Complete or Partial Androgen Insensitivity Sydrome (PAIS or CAIS) have been told that their "ovaries"—which were in fact testes—had to be removed because they had not developed properly; see, for instance, Morris 2006.

10   There are different opinions in the medical community about which conditions should be included in the term, and about how common (or rare) these conditions are. Anne Fausto-Sterling has estimated that more than 1.5 percent of all live births are intersex, assuming a very large figure for cases of late-onset Congenital Adrenal Hyperplasia (LOCAH); this figure, as well as Fausto-Sterling's definition of intersex, have been challenged (see Fausto-Sterling 2000: 53); for a challenge to Fausto-Sterling's numbers see Sax 2002. Sax wants to restrict the term "intersex" to cases "in which chromosomal sex is inconsistent with phenotypic sex, or in which the phenotype is not classifiable as either male or female," excluding conditions such as LOCAH, Klinefelter's syndrome (an additional X-chromosome in 47, XXY males), and Turner's syndrome (a missing second X-chromosome in 45, X females). Under Sax's narrow definition of "true intersexuality" the frequency of intersex births drops to less than 0.02 percent. If we discount Fausto-Sterling's high number for LOCAH, and take her remaining number as representative, we arrive at a rate of 0.2 percent.

11   A medical study conducted in Germany in 2006/7 about the long-terms effects of medical and surgical treatment for intersexuals had 69 participants (see Schönbucher et al. 2010). It is up to date one of the most comprehensive studies of its kind, and the majority of its participants were recruited through support groups. However, if we assume an intersex birth rate of 0.2 percent in a population of over 80 million, Germany's intersex population

also gay, lesbian, or transgendered. The vast majority of intersexuals is silent in public, while the "out" minority is divided on questions of identity and political allegiances.

Unlike the groups contained in the LGBT movement, intersexuals have no developed queer community. In some places, the LGBT movement has included intersex issues on their agenda—as evidenced by the expansion of the acronym to LGBTI or LGBTQI—and intersex activists may benefit from established connections between the LGBT movement and policy-makers (Turner 1999).[12] But some intersexuals reject all connections with the LGBT movement. Hence, if we understood "queer" to mean "identifying as queer" and "belonging to a developed queer community," intersexuality would obviously not be a queer identity.

Intersexuality as Medical Category

Intersexuals may not challenge the norms of gender dichotomy, but they obviously challenge the norms of sex dichotomy, since intersexuality is defined as the presence of both "male" and "female" sexual features in one individual.[13] The term covers a wide range of conditions, with external phenotypes ranging from the clearly female to the clearly male. Since intersex conditions encompass such a variety of phenotypes and since they generate different medical needs (and some generate none at all) it may seem misleading to subsume all of them under the label intersexuality.[14]

In 2006, the American and European endocrinological societies adopted the new term Disorders of Sexual Development (DSD) as a replacement for the previous terms "intersexuality" and "hermaphroditism." Those in the medical community argued that DSD would be a neutral, descriptive term, less stigmatizing than the previous labels. The switch from intersex to DSD was welcomed, for instance, by parents who want their intersexed children to be treated as normal boys and girls. Since the term "intersex" may be taken to connote a third gender and/or an atypical sexuality—a connotation which has been welcomed by some intersex activists,

---

would exceed 16,000 persons, meaning that well under 1 percent of all German intersexuals participated in this study and/or are active in support groups.

12   Turner even argues that intersex activism is deeply indebted to the LGBT movement.

13   These anatomical features can be the chromosomes (i.e., the presence of more than one chromosome set in one body, e.g., 45X/46XY), the gonads (i.e., the presence of both ovarian and testicular tissue, or underdeveloped "streak" tissue), or the genitalia (i.e., the presence of enlarged clitorises, so-called micropenises, fused labiae, empty scrotal sacks, short and/or narrow vaginas).

14   In other words, the term "intersexuality" may be as misleading as the term "hermaphrodite" which conjures up images of mythical beings with fully formed sets of male and female genitals. In a similar vein, "intersexuality" may be taken to imply the presence of clearly ambiguous genitals—which need not be the case.

primarily those associated with LGBT activism and/or queer scholarship—parents are predictably not inclined to accept such a label for their children.[15]

However, some intersex activists continued to use the old term, and they criticized the use of DSD, since it continues to label intersexuality as a disorder. These activists understandably worry that speaking of disorders of sexual development will merely perpetuate the pathologization of intersex bodies and intersex lives and undermine the single most important goal of intersex activism: to protect intersexed persons—and in particular intersexed infants and children— from unwanted and harmful medical interventions.

But even so, we may suggest that the almost exclusive focus of intersex activism on medical (mal)practice is precisely what sets intersexuality apart from other queer identities. Intersexuals want to be treated with dignity and respect by the medical community and by other human beings, and perhaps the way to achieve this goal is to view intersexuality as a strictly medical category, with no social and political implications. The idea is that if health care professionals treated only the medical issues in intersex conditions—and refrained from trying to address broader psycho-social issues through corrective surgery—intersexuality would become less stigmatized. Conversely, we may suggest that it is precisely the notion of intersexuality as a third gender or a third sex that contributes to the social stigma.

In support of this view, we may adduce the fact that many intersex support groups are organized around specific conditions—Congenital Adrenal Hyperplasia (CAH), Androgen Insensitivity Syndrome (AIS), Turner's syndrome, Klinefelter's syndrome—and not around intersexuality as a category.

Intersex Passing—Invisible Differences

The term "passing" has the connotation of a deliberate attempt to be perceived as something one is not, often in order to gain social or financial benefits or to avoid physical or psychological harm. In racist circumstances, a non-white person may have a strong incentive to pass as white. In homophobic circumstances, a queer person may have a strong incentive to pass as straight. But this notion of passing as a deliberate denial of one's identity presumes that one has a *social choice*: You can decide either to pass and hide your "true identity"—or you can be "out." Though the choice is not attractive, a black person in racist circumstances may choose not to pass; and a queer person may choose to be open about their sexuality even in homophobic circumstances.

Now we may suggest that in the case of intersexuals, passing is not a social choice, but a social reality that is reinforced by surgical and pharmaceutical means. Like, say, a learning disability, intersexuality is, in most situations, an invisible difference. The anatomical features which distinguish intersexed persons from others—enlarged clitorises, micropenises, sparse or lacking pubic hair, narrow or

---

15 See the epilogue of Reis 2009, especially pages 154-8.

absent vaginal canals—are usually hidden beneath clothes. The only persons who will usually notice these features are parents, lovers, and doctors. (And the stigma attached to intersexuality may indeed make it impossible for the intersexed person to reveal her/himself to a potential lover or a doctor.)

But regarding her/his public appearance, the intersexed person will pass by default. Not just will her/his unique anatomical features go unnoticed, s/he will automatically be seen as male or female, i.e., as *someone with an unambiguous bodily identity*. This type of passing requires little or no effort, and it would be wrong to understand it as the success of a deliberate attempt of the intersexed person to conceal her identity. Passing is effortless for the intersexed person because of the deeply gendered way in which we perceive other people. Whether we see them on the street, hear their voice, or smell their perfume, we immediately and invariably categorize other human beings as either male or female based on these impressions.

It irks us when we cannot figure someone's gender immediately. But even in such cases, we assume that if we knew *all the facts* about that person's body— e.g., if we could see beneath their clothes—we would know what their sex is, and by implication, what their gender is. Thus, because of the default epistemic assumption that human beings have anatomically standard bodies, intersexed persons have no choice but to be perceived as either male or female.

But intersexuality is not merely invisible within the male/female dichotomy; it is also invisible within the queer/straight dichotomy. Queer people—homosexuals in particular—have developed strategies to make their queerness visible by publicly challenging gender roles. This can be done through haircuts and hairstyles, clothing styles, accessories (or lack thereof), make-up (or lack thereof). However, if an intersexed person employed these strategies, this would not be perceived as a statement about her bodily identity. For instance, if a lesbian, intersexed, female-identifying person wears a short and practical haircut, baggy jeans and "male" shirts, and sneakers or boots, this would be perceived as a statement about *her sexuality and her gender role*, but not about her bodily status. The notion that there may be queer bodies underneath queer clothes is not part of our standard epistemic repertoire.

We also need to consider the following factor that contributes to the invisibility of intersexuality: public silence and ignorance. Intersexuality has only just begun to enter the media, entertainment, and higher education curricula as a topic worthy of discussion.[16] Compared to other queer identities, the public knows even less about intersexuality than about homo- and bisexuality, transgendered people, and

---

16   Intersexual characters were featured on the popular TV shows *House, M.D.* and *Grey's Anatomy*; and in the area of professional sports, the topic came into sharp focus when Caster Semenya, a South African middle distance runner, was accused of being a "hermaphrodite" after her resounding victory in the women's 800 meters at the Athletics World Championship 2009 in Berlin.

genderqueer behavior—and there are certainly fewer persons lobbying on behalf of intersexed persons.

Thus, given the near-complete invisibility of intersexuality, we may suggest that passing for intersexuals takes on a fundamentally different significance. But of course, despite this invisibility, there is always the option of being an out intersexual by explicitly and publicly labeling oneself—and we need to ask whether this process also has a different meaning for intersexuals.

Intersex Outing—Confronting Medical Trauma

Given that passing is effortless for most intersexed persons, and that few people would ever get to see the anatomical features in virtue of which the intersexual person differs from others, it is curious that it would ever be considered a necessity to alter or eradicate these features. And yet for the past half century, a medical treatment protocol has been in place which treats cases of intersexuality as a medical emergency and which regards cosmetic surgery on intersexed genitals as imperative, precisely because of the cases in which intersexed persons would be forced to reveal their identity. The need for cosmetic surgery is justified by an appeal to precisely those cases in which an intersexed person would be forced to reveal her/his differences—sexual relationships, and other contexts in which nudity in front of others is acceptable and expected (locker rooms, public urinals).

Both medical normalizing procedures and the practice of assigning a "gender of rearing" to intersexed infants at or shortly after birth are supposed to enable them to fit more smoothly into a deeply gendered world. They are tools supposed to *enable passing* as someone with an unambiguous sexual identity. But the medical tools in this repertoire have consistently failed[17] to achieve the desired results, creating more harm than good. Cosmetic genital surgeries on intersexed persons frequently result in extensive scarring and significantly decrease or destroy the capacity to feel sexual pleasure. Despite these surgeries, the anatomical differences of the intersexed person may still be obvious to a future sexual partner—assuming the partner is reasonably perceptive—and the intersexed person may feel abnormal *precisely because* s/he has been subjected to normalizing procedures and to medical scrutiny. Even patients who do not report negative results from cosmetic surgeries often complain that the pervasive secrecy surrounding their condition and humiliating treatment from health care professionals greatly contribute to shame and stigma.[18]

---

17   My use of the word "consistently" may be challenged on the grounds that we have very little data about the long-term effects of medical interventions on intersexed children and adolescents.

18   The types of surgeries which have been most vocally challenged by intersex activists are partial or complete amputations of the clitoris (clitorectomy), reconstructive surgeries to create or dilate the vagina in intersexed infants (vaginoplasty), and surgeries to reroute the urethra to the tip of the penis in persons with hypospadias, a condition in which

Unsurprisingly, the main focus of intersex activism has been on altering medical practice, and on helping intersexuals to come to terms with their experiences with the medical community. The major value of being out and organized for intersexuals is to find others who have had similar experiences and to overcome medical trauma (and share resources needed to address one's medical needs and get access to one's full medical records). And thus, we might suggest that outing in the case of intersexed persons is closer to "outing" oneself—i.e., coming to terms with one's experiences as—a victim of sexual violence than it is to outing oneself—i.e., embracing one's identity as—a member of a sexual minority.

Intersexuality is a Queer Identity

Let us turn now to the reasons for the view that intersexuality is a queer identity— framed as responses to the observations I offered in the first part of this essay.

Queer Bodies

I want to suggest that intersex bodies are queer in virtue of their very existence. These queer bodies challenge the norms of gender dichotomy in at least two ways: They undermine the idea that sex, as opposed to gender, is unambiguous and fixed. Intersex bodies are proof that the concept of sex is as flexible as the concept of gender. Decades of medical research attempting to define the true source of the sex dichotomy have left us with the sobering conclusion that there is no single source. Neither the gonads, nor the chromosomes, nor hormones can be singled out as unique markers of sexual identity.[19] There is no strict sex dichotomy; rather, bodies can be arranged on a continuum, ranging from the clearly male to the clearly female.

Secondly, intersex bodies undermine the norms of standard heterosexual sex. Many of these bodies are judged to be incapable of being sexually active and the possessors of these bodies are judged to be incapable of having sexual relations—despite the fact that these bodies are perfectly capable of giving and receiving sexual pleasure as they are. If we define sex as penile-vaginal contact and penetration, then, yes, some intersex bodies will not be capable of having sex. But there is no good reason why we should define sex in this narrow way. *At least* oral sex, anal sex, and mutual masturbation are all "real" sex; and perhaps the actual reason for deeming intersex bodies unfit to engage in sexual relations is the implicit delegitimization of "queer" sex, e.g., sex involving clitorises big enough

---

the urethra does not end at the tip of the penis, but along its shaft or at its base. (For personal accounts of the long-term effects of early corrective surgery, see, for instance, the stories assembled in Dreger 1999.)

19   See, for instance, the historical account of the attempt to determine the "true sex" of "hermaphrodites and to find the true source of sex dichotomy in Fausto-Sterling 2000.

to penetrate a vagina or penises not big enough to penetrate, and sex focusing on the use on mouths, hands, and anuses.

But what are we to make of the fact that many intersexual do not identify as queer and would not want their bodies regarded as queer? I suggest in response here that many intersexuals realize, even when they are not fully informed about their condition, that they are different from the norm—and they are reminded of that fact by medical attention and medical interventions which may in fact contribute to their uneasiness about asserting their differences. Conversely, as we will see below, medical attempts to normalize intersex bodies only make sense in a social and cultural context in which these bodies are regarded as queer. As Katrina Karkazis puts it: "[The] whole reason intersex even exists as a category is because these bodies violate *cultural* rules about gender" (2009: 5).

Just a Medical Issue?

The main focus of intersex activism has been on the medical (mis)treatment of intersexuals. It might thus seem obvious that intersex "identity" is a localized phenomenon, defined and limited by medical practice. However, this medical practice—and especially the treatment protocol which has been in place in the "Western" countries for the past decades—cannot be understood without reference to the broader cultural context.

Cosmetic normalizing procedures on intersexuals are not a medical necessity; and the birth of an intersexed infant is treated as a "psycho-social emergency" but it is rarely a real medical emergency. The reason newborn intersexed infants have been rushed off to the neonate ICU is often not because they need immediate intensive care, but because the doctors want to win time to determine the chromosomal, gonadal, and anatomic status of the child—and thus conjecture its likely future gender (Karkazis 2009: 6-8).

The standard medical practice which favored early surgical intervention is based on the idea that a person with ambiguous genitals—and by implication, an ambiguous sexual and bodily identity—will not be able to function in a deeply gendered society. Doctors invoke the prospect that the intersexed child will be mocked by peers for her/his appearance, that s/he will be unable to find sexual partners, and that s/he will suffer from simply being different. The doctors' opinion on these matters is informed *by cultural norms*, not by medical norms—cultural norms that determine what constitutes an "acceptable appearance" in the locker room, the public urinal, or in the bedroom.

The way in which sexual function was determined in the treatment of intersexuals is a point in case. Sexual function meant not the capacity to give and receive pleasure through genital contact (or manual-genital contact or oral-genital contact, for that matter). Sexual function was defined by the ability to penetrate or be penetrated—which is why, according to the standard treatment protocol, very small penises and very narrow and/or short vaginas were unacceptable. The same logic ruled out large clitorises, since the ability to penetrate and be penetrated in one body was also unacceptable.

Certainly the doctors did not have malicious intentions in acting on these cultural norms; they wanted to ensure that their patients could live satisfying lives. But the fact that these intentions were informed by *cultural norms* matters, since it means that medical (mis)treatment of intersexuals is *not* a localized phenomenon.

Queer Invisibilities

I suggested above that intersexuality is invisible in a standard heterosexual context as well as in a queer context. But the same is true for other queer identities. A lesbian, post-transition male-to-female transsexual may be read as nothing but a lesbian woman (while running the risk of being shunned by the lesbian community if she discloses her transition). A femme lesbian may be ignored by her "own" community, and regarded as unquestionably straight by everyone else.[20]

On the other end of the spectrum, "queer" looks and "queer" behavior are easily misconstrued as indicating a stable same-sex desire: a young man wearing mascara in public may be read as "effeminate, and therefore gay." Young women with "butch" looks will likely be read as lesbian. Since the gay-straight-continuum represents stable sexual desires and sexual practices, and not bodily differences and fluctuating desires and identifications, it is ill-suited to represent intersexuals, transsexuals, genderqueers, and bisexuals. And transsexuals and bisexuals in particular have complained about their under- and misrepresentation in the LGBT movement. (We should note another related point here: The fact that there is a tension between organized intersexuals and the LGBT movement—and between transsexuals/transgendered persons and intersexuals in particular (see e.g. Kaldera 2011)—does not imply that intersexuals are not queer.)

The presumed invisibility of intersexuals in a queer context is not a reason to single out intersexuality as a non-queer identity—for if this reasoning applied here, then it may also apply in the case of trans- and bisexuals, but both identities are commonly regarded as queer.

Queerness as Resistance

I suggested above that intersex outing may be closer to "outing" oneself as a victim of sexual violence than to outing oneself as a member of a sexual minority (and embracing this identity). Intersexuals are not (yet) celebrating their identity as a group; instead, they give each other support to cope with and overcome their medical histories.[21] Certainly there is a difference between support groups with just

---

20   On this problem, see the contribution by Alice MacLachlan and Susanne Sreedhar to this volume.

21   Sharon Preves (2003) suggested that there is an emerging intersex pride. However, this pride can certainly not compare in magnitude and expression with the established gay

a few dozen members and large LGBT organizations able to mobilize thousands for parades and demonstrations.

We should not forget, however, that other queer movements were born out of resistance to violence and pathologization. Since the invention of the term "homosexuality," same-sex desire was regarded as a disorder, and it is still regarded by some as a curable illness. Transsexuality is listed under "gender identity disorder" in the *Diagnostic and Statistical Manual of Mental Disorders* (DSM), and homosexuality was listed as a disorder in the DSM until 1973 ("ego-dystonic homosexuality" was only removed from the DSM in 1987). Homosexual persons, or persons merely suspected of being homosexual were in the past subjected to drastic medical interventions: clitorectomies for lesbian women, chemical castration for gay men (the most prominent member of the latter group was probably Alan Turing). In the case of homosexuals in particular, pathologization and medical malpractice obviously seems to be just one aspect of general societal disapproval and oppression. We count list here countless other instances of violence against and shunning and silencing of queer people: school bullying, homophobic slurs, assaults, "corrective rapes," and so forth.

And thus being out for queer people is not merely celebrating one's identity and becoming part of a community, it is also a way of resisting societal oppression. In the case of white, middle- or upper-class queers in affluent countries, it may not feel that way anymore—but we should not forget that in many other contexts, being out or being outed as queer can be dangerous and even life-threatening.

Yet once again, we could suggest that the situation for intersexuals is different, since they are "merely" resisting the medical establishment. But this suggestion overlooks the fact that the medical reaction to intersexuality is informed by the judgment that intersexed genitals are socially unacceptable—and that the particular social unacceptability of intersexed genitals fits into the broader social unacceptability of queerness, broadly construed. A recent example for a potential intersection of the medical treatment of intersexuals and societal shunning of queer sexuality is the dexamethasone controversy: Dexamethasone—or "dex" for short—is a drug that is thought to reduce the virilizing effects of elevated testosterone levels in female fetuses with CAH when given to the pregnant mothers. Since some studies have associated the elevated testosterone levels in CAH girls and women with an increased incidence of homosexual desire, critics have branded this as of now still experimental treatment as a prevention not just of intersexuality but of homosexuality as well.[22]

Generally speaking, the attempt to eradicate the signs of intersexuality by surgical and pharmaceutical means would not make sense without a social and cultural context in which intersexed bodies are deemed freakish (and in which, indeed, the existence of intersexed bodies is denied—most people do not know about the appearances or the frequency of intersexuality). Hence, intersex activism

and lesbian communities.

22   For a recent journalistic account of the controversy, see Wetzstein 2010.

is not merely opposition to a specific medical practice; it is opposition to societal conditions which make the medical practice in question possible and intelligible in the first place.

Conclusion

There are good reasons why intersexuals are hesitant about associating with the LGBT movement and about claiming concepts such as "queer": They fear appropriation and misrepresentation of their concerns from a larger, established community, and they fear that by using the vocabulary of non-standard sexuality, they would make themselves vulnerable to further stigmatization and pathologization.

I have suggested here that these fears are understandable, but ultimately not compelling. It seems to me that the stigmatization and pathologization of intersexuals and their bodies can be overcome only if intersexuals are able to reclaim their differences and thus their "queerness." Despite the slowly growing influence of intersex organizations, the obstacles to this process of reclaiming are extremely daunting. Intersexuality is still subject to pervasive stigmatization, shaming, and secrecy; intersex activists are still being branded as radicals, especially by the medical community. The intersex movement, even though it is very small, is already experiencing internal strife about issues such as early gender assignment and its association with the LGBT movement.

It is difficult to make conjectures about the future of intersex movement, since it is so young and so small. It may dissipate or disappear, or it may grow into a stronger community over time. If the latter happens, then intersexuality could develop into a stable, socially represented identity. But for now, intersexuals and the queer identities represented in the LGBT movement at least have the same general goal: to reduce discrimination and violence against and increase acceptance of non-standard, i.e., non-heteronormative, sexual identities and sexual practices. And this, I think, should count for something.

Comments on Behrensen "Passing Bodies: Are Intersexuals Queer?"

Samantha Brennan

In "Passing Bodies: Are Intersexuals Queer?" Maren Behrensen makes a compelling case for the queerness of intersexual identities. Behrensen also argues that passing and outing are not fundamentally different for intersexuals. Structurally, Behrensen's argument takes on the arguments against these two theses and shows how they are lacking. There's a lot here to agree with. In particular, I found her responses to the arguments against the queerness of intersex identities compelling. I also agree with the critique of the arguments for the difference in passing/outing experiences. However, in my response to Behrensen's argument I'm going to focus on the former. I am going to talk more about the relationship between intersex identity and queer identity not because I think this is more interesting but rather because it's where I think we might have some disagreement. What I am going to say is that while the arguments against the queerness of intersex identities fail we are still left needing a positive argument in favour. Behrensen has made room for these arguments, opened up a space for the queerness of intersex identities, but all that's been established is queer potential. Further, I think that's a good thing. It's appropriately respectful of the gap between intellectual work and activism.

What is it for an identity to be "queer"? The definition adopted for the purposes of the argument are sexual behaviors, appearances, or practices that challenge the norms of gender dichotomy. But is that all? Behrensen considers and ultimately rejects another condition, namely that in addition the queer person must identify as queer. Behrensen rejects this because if identification were a necessary condition we could answer the question about the queerness of intersex identities simply by asking. Intersexual organizations tend not to identify as queer and so it would not matter if the first condition were met or not.

I think Behrensen is correct about the first condition and correct in the assessment of arguments against it. They are bad arguments. But I am still hung up on the identification condition. In what follows I address the issues around queer identification and raise some questions about its necessity. (And let me stress, my arguments are at this juncture simply because I agree with everything in Behrensen's argument up to this point.)

I'm simply loath to identify anything or anyone as queer who does not themselves endorse that label. Some bisexuals, for example, welcome the label "queer" as getting us beyond debates about the details of particular attractions and affections. At stages in my own life, I've quite liked the term. I would describe myself as attracted to masculinity but not so fussed about what particular biological package it comes in. But at other times, queer seems to risk losing bisexual identity within this very large tent. If we start including non-monogamous heterosexuals and kinky people of all persuasions as queer as well (see especially recent discussions of queer heterosexuality)—and in some moods I quite agree, "the more the merrier"—the worry is that we lose out on particular details that matter to us for a wide range of reasons. And there are many other reasons why an intersex person might not prefer to identify as queer. For example, political progress for one group or cause might be hurt by tying it to another. I am not persuaded that we all need to be together all of the time. Sex workers and the LGBT movement, for example, might find common cause on some issues but it does not follow that we need a common label.

One might argue against the medical management and surgical/hormonal treatment of intersexuality without seeing any connection between intersexuality and queerness. (And again that does not mean it is not there.) I'm thinking here of children's rights advocates who object to decisions being made for children, at an age when it is impossible to consult or involve them, whose primary moral complaint is against the medical treatment of intersex infants and children. Not all intersex persons or allies will see the value in identifying as queer. And I'm not persuaded that we have the arguments at hand to persuade them that they ought to. Of course, not all gays, lesbians, bisexuals, transgendered or transsexual people will see value in a queer identity either. Some LGBT advocacy organizations are more mainstream than others.

The strongest points in Behrensen's argument concern the similarities in the medicalization of homosexuality and of intersexuality. Many people think that what sets intersex identities apart is the focus of intersex activism on medical malpractice and on the mistreatment of certain particular conditions. But the history of homosexuality is tied to the history of its medical treatment. There is a difference in degree not kind. While I think Behrensen is right that the arguments *against* the queerness of intersexuality fail, I also think that what's been opened by the argument is the queer potential of intersexuality. A case is also made for the endorsing of this potential but whether that potential is taken up will depend on the political thought and actions of individual intersex persons and the intersex community.

Behrensen's position is much stronger though. What's argued for is the very strong claim that intersex bodies are queer in virtue of their very existence "since they undermine both the male/female and straight/queer dichotomy." Intersex bodies undermine the idea that biological sex is fixed, determinate, and binary. Likewise, intersex bodies challenge traditional understandings of sex as heterosexual intercourse since some intersex bodies may not be capable of sex so understood while being perfectly capable of giving and receiving sexual pleasure. Further, the cultural norms of how sex is understood informed medical practice. Surgeries and medical treatments had heterosexual intercourse as the goal, even if achieving this meant making sexual pleasure unattainable. Can we understand this at all without understanding the cultural dominance of heterosexuality? No. Does that make intersexual identities queer, even in the absence of endorsement, I am not so convinced.

Comments on Brennan's "Those Shoes Are Definitely Bicurious"

Maren Behrensen

Samantha Brennan's argument is very rich and broad in its scope, so I will limit myself to raising some questions connected to some specific observations offered in it. A central theme of the argument is recognition as a right[23] and a political goal of queer communities, and fashion as a visibility strategy, which may aid in this quest for recognition.

As Brennan notes, "recognition" can mean at least two different things here: "First, there is recognition by one's own group ... Second, there is recognition

---

23   I am not quite sure what a right to recognition would entail.

by a larger community and this can be more difficult to accomplish as it requires education of the part of the larger group" (see Brennan, this volume) The second kind may be more difficult to accomplish generally, but both actually seem to require a kind of education. She also points out that being able to dress in order to be recognized by one's own queer peers requires knowledge and training, and it can be an arduous trial-and-error process—and the "errors" may be similar to the one's that can occur in dressing for one's professional role. A "casual" professional dress for a young academic may be just as hard to achieve as a "casual" queer look—and both may require, for instance, that one has the money to pay for quality haircuts, the right brands of clothes, the right brands of shoes, etc.. If one is not able or willing to invest in these things, then one is easily mistaken—for example, when I appeared with jeans, a plaid shirt, and a Red Sox hat at the Human Resources office of the school where I am teaching to do some paperwork, I was initially mistaken for a sports coach.

It seems to me that the issues raised by the problem of "recognition" and the related concept of "sexual citizenship" are at least conceptually distinct—and I would like to hear more about whether Brennan thinks that they are also practically distinct. Consider the following cases:

1. A bisexual woman who will not be recognized or accepted by other queer women.
2. Bisexual styles are not recognizable by the wider public; as a consequence, bisexuals remain invisible in public spaces.
3. Wearing a queer style in public bears the risk of verbal abuse, shunning, or violence; as a consequence, bisexuals remain invisible in public spaces.

It seems to me that Brennan deals mostly with 2) in her argument—the near-complete absence of bisexual styles and thus a near-complete public invisibility. Cases 1) and 3) are not the main focus of the argument, and I wondered what bearing bisexual visibility in the context of 2) might have on the other two.

The first case concerns recognition within an (established) queer community, the second concerns the visibility of (established) queer communities in a wider social context, and the third concerns safety in expressing non-standard gender identities. Brennan mentions that she observed on her travels that in some countries no one appeared to be queer—I wondered how much of it may have had to do with the specific "queer dress codes" of the society in question, and how much with (severe) legal, social, or economic penalties for dressing queer.

The three visibility and recognition concerns could at least potentially come apart. Visibility within the queer community may be no issue, even if the community itself has to hide (think of secret signs such as earrings in the pre-Stonewall era). And visibility in the wider social context may require other strategies than visibility within one's own community (e.g., the "hanky system" would seem to be a fairly inefficient strategy to bring about wider social visibility, no matter how well it works within the leather community).[24] I would like to hear more about how the different strategies that could be adopted in the response to the problems of visibility and recognition are related.

The scenario in 3), in contrast, appears to raise issues of citizens' rights and human rights proper. A state that cannot or will not keep all its citizens safe from abuse and attacks fails to achieve its moral purpose. Conversely, being protected in the expression of alternative gender identities would appear to be a matter of equal standing before the law. Furthermore, it would seem that in modern states, which for the most part encompass anonymous mass societies, recognition takes on a fundamentally different meaning than "being visible to one's own group" or even "being visible in public spaces." Recognition may require more than the visibility of queer individuals in public spaces—it may require, for instance, the visibility of groups in the media and in the political realm through representative spokespersons or icons (an example of which would be the coverage of Rachel Maddow as a butch fashion icon).

Equal protection by and equal standing before the law can be enforced, at least in principle (of course, legal systems may in practice fail to protect queer individuals; sadly, there are too many examples of this). But recognition cannot be enforced; it could only be fostered through, for instance, education. Again, I would like to hear more about whether fashion also has a role to play in fighting for and asserting equal protection and equal legal standing for queer individuals. Is this role the same as in the quest for recognition and visibility?

Let me move on to a point that does not concern the relation of queer individuals and communities to the society-at-large, but the internal politics of these communities. Brennan notes briefly that some lesbian styles may not be known or not be affordable for working-class dykes—the brand of jeans that one is supposed to wear, for instance, may quite simply be too expensive. It seems to me that behind this remark lingers a rather grave, general concern with fashion as political strategy. Fashion does not only make a "visibility statement" and allows others inside or outside my group to identify me as a member—fashion also communicates to others that they are not like me, that they do not belong to my group. Fashion is not only a means of recognition, it is also a very powerful tool of exclusion. Consider uniforms: All uniforms denote a specific social status and social role that not everyone is entitled to—military uniforms, for instance, denote a strict social divide between civilians and soldiers. To cross this divide by "dressing up" as a soldier would, in many cases, be seen as a social and cultural, if not legal offense.[25]

---

24   Brennan notes that "flagging" can be read as a sign of queer pride, and not just a sign of particular sexual preferences within a specific queer community. That is certainly true—however, I would suggest that by itself, this particular visibility strategy will not have the desired political or legal effects.

25   Of course being dressed as a soldier can have social disadvantages, too—most importantly when one's country is at war and one happens to be in a combat zone, dressed

Similarly, the dress codes that have been and still are imposed on women and men can be understood as a reinforcement of the social, cultural, and economic divides between men and women—otherwise, why would there be harsh social penalties for ambiguous gender presentation? This last point, of course, applies to all individuals—feminine men, transgendered persons, intersexuals—who transgress the boundaries of gendered fashion.

But if fashion can serve as a tool for exclusion, should this not make us worry about the use of fashion in queer communities? If fashion serves as a medium to communicate belonging among white middle-class lesbians, for instance, then it may at the same time exclude working-class dykes or non-white lesbians, insofar as the latter groups may not be aware of, not care about, or not be able to afford the requisite fashion items. What I want to suggest is that political philosophers have good reasons to be suspicious of fashion. And I would have to be convinced that the use of fashion *within* queer communities (and at their boundaries) differs significantly from the use of fashion in other social groups (and their boundaries), i.e., I would have to be convinced that it is not the case that one important use of fashion in both cases is the policing of these boundaries. And furthermore, I would have to be convinced that a bisexual style, if and when it comes into existence, would not have the same exclusionary effect. I do not deny that the transgression of gendered fashion norms has positive political potential. But what is outwardly transgressive can devolve into something inwardly repressive. How would a queer visibility/recognition strategy centered on fashion overcome these problems?

In a similar vein, I would like to raise the question of the limits of fashion in promoting visibility—in particular, how much can be achieved by fashion, and how much must be left to strategies of speaking out and explicit naming and labeling? I am thinking here in particular of identities who run the risk of being invisible (or hard to see/read) even in queer fashion, e.g., bisexuals or intersexuals. I cannot think of anything that would serve as a fashion statement to identify someone as intersexual—other than wearing a T-shirt that would explicitly announce that identity to others, for instance. When an intersexed lesbian female dresses butch, she's seen as a lesbian female—but not as an intersexed lesbian. In general, fashion statements seem to privilege stable, rigorous categories—dyke fashion usually indicates primarily stable homosexual desire, and neither homoerotic interest nor bisexuality. And yet it would seem that one important queer political goal is to get over the assumption of stable, rigorous sexual categories. Whether and how this can be achieved through fashion is still an open question for me.

---

in military gear—unlike the civilians in that zone, a soldier will be a legitimate target for enemy soldiers.

Reply to Behrensen

Samantha Brennan

In a pair of essays—the first published in a volume on philosophy and fashion and the second in this chapter—I have worked through some issues relating to rights of recognition and to visibility as a political strategy for the queer community.[26] In both cases, I have been interested in the politics of fashion and the ways in which visibility is easier for some to achieve than for others. Femmes were the focus of the first essay and my argument in this chapter looked at visibility as an issue for bisexuals, particularly bisexual women. Fashion is a communicative process and like visibility as a strategy it requires a knowledgeable audience. Bisexual women and queer femmes of all persuasions know what it is like to be misheard, misread, mis-seen and invisibility takes its toll, especially in the face of political cries for greater visibility. You can feel that not only are you not recognized by your community but also that you are failing to live up to your political obligations. In terms of fashion, it was a movie that first made me aware of the need for an appreciative audience for attempts at fashion to succeed. "Romy and Michele's High School Reunion," the story of two women who attended high school in Arizona in the 1980s, captured beautifully how one could be trying hard to be fashionable but succeed only in being seen as a misfit by one's peers. In my own life, there have been a few of these events, such as being asked by a kindly aunt whether I am wearing so much black in an effort to appear thinner. ("No, I'm an aspiring Goth! A fat-positive aspiring Goth!" But of course neither "fat-positive" nor "Goth" would have been words in her vocabulary.)

Once you start thinking about this phenomenon, you can see the many places it occurs. It is harder for poor women to wear ripped clothing as a fashion statement when people might see you and think you could not afford anything new. Trucker caps are not ironic if you are wearing them in an environment where people wear trucker caps seriously.

These two essays also were for me an experiment in writing about personal experience. This may be familiar ground for others in the volume coming from different disciplines, but as an academic philosopher I have rarely written about my own life directly. My essays on children's rights and family justice for example, make no mention of my own experience of parenting and that is the norm within my discipline. I have also very much enjoyed the collaborative approach to writing, undertaken in this volume. I appreciated and learned a lot from Behrensen's comments on my argument. Indeed, there were enough excellent questions raised that I started to think in terms of longer projects. If I end up trying to write a book it will be Behrensen's fault. I very much liked Behrensen's story of being mistaken for a sports coach instead of a young academic. Twinge of jealousy here. As an athlete of sorts, I sometimes wish someone would mistake me for a sports coach.

---

26   See Brennan 2011.

Today for me many of the issues related to mistaken identity relate to aging. As I approach 50 I'm aware that it's increasingly difficult to be seen as a sexual being at all. It is certainly harder to spot dykes as so many older women adopt short hair, drop the make-up, and sport comfortable shoes. And I now see why some older women wear stereotypically "sexy" outfits. I certainly noticed the 70+ year old woman at the airport with the white blonde bob, dressed in a red leather jacket and miniskirt. She was screaming sexuality but I suspect that after 70 you have to scream in order to be heard at all.

But to whom are the bisexuals in my essay screaming? Behrensen raises the question of visibility to whom. Who is it I want to be recognized by? The question of audience is an important one. There is a difference between being visible to peers, to my community than there is being visible to the general public. I am interested in both topics though I think I could have more carefully distinguished these two questions. There are also likely, as Behrensen mentions, important connections between the two. There are connections between bisexual invisibility in the queer community and bisexual invisibility in the public and wider political realm. If our community representatives do not see or hear us, then it is hard for them to represent us. Behrensen mentions a third possibility, choosing not to be visible because of violence and the risks of appearing queer in public. This possibility I did not consider at all. It's an important issue that I overlooked though it likely was not an issue in the places I'd travelled where I could not recognize queer people. In those countries—Germany, Sweden, Australia—I just could not read fashion trends and clothing norms. I think the problem was my ignorance and not one of political repression.

Two other themes come up in Behrensen's comments: the politics of visibility and the politics of fashion. In both cases, I share some of the worries Behrensen raises. Not all identities are equally visible, nor is it easy to see how they might become so. This is part of my skepticism about visibility as a political strategy. Behrensen mentions intersex as an invisible queer identity but there are others as well. Not everyone who is kinky, for example, will choose to wear their kink identity on his/her sleeve and not at all poly-amorous people choose to be "out" to the world at large. You might be out as a lesbian at work and not feel the need to share other aspects of your sexual identity. There are degrees of "out" and degrees of "visibility" and negotiating these degrees does not automatically make one a coward for failing to reveal all aspects of one's identity. This shows a tension between visibility as an individual strategy and visibility as a political issue. We might want to raise awareness about sexual minorities without always insisting that the best route to doing this is by having individuals come forward. And if they do come forward the burden of recognition, of explanation, surely ought not to fall on individuals alone. Nor is this issue an issue just for the queer community. Disability theorists also write about visibility as a strategy and encounter the same challenges with invisible disabilities.

On the subject of fashion, I share many of Behrensen's worries about accessibility, class, and exclusion. Where we perhaps differ is in taking fashion seriously as a subject for academic discussion. I do not think we make the problems presented by fashion go away by ignoring them. In particular, when academics think of ourselves "above" worrying about fashion I think we reveal our own particular class privilege. We need to take fashion seriously, to theorize about it, in order to see how it works and the role that it plays in our social and political lives. Do we need a lesbian aesthetic or a bisexual fashion trend as part of the path to greater visibility? Perhaps not. But such patterns exist whether or not we intentionally set out to make them so. My only endorsement here is a very limited one, fashion as worthy of academic study, in particular as a topic that ought to be of interest to political philosophers. I think once we understand the role community plays in fashion and the communicative function of fashion, the political importance of fashion is easy to see. I also think it can be fun, but that is a topic for another essay.

Reply to Brennan

Maren Behrensen

Brennan expresses two main concerns about my argument:

1. I have opened up philosophical space for the queer potential of intersex identities, but I have not shown that intersexuality *is* in fact a queer identity.
2. I completely disregard the "identification criterion" for queerness, i.e., I seem to impose a label on persons who may want to reject this label for good reasons.

I think that a quick answer to the first concern could simply refer to the issue, which triggered the second: I claim in my argument that intersexed bodies are "queer in virtue of their very existence." If I am right about that, then it looks as if I have shown that intersexuality is a queer identity. But I may have moved too quickly here with my argument: In order to have an identity, it seems that one must have been *identified as something*, either by others, or by oneself. And if many intersexuals refuse to be identified as queer, and if they are often not identified as queer by others, then we cannot impose that identity on them by simply referring to some of their bodily features.[27] And thus the way in which I

---

27   Indeed, I may be doing to intersexuals what others have been doing to human females for most of recorded history: taking some of their bodily features—the fact that they have vaginas, breasts, and a specific mixture of hormones, or that their brain is assumed to be "wired" in a certain way—and legislating that because of these features, their social role ought to be a certain way—i.e., they should present as the gender *woman*, with its very specific social and cultural expectations and restrictions.

claim that intersexuality *is* a queer phenomenon violates the identification criterion for queerness.

Like Brennan, I'm loathe to push a label onto someone who does not endorse it; and like Brennan, I see the political risks in broadening the label "queer": losing particular identities in an umbrella term, and stretching the boundaries of the term "queer" so far as to render it meaningless.

However, I suspect that the real problem is not with the term "queer," but with the term "identity." And so perhaps I should follow up on my suspicions about the term "queer identity" I had so quickly dismissed in the original essay. The use of the term "queer" was, at least in some circles, initially motivated by a desire to escape the constricting forces of identity talk.[28] When we say that someone has this or that identity, we seem to imply that whatever the thing is that determines their identity, it must be of great importance for who they are—and that it will allow us to predict their behavior with relative ease. It is not hard to see why some gays and lesbians, for instance, rejected this implication. They refused to accept that their homosexuality was the most important thing about them; and they thought that it would be politically and psychologically detrimental if someone's homosexuality was taken to be a definitive marker of their identity—not merely because forces outside of the gay and lesbian community could use this implication to brand gays and lesbians as a sick, disgusting, uncivilized "other," but also because persons within the community could use it to legislate a "proper way" to be gay or lesbian (and exclude, for instance, transgendered or bisexual or intersexed people).[29]

Indeed, it *should* seem odd that we speak about queer—lesbian, gay, transgendered, bisexual, intersexual, etc.—identities, as if a person's sexual preferences and practices, or the constellation of their genitalia and hormones tells us something of utmost importance about that person. If you have spent some time with me, for instance, you will realize that my love of sports is probably much more descriptive of my social identity than anything you might learn about my sexual behavior or my body, or the fact that I am a German citizen, and perhaps even the fact that I am a philosopher (whatever that means). So I think that what is worrisome about calling intersexuality a queer identity is the potential for reducing intersexual persons to their intersexuality.

And this is indeed what doctors have done in the past, especially since genital surgery became common practice in the 1960s and 1970s. Medical discourse has reduced intersexuals to freaks, unfortunate accidents, and threats to the hetero-

---

28   One significant way in which "queer" avoids the constricting forces of identity talk is that it leaves unclear to which aspect of their bodies or their behavior the queer person is referring. When we hear "gay" or "lesbian," we assume that we now know that the person who has labeled him/herself in this way exclusively sleeps with men/women. "Queer" does not allow us to make this assumption.

29   These appear to be the two main worries that informed Judith Butler's hesitation to accept the "sign" *lesbian* for public, political causes. See Butler 1993.

sex-dichotomous norm.[30] Surgical and pharmaceutical interventions have reduced intersexed genitalia, intersexed sexuality, and by extension intersexed persons to a problem that can and should be fixed—something that appears so monstrous, so unacceptable, that "cutting is a kindness" (Chase 1999: 150). In fact, to the medical practitioner, it may seem as if the fixing of the body signifies the intersexed individual's entry into personhood—since an unsexed individual does not count as a person.[31]

Intersexuals, of course, respond to this attitude by pointing out that they are *persons* to begin with, that their *personal identity* cannot be reduced to a medical condition, and that they do not need medical interventions to *become persons*. And this is the point where, I think, the dialog between Brennan and me would turn to political strategy: Is the best strategy to resist oppressive reductionism about social identities to denounce such identities altogether (as some have done who employ the term "queer")? Or is the best strategy to reinterpret these identities and usurp their meaning (as has happened with labels such as faggot, dyke, homosexual)? I am wary of identity talk in general, but as a matter of political strategy, it can certainly be effective—in particular insofar as it can reverse the effects of being labeled and being identified as something *by others*. My hope is that intersexuals will one day be free to speak about their intersexuality with pride, not shame. The realization of this hope will presumably require that intersexuals are able to take back the labels that have been used to silence them and to justify their "normalization."[32] When this happens, I think that it will be much like the reinterpretation of terms and identities that has happened and is still happening in other queer communities. And this potential for reinterpretation could perhaps be called the *queer potential* of intersexuality, if we want to avoid imposing an *identity* on people.

---

30   Cf. Reis 2009, chs 2 and 3.

31   Instead of quoting professional philosophers here, I will refer to one example from law, and one from science-fiction. Law: The German *Personenstandsgesetz* (Law on Civil Status) requires that every infant born in Germany be assigned a gender within seven days after its birth. Fiction: Ursula K. LeGuin describes a world ("Winter") whose human inhabitants have no sex-distinction. They develop sexed features, i.e. genitalia and reproductive organs, only when they enter their monthly state of sexual arousal ("kemmer") and whether they develop male or female features is determined entirely by the unique sexual dynamic between them and their partner. An earthling who is sent to Winter as a first observer has this piece of advice for future envoys ("Mobiles"): "The First Mobile, if one is sent, must be warned that unless he is very self-assured, or senile, his pride will suffer. A man wants his virility regarded, a woman wants her femininity regarded, however indirect and subtle the indications of regard and appreciation. On Winter they will not exist. One is respected and judged only as a human being. It is an appalling experience" (1969: 66).

32   In this spirit, the Intersex Society of North America's first newsletter was called "Hermaphrodites with Attitude."

References

Andre, A. http://www.bilerico.com/2011/09/what_does_a_bisexual_look_like. php.

Brennan, S. 2011. Fashion and Sexual Identity, or Why Recognition Matters, in *Fashion and Philosophy*, edited by J. Kennett and J. Wolfendale. Hoboken, NJ: Wiley-Blackwell.

Butler, J. 1993. Imitation and Gender Subordination, in *The Lesbian and Gay Studies Reader*, edited by H. Abelove, M.A. Barale and D. Halperin. Routledge: London, 307-20.

Chase, C. Surgical Progress is not the Answer to Intersexuality, in *Intersex in the Age of Ethics*, edited by A.D. Dreger. Hagerstown, MD: University Publishing Group, 147-60.

Cordes, D. http://www.bilerico.com/2011/11/why_i_flag_its_not_just_about_sex. php#more.

Dreger, A. 1999. *Intersex in the Age of Ethics*. Hagerstown, MD: University Publishing Group.

Elizabeth, R. 2009. *Bodies in Doubt: An American History of Intersex*. Baltimore, MD: Johns Hopkins University Press.

Fausto-Sterling, A. 2000. *Sexing the Body*. New York: Basic Books.

GLBTQ Encyclopaedia of Culture, http://www.glbtq.com/.

Green, L. 2011. Sex-Neutral Marriage. *Current Legal Problems*, 64(1), 1-21.

Hemmings, C. 1997. From Landmarks to Spaces: Mapping the Territory of a Bisexual Genealogy, in *Queers in Space: Communities, Public Places, Sites of Resistance*, edited by G.B. Ingram, A. Bouthillette, and Y. Retter. Seattle, WA: Bay Press.

Kaldera, R. 2011. *Dangerous Intersections: Intersex and Transgender Differences* [Online]. Available at: http://www.ravenkaldera.org/intersection/ DangerousIntersections.html [accessed: July 15, 2011].

Karkazis, K. 2008. *Fixing Sex-Intersex, Medical Authority, and Lived Experience*. Durham, NC: Duke University Press.

Leonard, S. 2002. How common is intersex? A response to Anne Fausto-Sterling. *The Journal of Sex Research*, 39(3), 174-8.

LeGuin, U.K. 1969. *The Left Hand of Darkness*. New York: Harper & Row: New York.

Morris, S.G. 2006. Twisted lies: My journey in an imperfect body, in *Surgically Shaping Children*, edited by E. Parens. Baltimore, MD: Johns Hopkins University Press, 3-12.

O'Neill, O. 1996. *Towards Justice and Virtue*. Cambridge: Cambridge University Press, 40-1.

Phelan, S. 2001. *Sexual Strangers: Gays, Lesbians, and Dilemmas of Citizenship*. Philadelphia, PA: Temple University Press.

Preves, S. 2003. *Intersex and Identity: The Contested Self*. New Brunswick: Rutgers University Press.

Reis, E. 2009. *Bodies in Doubt: An American History of Intersex.* Baltimore, MD: Johns Hopkins University Press.

Rooke, A. 2007. Navigating embodied lesbian cultural space: Toward a lesbian habitus, space and culture," *Space and Culture*, 10(2), 246-7.

Russo, J. 2007. Hairgate! TV's coiffure controversies and lesbian locks. *Camera Obscura*, 22(65), 166-72.

Samuels, E. 2003. My body, my closet: Invisible disability and the limits of coming-out discourse. *GLQ: A Journal of Lesbian and Gay Studies*, 9(1-2), 233-55.

Savage, D. 2011. Bisexuals: You need to come out to your friends and spouses—now. *The Stranger*, June 21. http://www.thestranger.com/seattle/bisexuals/Content?oid=8743322.

Schönbucher, V., Schweizer, K., Rustige, L., Schützmann, K., Brunner, F. and Richter-Appelt, H. 2010. Sexual Quality of Life of Individuals with 46, XY Disorders of Sex Development. The Journal of Sexual Medicine. doi: 10.1111/j.1743-6109.2009.01639.x.

Turner, S. 1999. Intersex identities—locating new intersections of sex and gender. *Gender and Society*, 13, 457-79.

Vernallis, K. 1999. Bisexual monogamy: Twice the temptation but half the fun? *Journal of Social Philosophy*, 30/Winter. 347-68.

Walker, L. 2001. *Looking like What You Are: Sexual Style, Race, and Lesbian Identity.* New York: NYU Press.

Weeks, J. 1998. The Sexual Citizen. *Theory Culture Society*, 15, 35-52.

Wetzstein, C. 2010. Critics of doctor Deplore 'cure' for lesbianism in Utero—lack of formal study faulted. *The Washington Times* [online], 7 July. Available at: http://www.washingtontimes.com/news/2010/jul/7/critics-of-doctor-deplore-cure-for-lesbianism-in-u/?page=1 [accessed: July 15, 2011].

Chapter 7

Transgender Identity and Passing Authentically

Christine Overall and Karin Sellberg

Introduction

Christine Overall and Karin Sellberg create a critical dialogue on personal and generic identity. Overall focuses on understanding identity and passing through an examination of transgender and cisgender identity. For trans people, to pass is to live authentically. Sellberg illustrates her argument that identity is performative by examining plays that challenge essentialist accounts of what it is to be a person, and an individual. Sellberg uses the example of Myra/Myron Breckinridge to call into question whether gender identity is a necessary component of a person's self.

Gender, Aspirational Identity, and "Passing"

Christine Overall

Some people think that trans persons, who transition from one gender to another, are somehow engaged in deliberately deceitful behavior: They are (supposedly) deceptively engaged in "passing," a deliberate attempt to be interpreted or read as a member of the wrong gender. Their "real" identity is thought to be that which they were assigned at birth, presumably on the basis of their genitalia. As Paisley Currah and Lisa Jean Moore put it, "it is precisely because some transsexual women and men can pass in their new gender, can traverse many social, economic, even intimate landscapes as 'the other sex,' that authorities believe 'the public' must be protected from fraud" (2009: 119).[1]

---

1   To take just one highly significant example, in 1965 the New York Academy of Medicine's Committee on Public Health advocated that an application by a transsexual woman to change the sex indicated on her birth certificate should be denied because of "the public interest for protection against fraud" (quoted in Currah and Moore 2009: 118). A more recent example is the murder in 2002 of Gwen Araujo, whose killing was rationalized by the murderers and their families on the grounds that Araujo deceived them in presenting herself as a woman (Bettcher 2007).

Trans people violate one of the most fundamental social rules: that gender self-presentation must be conventionally consistent with one's genitalia. We are simultaneously required to cover up our genitalia and then to advertise their existence indirectly, using gender indicators such as our clothing, our ways of moving, talking and sitting, and our other activities. As Talia Mae Bettcher puts it, "[S]ystematic symbolic genital disclosures are secured through the very items designed to conceal [the] sexed body" (2007: 53).

Anyone who declines, or is suspected of declining, to maintain a conventional consistency between genitalia and gender presentation is seen as deviant. "[G] ender presentation literally signifies physical sex. If it is true that trans people who 'misalign' gender presentation with sexed body are deceivers or pretenders, then those who 'correctly' align presentation with body tell the truth" (Bettcher 2009: 105). Hence, trans persons are regarded as deceptive and deliberately passing" as someone they are not, whereas cisgendered persons (whose gender identity is considered to be consistent with their genitalia of birth) are regarded as revealing and acting upon their "real" identity. The result is that trans-identified persons may be "punished" by bigots who wish to push trans persons into what they (the bigots) regard as appropriately non-"deceptive" self-presentation and behavior.[2]

Of course, trans people themselves, and their allies, do not think that trans-identified persons are engaged in fraud or deceit. I[3] believe their view is correct, and this argument aims to show why it is correct; that is, it aims to provide a philosophical foundation for refutation of the "fraud and deceit" claims.[4] There is nothing inherently ethically problematic about gender "passing," and those who do not engage in gender "passing" ought not to be considered somehow more moral than those who do.[5] I will first show that the idea that there is something ethically wrong with gender "passing" is based upon two ontological errors. Indeed, I place the word "passing" in quotation marks to indicate that the use of the term is founded on metaphysical misunderstanding. First, it is based upon an incorrect view of gender identity. Second, it is based upon false assumptions about the supposed contrast and differences between trans-identified and cisgendered

---

2   Unfortunately, "coming out" (repeatedly) and being out *as* a trans person, as some individuals do, does not necessarily save them from mistreatment up to and including violence.

3   I write as a cisgendered person. I am grateful to the many brilliant and brave trans and genderqueer folk from whom I have tried to learn.

4   Talia Mae Bettcher writes that she is "not interested in defending trans people against charges of deception. Rather, it is a starting point of my work that trans people live morally acceptable lives" (2007: endnote 14). My own interest in arguing against the charge of deception arises *not* because I do not assume that trans people live morally acceptable lives but because I *do*, and I think it is worthwhile to show that charges of deception in gender presentation are false and unfair.

5   A quite different issue is whether trans persons have a moral responsibility (always? sometimes?) to be out *as* trans persons (Green 2006 [2000]; Stone 2006 [1991]). I do not discuss it here.

persons. I will then provide a positive argument in support of the entitlement of trans persons (and every person) to identify with the gender in which they are most comfortable and at home.

Gender as Aspirational Identity

I suggest that there are, generally speaking, two kinds of social identity.[6] I call them acquired identities and aspirational identities. An acquired identity is a notable personal characteristic that has been permanently ascribed or earned and requires no further action on the part of its possessor in order to be maintained. For example, one of my acquired identities is university graduate. It is something I have accomplished and completed, and whatever else happens, I remain a university graduate.

Other identities are not acquired but are ongoing and what I call *aspirational*. An aspirational identity is a notable personal characteristic such that, if its possessor values it, s/he must maintain and reinforce it through ongoing action. One example would be the identity of mother, not in the biological sense of having gestated and given birth (that would be acquired), but in the social sense of caregiver for one or more children. The individual who values her identity as a mother in the social sense must continue to engage in what are considered culturally appropriate mothering behaviors. If she fails to, she is in danger of losing her identity, as when people say, "She's no mother," or "She's not a real mother." Another example is artist. Artist is an aspirational identity (in most cases) because if the would-be artist does not practice her art and continue to generate works of art during her lifetime, people are likely to say, "She was an artist, but she gave it up." With respect to aspirational identities, their possessor is always at risk during her lifetime, if not of failure, then at least of inadequacy; the possessor of an aspirational identity must always and continually prove herself.

To say that an identity is aspirational, however, is not to say that it is necessarily a matter of free choice. Within a given culture, some aspirational identities may be compulsory; some may be voluntary; and others may be forbidden. These requirements and constraints will be enforced in the usual ways—through training, validation, reinforcement, the absence of other options, ridicule, shaming, and abuse. In addition, to say that an identity is aspirational is not to say that it is necessarily experienced as being freely chosen. One may aspire, throughout a period of one's life, to a particular identity while perhaps feeling compelled to do so.

In my sense of the term, gender is an aspirational identity, a fundamental personal characteristic such that, if its possessor values it, s/he must maintain and reinforce it through ongoing action. One can aspire to exemplify a gender through bodily styling, self-presentation, and gendered activities, all of which

---

6   There may be more than two kinds, but these two, at least, are significant and are central to this argument.

must be ongoing for gender identity maintenance (Bartky 1990). This is not, of course, merely an individual and individualized activity (Shotwell and Sangrey 2009); it is a project undertaken in concert with, shaped by, and sometimes in opposition to the gender work of everyone else. One learns how to aspire to one's gender through cultural tutelage that includes role models, advertising, media representations, parental socialization, peer pressure, gender-segregated activities and facilities, and so on.

I call gender "aspirational" to acknowledge that gender identity is never complete and never finished; it is something that one renews each day. As Judith Butler so convincingly shows, gender is an on-going performance (Butler 1990); it is not a fixed characteristic, and certainly not a finished achievement, but rather an identity that can easily be called into question if one does not maintain it. Hence there are familiar accusations such as, "He's not a real man," and traditional prescriptions such as, "A true woman would ..." Thus, gender is something at which one must work. Sometimes the work is pleasurable, sometimes it is not pleasurable, but it is always a matter of labor directed toward a goal that forever recedes from one's reach: the goal of being—exemplifying—a fully appropriate manifestation of one gender or the other. In that respect, gender is the same for everyone.

Gender "Passing"

At least in theory it is possible to aspire to one gender or the other—either the gender socially defined as congruent with one's physical being (one's sex), or the gender socially defined as incongruent with it. What one aspires to may or may not match the conventional picture of what a person with one's particular body should aspire to; and it may or may not match the gender assignment one was given at birth. A cisgendered person is one who aspires to a gender identity that is conventionally considered consistent with her or his genitalia of birth. A trans person is someone who does not aspire to a gender identity that is conventionally considered to be consistent with her or his genitalia of birth. For both the trans person and the cisgendered person, gender is not optional, and each one must constantly act in such a way as to validate their aspirational gender identity.[7]

Because her or his gender aspiration is not conventionally considered to be consistent with her or his genitalia of birth, the trans person may be considered to be "passing" and hence deceptive, whereas the cisgendered person is not. The very concept of "passing" assumes that there is something that one really is, at

---

7   There is, of course, a crucial material difference between the aspirational gender identity of trans persons and that of cisgendered persons. Most cultures make acting on one's gender aspirations relatively easy and safe for cisgendered persons, but both difficult and dangerous for trans persons. So one obvious important difference between the situations of a cisgendered person and a trans person is that the trans person is much more likely to be at risk of harm for the sake of her gender aspirations than the cisgendered person is.

heart, in one's essence, in one's innermost being, and that something is being hidden. "In this framework, gender presentation (attire, in particular) constitutes a gendered appearance, whereas the sexed body constitutes the hidden, sexual reality" (Bettcher 2007: 48).

But as three decades of feminist critique and psychological evidence have shown, there is nothing inevitable or necessary about the connection between genitalia (or other supposed markers of sex) and one's gender. There is nothing about the possession of a penis or a vulva that makes some appearances and behaviors inevitable and others inconceivable. The progress of feminism is its success in showing, with respect to more and more contexts (education, employment, childcare, civil rights, economic capacity, political office, etc.), that one's genitalia, *per se* (that is, in and of themselves, independent of one's other characteristics, including reproductive status, sexuality, age, and health) are not salient in 21st century Western nations (even if social forces sometimes continue to treat them as salient). The gradual and as-yet incomplete process of the decline of sexism and the success of feminism reflects the growing recognition of how seldom one's genitalia are relevant to social interactions; for almost all situations in which human beings find ourselves, our genitalia do not matter. Hence, on an ontological level, there is no "reality" of gender identity. Or more accurately, to the extent that gender is "real," it is a social process, one that is not inevitably grounded in given genitalia or chromosomes but rather is developed and maintained through activity.

So the first reason that gender "passing" is not deceitful or fraudulent is that genuine deceit and fraud must be based on misrepresentation. Yet the trans person is not engaged in misrepresentation: Far from being deceitful, her/his gender aspirations are in fact quite public; s/he is manifesting the gender with which s/he identifies.

Gender is what gender does; the trans person is engaged in doing gender, just as the cisgender person is. It may appear, however, that a difference between the cisgendered person and the trans person has to do with the continuity or discontinuity of their gender aspirations. That is, the accusation against trans persons of deceit and fraud depends in part upon a contrast to the behavior of cisgendered persons. There is continuity, it might be thought, in the cisgendered person's gender aspirations, whereas there is discontinuity in the gender aspirations of the trans person, who may change her gender presentation and behavior. This apparent discontinuity may lead people to think there is a real question of "passing" with respect to trans people that does not exist with cisgendered people.

I think this belief is a mistake. In many cases, both the continuity of cisgendered people's lives and the discontinuity of trans people's lives are only apparent. Both cisgendered and trans persons may vary, over the course of their lives, in terms of their affiliation to their assigned gender and to their aspirational gender.

For example, while some trans persons adopt their new gender identity part way through life, there are others who say they have always felt, or have felt for a long time, that the gender assigned to them on the basis of their genital characteristics was a mistake. They have a lifetime of aspiring to and acting on a gender that is not consistent with the gender stereotype imposed on persons with their genitalia. Hence, ostensibly new manifestations of their gender are the result of aspirations that have been growing and developing for many years. For them, there is no discontinuity in aspirational gender, and their rejection of their assigned gender does not represent a change in gender identity but rather their taking action on their aspirational gender, which has not changed.

On the other hand, while some cisgendered persons never question the nature of their gender affiliation, others do. A cisgendered woman who does not reject her assigned label of "woman" may nonetheless change, maybe even substantially, her woman-ly aspirations. That is, over the course of her life, she may make big changes in the kind of woman she wants to be. I think this is the case, for example, with many women whose lives were profoundly changed by feminism at various points in its history. There have also been cases where persons with the assigned gender of woman have chosen to go off to war, to reject marriage and procreation, to have a sexual relationship with a woman, or to get an education—all behaviors that were incompatible with their assigned gender at the time, and therefore represent a substantial gender discontinuity. Such individuals may even have presented themselves, in public, as men, even while they continued to identify as women.

Thus, there may be continuity in some trans persons' gender aspirations, and discontinuity in some cisgendered persons' gender aspirations. "Passing" may seem to be both inevitable and fraudulent for some individuals (those who are trans), while for others, "passing" may seem to be unnecessary and even impossible (for those who are cisgendered). Both of these assumptions are false. The alleged contrast between cisgendered and trans persons is not sustainable. For both, gender is an ongoing aspirational project, not a settled and unchangeable identity.

In addition, both cisgendered and trans persons may in some cases decide to seek surgery in order to perform their gender identity (although the conditions, requirements, and criteria of access to such treatments are not the same for trans and cisgendered persons). For example, some cisgendered women seek surgery to enlarge the size of their breasts, or to reshape their genitalia (in an operation called labiaplasty) in a way they believe to be desirable for authenticating and enhancing their membership in the gender to which they aspire. Similarly, some trans people seek surgery in order to remove their genitalia and/or to surgically develop genitalia conventionally associated with persons of the gender to which they aspire. Moreover, some of both cisgendered and trans persons may seek hormonal treatments of various sorts in order to enhance their experiences of or confirm their membership in the gender to which they aspire. For example, cisgendered women may use, at different times in their lives, contraceptive pills and so-called hormone replacement therapy. Cisgendered men may take testosterone. Trans men may take androgens and trans women may use estrogens and progestogens.

Nonetheless, trans persons, it might be argued, are *specially* caused by their hormones or their brains to reject the dictates of their genitalia and seek out a different gender. It is these physical forces, some may argue, that lead to what they regard as deception by trans-identified individuals but not by cisgendered persons. Trans persons are biologically motivated to act upon gender aspirations that are incompatible with what their genitalia would normally dictate.

In response, I'd say that the role of the body with respect to our gender aspirations—of any sort—is probably quite complex. We are embodied beings. How we are in the world, and the kinds of ways we feel, are at least in part a product of our bodies—their physical structure, their hormones, their capacities, their muscular development, their state of immaturity or maturity, their health, their impairments, etc. I agree with Riki Lane's recent argument that "while arguments for a biological role in gender development need careful scrutiny, they should not be rejected out of hand, especially when they stress nonlinearity, contingency, self-organization, open-endedness, and becoming" (Lane 2009: 137). Our bodies certainly endow us with particular proclivities, tendencies, wants, needs, weaknesses, and strengths.

Yet if, as feminists have argued for at least four decades, gender is acquired, learned, then our bodies do not *directly* give us gender, although they may well make one gender easier and more comfortable to acquire than the other. Determining what aspiration to have is not a matter of consulting some primordial, infallible, indubitable sensation inside. If there is such a thing as feeling like a girl or feeling like a boy, that feeling is not the same as having a feeling of hunger, pain, or fatigue. A girl does not have to learn what "hunger," "pain," and "fatigue" mean in order to feel hungry, in pain or tired, but she does have to learn what "girl" means before she can feel like a girl. She has to observe girls and women, watch role models, be tutored in whatever stereotype of girlhood currently prevails, and practice being a girl. Our bodies are shaped by our social environments and we also participate in shaping our bodies. Because gender is aspirational, one is always working at it, and one is never finished with it. So feeling girl-like, or like a girl, is very different from feeling hungry, tired, or in pain, and one's body does not impose one's gender in any culturally-unmediated fashion.

I suspect that *if* hormones and brain structures influence gender aspirations in trans people, then they also influence gender aspirations in cisgendered people. Since gender is *thought* to take its meaning from biological sex, our gender aspirations—whether we are trans or cisgendered—are perhaps reinforced by some bodily cues and called into question by others. What one aspires to is likely to be partly a function of what one's body is like, and partly a function of one's socialization, always remembering that human beings are not merely passive recipients of socialization but active participants, with varying degrees of choice and autonomy.

I regard it as legitimate to ask why people—both trans *and* cisgendered—have the gender aspirations they have. Why, for example, are some cisgendered women conventionally feminine while other cisgendered women are not? I suspect that discovering the causes of gender aspirations would be no less and also no more complex than explaining the causes of other significant and life-defining human wants and aspirations. Why do some women deeply want to be mothers and others just as wholeheartedly do not? Why do some people feel called, and sometimes very early on in life, to artistic pursuits, or to athletics, or to spiritual activities? Why are some people ambitiously entrepreneurial, whereas others are uncompetitive and non-materialistic?

Hence, I regard the claim that trans persons' gender aspirations are caused by specific brain structures or hormone patterns as entirely inadequate, even if partially true, to show that trans persons are specially caused to engage in gender deception, since I see no reason to suppose that cisgendered persons' gender aspirations are independent of their brains and hormone patterns.

The Ethics of Gender Presentation

From an ethical perspective, there is no true obligation to ensure that one's gender reflect and reveal one's genitalia. There is no *prima facie* obligation to "do" one's gender in any particular way, and certainly not in a way that is considered conventionally consistent with one's genitalia.

Although I do not have room here to do justice to the subtleties of her ideas, I take from Bettcher (2009) the idea that every one of us, whether trans or cisgendered, has First Person Authority (FPA) with respect to our gender. Bettcher explains that this is primarily a moral claim, not so much an epistemic one (2009: 99). That is, it is not a statement about how we know what gender we are, but rather a statement about who is entitled to legislate on our gender. As the International Bill of Gender Rights states, it is "fundamental that individuals have the right to define, and to redefine as their lives unfold, their own gender identities, without regard to chromosomal sex, genitalia, assigned birth sex, or initial gender role" (quoted in Currah and Moore 2009: 123). One's gender is not so much something about which one has infallible knowledge, as it is something over which one has moral authority. That is, our FPA with respect to our gender is concerned with what we believe ourselves to be, want ourselves to be, and aspire to be.

No one, therefore, is entitled to assign or impose a gender upon another functioning, autonomous human being.[8] There is no one else who is better placed to determine an individual's gender than the individual her- or himself. Gender is one of the central elements of most people's identities; if others do not accept my gender aspirations, then in effect they are not accepting me as a person. They are engaging in one of the most fundamental forms of disrespect: what Bettcher calls the "Basic Denial of Authenticity" (2009: 105). As Bettcher expresses it, seeing a trans person as a "deceiver" with respect to her/his gender "constitutes considerable emotional violence against transpeople through its impeachment of moral integrity and denials of authenticity" (2007: 47). Therefore, respecting everyone's FPA with respect to gender obviously promotes people's comfort,

---

8   We should therefore assume that the assignment of gender to infants is at best provisional only, until the child reaches the age of being able to decide for her- or himself.

safety, wellbeing, and flourishing. Moreover, policing gender and attempting to enforce gender against the aspirations of some individuals is bound to be inadequate and unsuccessful, unless the policing attains totalitarian depths. The long history of trans people, queers, and other gender non-conformists shows that people will go to great lengths to act on their gender aspirations; they can only be slowed down by enforcement—everything from public ridicule and shaming to physical assault, incarceration, and murder—that is utterly incompatible with a free, just, responsible, and democratic society.

Conclusion

I conclude that gender "passing" is not inherently wrong. The belief that it is wrong is founded on a mistaken ontology of gender, and on an unfounded assumption that trans persons are significantly different from cisgendered persons with respect to gender: both how and why they aspire to their gender, and the nature and extent of their commitment to their gender. Moreover, according to the well-founded principle of first person authority with respect to gender, each one of us has a legitimate prerogative to determine our gender, an authority that is entitled to respect. There is no moral obligation whatsoever to make one's gender aspirations, self-presentation, or activities conventionally consistent with one's genitalia.

Pro-passing, Transgender Identity and Literature: (Post-)Transsexual Politics and Poetics of Passing

Karin Sellberg

Queer theory and transgender studies have often been presented as opposing discourses. Whereas the canonical queer texts of the 1980s and 1990s aim to eradicate gender differences and emphasize change, transgender studies usually develop positions that define or reify them. Yet, there are some writers who strongly resist this disciplinary division. The queer transgender theorist and performance artist Kate Bornstein and Gore Vidal's protagonist Myra Breckinridge in *Myra Breckinridge/Myron* embrace both a sense of gendered identity and an awareness of its continual and multidimensional change. They thus seize the opportunity to create something that reconditions both traditional and queer conceptions of gendered selves. Gendered absolutes and transgender interventions become the generators of new connections and new narrative spaces.

It is the development of such changeable gendered spaces that I will discuss, the negotiation of which appears through a continual politics and poetics of passing—both in the traditional binary gender sphere and the various alternative gender continuums developed in queer and transgender communities. In "The Empire Strikes Back," a canonical queer approach to transgender studies, the male-to-female (MTF) transsexual Sandy Stone argues that transgender should be considered less in terms of an identity, a type of gender, and more in terms of a "genre": "a set of embodied texts whose potential for *productive* disruption of structured sexualities and spectra of desire has yet to be explored" (1991: 231). Stone complains that "[t]he most critical thing a transsexual can do, the thing that constitutes success is to 'pass'" (ibid.). Transsexuality has become an attempt to rewrite the body/space according to the correct genre, thus erasing all traces of its subsequent history. According to Stone, this reductively simplifies the transsexual body, and robs it of its potential for textual exchange and communication.

Stone advocates a posttranssexual approach, where "transsexuals must take responsibility for *all* of their history" (1991: 232) and open up themselves to "the *intertextual* possibilities of the transsexual body" (ibid.: 231). According to Stone, the urge to pass as a "real" man or a "real" woman closes off all opportunities to communicate through the really queer "real" transsexual body. This conception of passing is itself rather restricted, however. As Kate Bornstein shows in *Gender Outlaw* (New York, 1995) and *My Gender Workbook* (New York, 1998), queer and transgender bodies are also negotiated through various passing acts, in order to become recognizable *as* bodies. Communication requires linguistic rules and there can be no text entirely free from generic prescriptives. Also an MTF transsexual, Bornstein's experiences have taught her to take advantage of passing's possibilities—of finding the freedom within the form. Passing, for Bornstein, is a way to open up the textual body space to new gendered discourses.

Bornstein bases a large amount of her gender approach on the theories of Judith Butler, who argues that gender is inherently performative: "gender is an identity tenuously constituted in time, instituted in an exterior space through a *stylized repetition of acts*" (Butler 1990: 179). However, these continual passing acts are internalized and embodied by the subject as well as his/her surroundings. Both in *Gender Outlaw* and *My Gender Workbook*, Bornstein portrays passing as a gendered performance that not merely reconditions the performer's body, but also significantly affects his or her surroundings. As Judith Halberstam recognizes in *Female Masculinity* (Durham, 1998), once a subject passes as a gender, he/she also has the power to reorganize that gender (1998: 29). Bornstein gives several examples of characters who take part in such interventionist acts of passing, and one of them is Gore Vidal's Myra Breckinridge:

> People have underrated Gore Vidal's *Myra Breckinridge* ... I think it has a lot
> to do with the point Vidal makes: that the existence of transgendered people –
> people who exist sexually for pleasure, and not procreation – strikes terror at the
> heart of our puritanical Eurocentric culture...I think he was on the mark, and I'd
> be proud to call Myra my sister. (Bornstein 1995: 78)

Myra's hedonistic sexuality is not necessarily her most awe-inspiring feature. Apart from being a transsexual terrorist and a megalomaniac feminist separatist, Myra is the perfect passing act. She is the epitome of sexualized femininity. Throughout both *Myra Breckinridge* and *Myron*, the protagonist is portrayed in superlative and decisively corporeal terms: "Myra Breckinridge is a dish" (Vidal 1989: 5), possessing "superbly shaped breasts" and "perfect thighs" (ibid.: 4 and 5), and she uses these body parts and her seductive feminine wiles to manipulate her way into the inner sanctum of American masculinity, which in *Myra Breckinridge* is Hollywood (ibid.: 18).

As Marjorie Garber shows, Vidal's Myra Breckinridge is thus a transgender image of power (1992: 114). Myra, like one of Leslie Feinberg's transgender warriors, is the model of transgender and/or feminine opposition to patriarchal society. Bornstein argues that "Vidal positions Myra as the voice and agent of doom for the traditional American male" (1995: 78). *Myra Breckinridge's* plot, which is narrated in diary form, follows the newly transitioned MTF transsexual Myra as she penetrates a stronghold of patriarchal values, her uncle Buck Loner's Academy for young aspiring actors in Hollywood, and claims a new surgically feminine space. She states that "I am the New Woman whose astonishing history is a poignant amalgam of vulgar dreams and knife-sharp realities" (Vidal 1989: 4) and "I too want a world and mean to have it. This man [Buck Loner] – any man – is simply a means of getting it (which is Man)" (ibid.: 18). This belief and desire results in the sadistic rape, not merely of a man, but of her masculine counterpart—the epitome of the American man, which here is represented by the young actor Rusty Godowski (Ibid: 149-50).

Kate Bornstein reads the novel's image of the transsexual as powerful and triumphant. Myra is strong and ruthless. She becomes the woman she wants to be and she shapes the world around her in accordance with it. Yet, Vidal's portrayal of her is ambiguous. Marjorie Garber notes that the image of the transsexual in *Myra Breckinridge* is idealized and radically inhuman. She is a "reified figure for blurred gender" (Garber 1992: 114) which Vidal "readily appropriate[s] to problematize sexual stereotypes" (ibid.). The sexual stereotypes are also reified, however. Myra represents an element of the sexual indistinctness that outlines the distinctions. She becomes the "emblem of fear and desire—the fear and desire of the borderline" (ibid.: 16) that holds up the binary structure.

Garber thus acknowledges that although Myra challenges patriarchy and gender normativity, her own performance and interaction within the gender sphere remains strictly binary and hyper-sexualized. However, this is one of the reasons why Bornstein chooses to identify with her. Myra's narcissistic appreciation of her perfectly feminine "too lovely for this world" (Vidal 1989: 41) body signals a sense of self that is entirely based on sex and power. Myra's passing acts are portrayed as continuous seduction rituals (directed towards herself as well as her surroundings), the structural inevitability of which become empowering. Bornstein, who defines herself as a sado-masochist (S/M) dyke, sympathizes with the embrace of ritualistic sex roles. In the transgender chapter of *On Our Backs Guide to Lesbian Sex*, Bornstein describes the liberating possibilities of S/M practices:

> What I've found in S/M is the rawest expression of power: I am, you're not. I do,
> you receive. It is a constructed binary that is honored by both of the participants.
> When you give yourself consciously to that sort of thing, it's like any other
> discipline, you achieve an ecstatic place from that. (Bornstein 2004: 223)

Bornstein further explains that she prefers to partner up with women who identify
as "old school butches." She wants a sexual partner who adheres strictly to a
traditional masculine gender role to perform her feminine gender role against. She
describes the sexual interplay as a ritualistic dance:

> When an old-school butch starts flirting with me, it's a recognizable dance, it's
> in my blood. And I just follow myself there, I follow her and she's just ... It's a
> dance of identities, and a very, very structured dance. Like any great dances, you
> have to learn the steps. (Ibid: 222)

In the same chapter of *On Our Backs*, female-to-male (FTM) transsexual Patrick
Califia's describes how he found himself increasingly attracted to overtly feminine
femme lesbians during his transformation into a man. He recounts how "this
surprised me because I bought into the idea that if you are a transsexual man, you
must on some level have negative feelings about the female form" (Califia 2004:
199). Califia deduces that the fact that his bodily shape no longer invokes him
to perform the feminine role helps him to appreciate it as a role: "Polarization.
The more masculine my body has become, the more comfortable I feel putting
my skin against Her" (ibid.: 202). The presence of a traditional feminine part in
the ritualistic gender game helps him to perform a traditional male part, and in
the process affirm his progress in passing as, and *becoming* a man: "By taking
pleasure from me, a femme confirms that I am not deficient ... In some ways,
a femme is my dick, because when she gets off around me, she makes what I
have seem valuable to us both" (ibid.). Califia thus describes the performance of a
gendered sex act which cathartically transforms him into a man.

   The performativity and mutuality of this transformative passing act is essential.
Similarly to Sandy Stone's reading of gender as genre, the strict femme-butch
dynamic here becomes a form of language. For Bornstein and Califia, like for
Judith Butler, language is not merely a means of expression, however: it is a
type of self-formation. This is because of its inherent performativity. As Judith
Halberstam shows, seductive and sexual interplay is liberating because it is a
matter of performance; a reiteration of preconceived roles. It gains its power as
an experience because of the power that has been invested in the performance's
signification. Because the roles have been played out before, the sex act is
simultaneously a performance of a character's self and a performance of something
outside of him/her (Halberstam 1998: 111-39). It deconstructs the boundaries
between self and other; the player and what is played.

   In accordance with this conception, Bornstein explores her gendered language
in terms of an "outlaw" theatre, where actors take on numerous differently

gendered roles and create new transgressive and sexually challenging narrative spaces. Passing for Bornstein is thus also strictly performative: "[t]ransgender is simply identity *consciously performed* on the infrequently used playing field of gender" (1995: 124).[9] Bornstein's conception of S/M is also channeled through the idea of radical performance:

> Sadomasochism intersects gender at the point of performance. We perform our identities, which include gender, and we perform our relationships, which include sex ...S/M is simply a relationship more consciously performed within the forbidden arena of power. (ibid.: 124)

Bornstein's S/M is a play of previously formulated and often reiterated identities performed in order to form new spaces. In *My Gender Workbook*, Bornstein quotes a chain of conversations she has during one evening signed onto an S/M internet chat room. She creates a number of radically gendered, transgendered, dominant and submissive personas in separate conversation windows with separate partners. Each of these encounters produces something different and as they are brought to a close at the end of the evening, Bornstein transcends her own spatial boundaries as their collective meeting point:

> I sign off. My screen goes dark. And everyone I was, all the different roles I was playing, they're floating out in front of me. All of my identities, everything I can be, is ready to be picked from some tree called me that never bears the same fruit twice. That's what I've been talking about, honey. That's what happens when I post hard. (Bornstein 1998: 224-5)

At the end of her chat room session, Bornstein creates less of a subjective space for herself than a more general transformative concept. She explains that for her the term transgender should be read as "transgressively gendered" (Bornstein 1995: 134). Bornstein, as the transgressive transgender body, passes through and *passes as* differently gendered identities in order to connect and transform them. Bornstein's various identities-in-becoming are the means by which identity narratives are connected, conditioned, revisited, and reconsidered. Her urge to identify is an urge to become connected and a desire for affirmative reconsideration of previous conditions. Connective experiences are revisited and reformed into possibilities for positive change.

Although Bornstein emphasizes the performativity of her passing acts, it would be incorrect to assume that these are *merely* a performance. As Judith Butler decrees, there is no "stable identity or locus of agency from which various acts follow" (1990: 179). Bornstein does not claim to base herself in some "real" self beneath her gendered attributes. Her transformations are fully embodied and her sense of self is continually changing along with her new forms. It would also be

---

9   My emphasis.

incorrect to claim that Bornstein's various passing acts are unconnected. Each new performance is an extension or progression of its predecessors—and each of her previous personas remains present within the power play that sustains the transgressive urge. Bornstein continually transgresses the boundaries of her roles and challenges the role of these boundaries.

Gore Vidal also constructs a transformative power relationship between Myra and her predecessor/successor Myron Breckinridge. Although Myra, despite certain phallic performances,[10] remains coherently feminine throughout most of *Myra Breckinridge*, the sequel *Myron* portrays a heroine whose gender coherence is more disrupted. Myra continually disappears and reappears; she blanks out for a few days and the radically masculine Myron takes over control of the body. These two characters are portrayed as gendered polarities of one original subjectivity. Myra recounts how the original incarnation, a sexually confused and gender dysphoric Myron Breckinridge contacted Dr. Randolph Spenser Montag about his condition and was transformed into her present form. Myron was effeminate, homosexual and weak-minded, all traits which Dr. Montag did not believe belonged in a male body: "There is no middle range" (Vidal 1989: 86). He "convinced Myron that one ought to live in consistent accordance with one's *essential* nature" (ibid.: 87), and thus Myra was born as the distilled femininity of Myron's complex subjectivity. The Myron that later reappears in *Myron* is no longer weak-minded and effeminate: he is a homophobic Republican "all American" (Vidal 1989: 218) Christian Scientist with a wife, a ranch, and a respectable job (Vidal 1989: 211-13).[11] Myron is portrayed as the distilled masculinity that was repressed and banished from Myra/Myron's body when Dr. Montag performed his surgical and methodical gender polarization.

The new Myron first appears after Myra loses her breast implants in a traffic accident in *Myra Breckinridge* (Vidal 1989: 210). Once more the significance of the character's bodily markers is emphasized. Myra's last words are: "Where are my breasts? *Where are my breasts?*" (ibid.).The pivotal markers are not just gender specific—they are also insignia related to Myra's feminine sexuality. When Myra first wakes up at the hospital she has developed facial growth due to lack of hormone treatment and she is told that her hair has been cut off. This does not truly disturb her. It is the removal of her sexually charged breasts that reverts her to Myron's masculinity. Myron's definitive claim over the body is made through the surgical addition of a phallus in *Myron* (Vidal 1989: 248). Myron and Myra subsequently perform their power struggle through the addition and removal of genitalia and mammaries on their body.[12]

---

10   In *Myra Breckinridge*, Myra uses a penile prosthesis to rape the young 'stud' Rusty Godowski (Vidal 1989: 147)

11   The latter description comes from *Myra Breckinridge*.

12   Throughout *Myron*, Myra adds breast implants and Myron removes them. Myra manages to rid herself of Myron's phallus, which he is unable to restore, but Myra is also unable to restore a new vagina.

In accordance with Bornstein's sexualized gender play, Myra and Myron Breckinridge locate their power struggle in the sexuality of their gendered bodies. When Myron first appears in *Myron*, he is less concerned with his effeminate hips, legs, and facial features than with his female genitalia and his lack of a functioning phallus. When Myra is subsequently resurrected, she notes:

> Between my still gorgeous legs, within that sacred precinct where the finest of Scandinavia's surgeons once fashioned a delicate vagina as cunningly contrived as the ear of a snail, that son of a bitch Myron has not only removed the delicate honeypot of every real American boy's dreams, but replaced it with A Thing! A ghastly long thick tubular object ... This cock has got to go! For one thing the overall effect is ghastly, since Myron was obviously too cheap to buy a pair of balls. (Vidal 1989: 248)

Whether male or female, Myra's and Myron's body is sexual, and as such it channels a great amount of power. Vidal notes in one of his essays that sex always involves power (Vidal 1999(b): 98). Myra considers her subjective defeat of Myron and her sexual defeat of Rusty in *Myra Breckinridge* in a similar light: "Having already destroyed subjectively the masculine principle, I must now shatter it objectively in the person of Rusty" (Vidal 1989: 113). All the heterosexual relationships in *Myra Breckinridge* and *Myron* are power struggles: the radically feminine Myra and the hyper-masculine Myron consistently claim the position of the Mistress/Master. The concept of mastery is directly reflected by sexual penetration. The phallic device here becomes a dual mark of power: Myra with her strap-on dildo is powerfully and overtly female in her possession of Rusty; and Myron is masculine and conventionally powerful in his relationship with his wife. As one of the characters notes: "there's only room for one star in any bed" (ibid.: 73). This is portrayed in relation to the earlier effeminate Myron, or as Myra calls him in *Myron* "Myron the First," (Ibid: 277) who according to both Myron and Myra in *Myra Breckinridge* was a "fag" (Ibid: 66), who "invariably took it from behind" (ibid.: 77). The polarized Myron and Myra are sexed extremes and thus become sexually powerful. This is portrayed as a reaction to the original Myron's impassivity: "I had avenged Myron. A lifetime of being penetrated had brought him only misery. Now in the person of Rusty, I was able, as Woman Triumphant, to destroy the adored destroyer" (ibid.: 150).

The heterosexual relationships in *Myra Breckinridge* and *Myron* are similar to S/M exhibitions of power. However, Bornstein points out that the categorical nature of the polarized power struggles of mastery and submission played out in S/M often tend to obscure the gender binaries: "S/M play can accommodate any combinations of sex, power, and gender play. When the play reaches the point of almost purely dealing with power, then many S/M players agree that gender has in fact been done away with" (Bornstein 1995: 122). In *Myra Breckinridge* and *Myron* the power struggle is strictly gendered throughout. The concept of power is equated with gender: sex not only is power—power is sex. Rather than to evolve into a matter of pure power, Myra and Myron's contention progressively becomes more purely sexual. Myra's only mission in *Myra Breckinridge* is to crush "the masculine principle" (Vidal 1989: 113) and Myron's primary pursuit is to suppress the image of the powerfully feminine in Myra. If this binary power struggle were to dissolve, the concept of Myra/Myron would disappear. Myra indicates as much when she believes that she is on the brink of final victory: "But who am I? What do I feel? Do I exist at all? This is the unanswerable question" (ibid.)

The gendered absolutes are thus not portrayed as functioning subjectivities in *Myra Breckinridge* and *Myron*. In *Myra Breckinridge*, Myra establishes that her role as the image of the "Woman Triumphant" (Vidal 1989: 57) is to become the transformative element that leads the society she inhabits into a new age. In *Myron*, she considers herself "the creatrix of this world" (Vidal 1989: 333). Her ultimate goal is to, like Halberstam suggests, reorganize the gender sphere from within and form the basis for a society that is "more open, less limited, abandoning old-fashioned stereotypes of what is manly and what is feminine" (Vidal 1989: 123). After she successfully destroys the masculinity of Rusty in *Myra Breckinridge*,[13] Myra sets out in *Myron* to create a whole "new race of beautiful, sterile, fun-loving Amazons" (Vidal 1989: 294). She produces silicon for breast implants in her closet, and subsequently implants breasts on young beautiful male victims after she has abducted, raped and surgically castrated them in her hotel room (ibid.). Although Myra is finally defeated at the end of the novel, Vidal indicates that Myra's mission has partially succeeded, when the still chauvinistic and homophobic Myron announces that the next Republican President is a "fun-loving Amazon" (ibid.: 416).

Although Myron succeeds to take possession of the shared body in the end, Myra and Myron's polarized play, like Kate Bornstein's "hard posting," becomes a transformative principle. The fact is that Myra/Myron Breckinridge changes the minds and the bodies of others even more often than he/she changes his own. There is not a single character throughout the course of the two novels that is unperturbed by the protagonist's presence. In *Myron*, Myra manages to transform herself into a gender icon. She decides that new gendered becoming requires a reconsideration of traditional gendered spaces through its generative media: 1940s Hollywood cinema.[14] She manages to get hers and Myron's body transported (literally sucked into the television) onto the set of the 1948 production of *Siren of Babylon*, starring Bruce Cabot and Maria Montez. Once there, she transposes hers and Myron's being into Maria Montez and in Montez's body she redirects the Hollywood industry and resurrects the glamorous and overtly feminine personas

---

13 Myron points out that he is sad to say that Myra's 'effeminization' of Rusty seemingly was successful. He regretfully states that Rusty now is "a complete homosexual" (Vidal 1989: 212).

14 Vidal states in an interview that he believes the Hollywood of the 1940's, 'when everybody went to the movies' to have had the capacity to radically change the course of history (Vidal 1999(a): 248).

that were slowly drifting out of fashion. Myra not merely becomes the image of femininity, she *becomes* femininity itself: "Once I have restored Hollywood to its ancient glory (and myself to what I was!), I shall very simply restructure the human race in my image" (Vidal 1999(a): 250).

Interestingly, Bornstein's use of Myra in *Gender Outlaw* indicates that the character's iconic status goes beyond the bounds of Vidal's fiction. Bornstein not merely refers to Myra as a character who passes perfectly, but as a feminine and transgender role model—somebody to *pass as*. Myra is the embodiment of the type of subjectivity that Bornstein attempts to formulate, and each reference and emulation of her is an attempt to harness her transformative power. She is a character whose continual subjective transpositions produce wide-reaching disruptions in the social structure and thus produce not merely personal and specific, but social and general change.

Comments on Sellberg's "Pro-Passing, Transgender Identity and Literature"

Christine Overall

In Karin Sellberg's argument, the fictional Myra Breckinridge is described as "the model of transgender and/or feminine opposition to patriarchal society" (see Sellberg, this volume). According to Sellberg, trans writer and activist Kate Bornstein "refers to Myra ... as a feminine and transgender role model— somebody to *pass as*. Myra is the embodiment of the type of subjectivity that Bornstein attempts to formulate, and each reference and emulation of her is an attempt to harness her transformative power" (see Sellberg, this volume, Sellberg's emphasis).

I have a good idea of what a *feminist* opposition to patriarchal society is: It would be political resistance built upon a rejection of the harms of compulsory gender. But I don't know what a "*feminine*" opposition would be. Is it supposed to be opposition by people who happen to be women? Or by people who happen to be feminine? Is it a particular *kind* of opposition—one that is, perhaps, soft, or devious, or seductive? If the latter, then I wonder whether the end justifies the means: whether the goal of ending patriarchal society justifies the use of methods that may be less than admirable.

This moral question reaches heightened importance when we consider more of the details about Myra that are provided in Sellberg's argument. I find it unconvincing that Myra Breckinridge, at least in terms of her characteristics as they are presented in Sellberg's contribution to this volume, could be a desirable role model for any kind of progressive resistance. Either Myra is a role model in some sense so metaphorical that I can't figure it out, or she is no role model at all.

I have two major objections to seeing Myra as a role model: A moral objection and a metaphysical objection.

I begin with the moral objection. Myra is described as a "transsexual terrorist and megalomaniac feminist separatist" (see Sellberg, this volume), with "a sense of self that is entirely based on sex and power" (see Sellberg, this volume). Myra "produces silicon for breast implants in her closet, and subsequently implants breasts on young beautiful male victims after she has abducted, raped, and surgically castrated them in her hotel room" (see Sellberg, this volume). I understand entirely the importance of resistance to gender conformity and compulsory gender (Overall 2000), and I believe that separatism has an important role to play in the history of feminist activism (Frye 1983: 95-109). But I do not see the value of terrorism and megalomania, or of a selfhood based entirely on sex and power. Not all types of resistance and non-conformity are morally valuable. It *matters* what form "opposition to patriarchal society" takes. In particular, I don't see "sadistic rape" (see Sellberg, this volume) as in any way exemplary, at least if the term denotes a literal action. If anything, and in addition to its violence, it merely reiterates the trope of sexual conquest and defeat as, respectively, masculine and feminine. If, however, "sadistic rape" stands for a non-harmful element of S/M sex play (see Sellberg, this volume), then I need to know how it has positive effects outside the private realm of sexual interaction. Sexual practices can be individually liberating, and sometimes they can have constructive social consequences, but it's an empirical question as to whether any particular set of sexual practices is socially transformative. What is the evidence that "sexed extremes" (see Sellberg, this volume) have a positive effect on power outside the bedroom? On the other hand, if the term "sadistic rape" is meant to be entirely metaphorical, I need to know why it is a good metaphor for the process of transforming gender and ending gender oppression. Its figurative value is not self-evident. So my moral objection to seeing Myra Breckinridge as a role model is just that some of her central characteristics, as depicted in Sellberg's argument, are execrable if interpreted literally, and of unproven effectiveness if understood in the context of sex play or in metaphorical terms.

My metaphysical objection to seeing Myra as a role model arises from an assessment of the two concepts of selfhood that are presented in the argument. One such concept is typically post-modern; the other is highly essentialized. Neither one is plausible, but the essentialized identity attributed to Myra Breckinridge makes her particularly inappropriate as a role model.

According to Sellberg, Bornstein "passes through and *passes as* differently gendered identities in order to connect and transform them. Bornstein's various identities-in-becoming are the means by which identity narratives are connected, conditioned, revisited, and reconsidered" (see Sellberg, this volume, Sellberg's emphasis). Sellberg writes, "Bornstein does not claim to base herself in some 'real' self beneath her gendered attributes" (see Sellberg, this volume). But I must register some skepticism about this rather familiar model of the self. Although I have a lot of admiration for Bornstein's writings and political leadership, I have doubts about the degree to which the ascription of a large number of identities is really accurate—for her or for anyone.[15] One piece of counter-evidence is that, arguably, there is a consistency and constancy both in Bornstein's political and philosophical views and in her literary style. They are not random and constantly changing. This consistency and constancy is evidence of a self that, if not "real" (whatever that may mean), has characteristics that are stable and persistent through time, no matter what experiments with impersonation and passing Bornstein may make. I am sure it is true, as Sellberg says, that Bornstein's "*sense* of self is continually changing" (see Sellberg, this volume, my emphasis); that experience is familiar to many of us. We have a sense of being different on different days, or in different places or with different people. Moreover, I have no doubt that the self is complex and highly capable of evolution. But the fact of a *changing* self is not evidence of *multiple co-existing* selves, at least not in most people. Instead, each new version of a self grows out of and is caused in part by the previous version of the self. Often a new version of the self is desired and actively sought by the previous version, and hence can be understood in terms of characteristics of the previous version of the self. For these reasons, I find the typical postmodern view of selfhood unconvincing and contrary to the evidence, and I suggest that the phenomenological experience of personal change can be adequately accounted for without postulating multiple simultaneously-coexisting selves.

The second concept of selfhood that is referenced in Sellberg's argument is equally problematic, although for different reasons. Ironically, it is a selfhood belonging to the character Myra Breckinridge, whom Bornstein is said to admire and who is said to serve as a role model of opposition to patriarchal society. This concept of selfhood is highly essentialized, in that the self is encompassed by a few stereotypical characteristics that allegedly define and encapsulate the person who has them, characteristics departure from which is said to be psychologically dangerous for the person who has them.

We first see this essentialized version of selfhood when it is attributed to the fictional Myron, Myra Breckinridge's predecessor. It sounds like a veritable cartoon of gender convention: "Myron was effeminate, homosexual and weak-minded" (see Sellberg, this volume), according to Sellberg. Moreover, the fictional Dr. Montag convinces Myron "'that one ought to live in consistent accordance with one's *essential* nature,' and thus Myra was born as the distilled femininity of Myron's complex subjectivity" (see Sellberg, this volume), a femininity that apparently incorporates an effeminacy, homosexuality, and weak-mindedness that were not suitable for the male Myron. At the same time, Myra's "performance and interaction within the gender sphere remains strictly binary and hyper-sexualized" (see Sellberg, this volume).

Apparently Montag believes "'There is no middle range'" (see Sellberg, this volume) of gender characteristics; only the gender extremes, distilled masculinity

---

15   Similarly with respect to Judith Butler, whom Sellberg also quotes: I am inspired by Butler's work, but I have doubts that "there is *no* 'stable identity or locus of agency from which various acts follow'" (see Sellberg, this volume, my emphasis).

and distilled femininity, are real or important. Thus, the Myron who appears later, after Myra, is a "homophobic Republican 'all American' Christian Scientist with a wife, a ranch, and a respectable job" (see Sellberg, this volume). This combination supposedly represents "distilled masculinity"[16] (see Sellberg, this volume).

Ironically, then, given the transgender context, each of the two essential natures is deemed inappropriate for a body with one kind of genitalia but wholly appropriate for a body with the other kind. This stereotyping seems to be the opposite of progressive. For example, I see nothing wrong with males being "effeminate [and] homosexual,"[17] and I don't know why those characteristics are deemed to be more suited for persons with a vulva. On the other hand, weak-mindedness, insofar as I understand what it is, and homophobia would seem to be flaws for an individual no matter what genitalia she or he has.

Of course, a novelist can make a character be or do anything he wants, for purposes of the novel. What I am puzzled about is why Bornstein would endorse these characters, and what they illustrate about passing. Sellberg writes, "Myra's passing acts are portrayed as continuous seduction rituals (directed towards herself as well as her surroundings), the structural inevitability of which become empowering" (see Sellberg, this volume). I do not know what it means to say that a seduction ritual is "structurally inevitable," nor can I tell why and how this ritual is empowering.

Perhaps all of the activities and characteristics attributed to Myra and Myron are meant ironically, or as a morality tale. Indeed, the notion of "distilled" masculinity and femininity sounds like nothing but satire. If so, then I need to know how to interpret the irony or satire, and what I am supposed to learn from it. For the selfhood of the main characters in Vidal's novels seems just the opposite of what Bornstein advocates. On the one hand, we are told that Bornstein has no essential self, or that she believes she does not. Yet we are also told that she admires and identifies with literary figures who appear to have nothing but essential—and highly limited gender-stereotyped—selves. While postmodernists sometimes talk about the liberating potential of traditional gender, I think they should provide

---

16   Sellberg writes, "Myra with her strap-on dildo is powerfully and overtly female in her possession of Rusty; and Myron is masculine and conventionally powerful in his relationship with his wife" (see Sellberg, this volume). I have no idea why Myra is described as "female" whereas Myron is described as "masculine". There is a lack of parallelism between "female" and "masculine". If we substitute "feminine" for "female," the first clause seems false, since using a strap-on dildo and "possessing" a male to the point of sadistic rape does not seem particularly feminine. On the other hand, if we substitute "male" for "masculine," the clause in which it appears becomes, in part, trivially true; we know that Myron is male (by virtue of his genitalia).

17   "Myron points out that he is sad to say that Myra's 'effeminization' of Rusty seemingly was successful. He regretfully states that Rusty is now a 'complete homosexual'" (see Sellberg, this volume). So we are to suppose both that a vicious rape makes a man gay, and that being gay is regrettable.

empirical evidence of this potential, especially when as in Vidal's novels, it is tied so closely to genital characteristics (whether innate or surgically constructed).

In conclusion, for two reasons, one moral and one metaphysical, I am unable to understand why Myra Breckinridge is taken by Kate Bornstein to be a model of transgender and/or feminine opposition to patriarchal society. Instead, I believe feminist resistance is vastly to be preferred to feminine opposition to oppression.

Comments on Overall's "Gender, Aspirational Identity and Passing"

Karin Sellberg

The Oxford English Dictionary records a number of different connotations to the term "response," most of which emphasize its expressiveness as well as its derivative basis. It is the production of an "output provided ... as a result of a given input" (Oxford 1989: 4c); an addition to the original or an expression of where the original source may go as well as where it derives from. My response to Christine Overall's argument will thus explore the ways in which the text can be positioned in relation to the discourses that it comes out of, as well as the possibilities for further exchange. I will not challenge or dispute Overall's analysis of gender and passing, although its basic assumptions, aims and objectives differ crucially from mine.[18] Instead, I will investigate how Overall's argument itself *responds* to existing transgender studies. I will trace the ins and outs of the text's responsive representation and examine its relation to the responsive responsibility which current gender theory recognizes that gendered structures demand.

Overall's chapter aspires to prove that biologically inconsistent gender identities are not necessarily fraudulent (or "false") and that gender passing (as the expression of such an assumed fraud) is not inherently morally wrong. She interestingly provides an additional layer to the already multidimensional gender structure that transgender theorists such as Kate Bornstein, Stephen Whittle, Julia Serano, and Gayle Salamon have taken turns to construct.[19] Overall's new "aspirational" gender comes out of a neat construction of identity, which divides the concept into "aspirational" identity and "acquired" identity. The "aspirational" element implies an intrinsically progressive approach to being, which is certainly appropriate to current discussions of transgender experience. Gender identity is not innately present, but developed and constructed.

---

18   I believe that such an approach would be unsuitable for the constructive mode of this volume.

19   Kate Bornstein divides gender into "gender assignment," "gender role," "gender identity," and "gender attribution" in *My Gender Workbook* ; Stephen Whittle's extrapolates on the interaction between these in *The Transgender Debate* ; Julia Serano adds the layer of "experiential gender" in *Whipping Girl*; and Gayle Salamon adds a progressive element to the equation in *Assuming a Body*.

Overall acknowledges that gender identity is always to some degree "aspirational," in what has become known as cisgendered,[20] as well as transgendered people. In light of her reference to Judith Butler's *Gender Trouble* this is unsurprising. Butler, after all, argues that gender is formed through a "stylized repetition" of gendered acts (Butler 1990: 179).[21] I find the "aspirational" an interesting way to approach gender, especially considering the expressions of longing or the urge to belong to a gender often encountered in transgender autobiographies. What I would question, however, is whether Overall's "aspirational" identities are truly that different from "acquired" identities. Gender is certainly not a stable construct—it is continually reshaped and reconditioned in relation to the individual's interaction with his/her/hir social realities. Surely, there is an extent to which *all* social identities are, however. Overall may have acquired her identity as a university graduate, but this identity will change over time. It is entirely dependent on society's view of what the university and academia stand for. In the United Kingdom, for example, there has been a considerable inflation of the university degree. What used to be a class marker and a sign of superior knowledge two hundred, fifty or even ten years ago, has now become a commonplace.

The fact that there is a ceremonial bestowal does not necessarily mean that a true stability or sense of acquiredness will follow. If the university that issued Overall's degree were to lose its authority, the identity of university graduate would quickly be threatened by her peers. How many graduates from smaller independent universities have not been told that they do not possess a "real" degree? If this is something that matters to them, these graduates go to great lengths to verify and maintain their graduate identities.

In view of the volatility of social identities, I find the term "cisgendered" a bit too simplistic to be truly useful. As Overall acknowledges, all members of the social gender dynamic need to go to a considerable length to live up to the gender to which they aspire and there are many different degrees and levels of identification at play in gender passing. The term "cisgendered" attempts to bypass the discourse of "truth" and "falsity" in relation to gender,[22] but if broken down it rather re-establishes these definitions. The idea that there is one specified and unchanging gender identity which each subject attempts to pass as and a simple case of pass or fail in relation to their performance, merely redistributes the locations of the gender "truths."

Such relocation also occurs within a large amount of the transgender scholarship on gender, and by extension in Overall's engagement with their models. "Truth"

---

20   This has been a commonplace term in transgender studies at least since Serano's *Whipping Girl*. I am not entirely comfortable with the term, and I will return to the reasons for this further down in my response.

21   The fact that gender is performative is only one facet of Butler's argument, however. As I will explain later, she also argues against the very usage of "truth" and "falsity" in relation to gender, as well as their moral connotations.

22   See Serano's argument in favor of the term.

(or in Overall's case the absence of "falsity") comes to reside in the gender identity (or "aspiration" if you like) rather than the gender attribution. As a literary scholar, I have always found it curious that gender discourses persist in reiterating discourses of "truth" and "falsity."[23] The idea that there is a certain amount of fraudulence, artificiality, or fiction to anybody's gender is as despicable to many transgender theorists as it is to their radical feminist enemies. There is an inherent fear of make-believe and narrativization. Yet, as Bernice L. Hausman, Patrick Califia, and Erica Zander acknowledge, many transgender writers construct very definite coming-of-age or gender discovery narratives.[24] On the one hand, they are necessary in order to personally make sense of one's sense of belonging, and on the other hand, they are required in some countries in order to get permission to undergo sexual reassignment surgery.[25] Statements like "I always knew that I was a little girl/boy" thus almost become a necessary and prescribed opening to many traditional transgender autobiographies (Zander 2006: 231).

Erika Zander admits that she finds it hard to fit her gender narrative into this format, at least in unilateral manner, and she is not alone. Other transgender writers, like Kate Bornstein, claim that they have at various times constructed different gendered experiences or facts. I believe this is the way most of us relate to identities—it is not so much a question of whether we "truly" are what we say we are, but more a question of whether we can build a believable character or persona who can justify to ourselves, as well as the people around us that we belong to a certain identity category. I would thus argue, once more in accordance with Judith Butler, that when it comes to gender embodiment, transgender or otherwise, it is never really a question of "truth" and "falsity," but rather of what J. L. Austin (1976) terms "felicity" and "infelicity."[26] From this point of view, terms like "cisgender" are superfluous, as well as misdirected.

---

23 I speak here also as a person who has grown up with a transgender parent and within a transgender community where such definitions were never discussed.

24 See Erika Zander's *Transactions*, Bernice L. Hausman's *Changing Sex*, Patrick Califia's *Sex Changes: The Politics of Transgenderism*. Zander argues that these often attempt to articulate a gender coherency that is not necessarily there. She claims that the current requirement of a consistent gender identity within transgender discourses creates the need for the formation of these fictional selves, which Zander shows are often uncannily similar (2006: 231-2). As I have argued elsewhere, this is not exclusively the case for transgender identities, however. Founding narratives are an important part of the formation of most social and/or politicized identities. See Sellberg's "Transitions and Transformations."

25 See Patrick Califia's *Sex Changes* and Bernice L. Hausman's *Changing Sex*. In order to receive sexual reassignment surgery in the United Kingdom or the United States, the subject usually needs to give proof of a consistent gender identity.

26 A felicitous statement is neither "true" nor "false"; it is a statement that presupposes that the speaker sincerely believes in it and performs it according to convention. When Butler argues that gender is performative, she is in fact saying that gender is felicitous as long as the subject sincerely believes in his/her/hir gender performance and fully internalizes it,

This is where I would like to return to the concept of passing. Overall initially introduces the word in terms of its connotations to deception, "falsity" or unreality: "[t]he very concept of 'passing' assumes that there is something that one really is, at heart, in one's essence, in one's innermost being, and that something is being hidden" (see Overall, this volume). She then goes on to prove that this assumption is false and that passing as a gender is in many ways "as real" as being of that gender. My work, as well as the work of other literary and transgender scholars writing within the queer paradigm,[27] never found the unreal connotations of passing a problem to start with—they point to the performativity of gender. Passing, as it is used by most transgender subjects, implies felicity (although it is of course possible to pass even if your performance is infelicitous). The performance is both sincere and successful. To question whether a person's gender performance is "true" or "false" is thoroughly illogical.

Like Overall, I would argue that we all go through processes of gender authentication, but I would claim that this is because there is no such thing as a "real" or "true" gender. We all aspire to construct felicitous gender performances that are consistent with the way we conceive of ourselves. We thus all attempt to pass in various ways. The ideas of femininity and/or masculinity we want to *pass as* change over time in relation to both the changing social conditions and our own personal experiences and choices in life. As Judith Halberstam acknowledges, life is a continual progression of passing processes (Halberstam 2005: 5-15). We constantly find gendered images and ideas, which we aspire to pass as, and this may be perceived as confining, but as I attempt to show in my response below, an awareness of the power of passing and the performative interactions that follow, may help us to use this in constructive and even empowering ways.

In view of this, and in conclusion, I would argue that it is illogical to speak about the morality of gender.[28] A gender performance is neither right nor wrong—it is merely more or less consistent. By discussing whether passing acts are "false" or not, we are perpetuating a discourse that is, if not directly harmful, at least not particularly useful for transgender subjectivity. I believe that all moral discussions of whether we are aspiring to be the "right" kind of man/woman or not should be avoided. Gender may certainly be a matter of ethics, but not of morality.

---

and that he/she/ze performs it correctly. A felicitous gender narrative performatively creates and/or maintains the gender of its author and this never needs to be authenticated by a "true" biological reality as long as the gendered subject performs it with sincerity and credibility.

27   I refer here to scholars such as Judith Halberstam, Kate Bornstein, and Sandy Stone.

28   Incidentally, Austin introduces the terms "felicity" and "infelicity" because he disagrees with the moral connotations of "truth" and "falsity." He argues that a performative statement is never inherently right or wrong—it is a statement that is complexly related to the conditions of its particular social construction.

A Response to Sellberg

Christine Overall

I find that I agree with much, though not all, of Karin Sellberg's comments. What is odd is that throughout her response, she seems to think she is always disagreeing with me. Since I do not hold many of the views that she attributes to me, and indeed, since I say precisely the opposite of some of the opinions she ascribes to me, I am at a loss to know why she thinks I hold them.

I will, however, begin by considering two areas where we do definitely disagree.[29]

First, Sellberg makes the interesting claim that, contrary to my view, there is not much difference between what I call aspirational and acquired identities. Now I can concede that social identities could be conceptualized as being on a continuum. At one end are those identities, such as gender, that are entirely aspirational. Others, in the middle, are partially aspirational and partially acquired.[30]

But there are definitely some identities at the opposite end of the spectrum, those that are acquired and no longer aspirational. My example was university graduate. It is true, as Sellberg points out, that what it *means* to be a university graduate is not "stable" (see Sellberg, this volume). And it is even true that, in an extreme case, the status of a university may be threatened and the credibility of its degrees undermined. But my point was *not* that the social meanings of acquired identities do not change. Of course they do. My point was that there is nothing the *possessor* of an acquired identity needs to do, or even can do, in order to perpetuate that identity. Even while the meaning of "university graduate" gradually evolves, there is virtually nothing I need to do, or even can do, to keep affirming it and aspiring to it. If a university is concerned about the decline in the cachet of its degrees it can try to shore up its reputation, but for me, as a grad from years ago, there is nothing left for me to aspire to. I cannot re-take the same degree; and neither can anyone take it away from me.[31] I am simply not aspiring to being a university graduate in the slightest; that part of my life is over. In that respect,

---

29 This disagreement does not, I suggest, arise from the fact, *if* it is a fact, that we come from different intellectual "generations." Rather, the disagreement comes from our different methodologies and academic disciplines, and also in part from the various literatures that we use.

30 Take, for example, the identity of university instructor. That identity is acquired, once one is, let us say, tenured. But there is at least a minimum of activities in which one must engage, that is, a minimum of pedagogical and scholarly aspirations that one must possess, in order to keep being a university instructor.

31 It is hard for me to see how even someone with a degree from an unaccredited institution could "go to great lengths to verify and maintain their graduate identities" (see Sellberg, this volume), though I grant that it is possible, in a few cases, that the identity of university graduate could continue to be aspirational rather than (or perhaps in addition to) acquired.

my identity as university graduate is acquired, not aspirational, and hence very different from my aspirational identities. For I do still aspire, and am expected to aspire, to be a woman.

My second clear area of disagreement with Sellberg is in her rejection of the concept of cisgender. The recent recognition and interrogation of the category of cisgender is analogous to the explicit recognition and interrogation, in the twentieth century, of the concept of heterosexuality. Where previously there had been only a social and scientific focus on "the homosexual," it gradually became clear that it was more useful, not to mention politically and morally progressive, to consider the concept of "heterosexuality," and not blithely assume that there is a kind of default, unmarked, "normal" and unnamed category of sexuality that need not even be identified. Similarly, as long as there is a concept of trans persons, we need a concept of cisgender persons. It is a matter of putting a name to the politics of social reality. Instead of only having a concept of "trans" and assuming that everyone else belongs to some default, unmarked, "normal," and unnamed class, it is useful to explicitly identify the category of cisgender.

Sellberg is wrong to think that my deployment of the category of cisgender necessarily implies that there is "one specified and unchanging gender identity which each subject attempts to pass as" (see Sellberg, this volume). Obviously gender identities, whether trans or cisgender, are open to change, fluidity, ambiguity, and evolution. To have a distinction between transgender and cisgender identities is not to suppose that genders are inherently fixed; in fact, their non-fixity, for *both* those who are trans and those who are cisgendered, was precisely one of the points of my argument. It is, however, an indubitable, even while regrettable, social fact that Western society still distinguishes, broadly, between the identity of girl/woman and the identity of boy/man, and still requires that these social identities be aligned with, respectively, female genitalia and male genitalia. With respect to that latter requirement, some people are clearly cisgendered, because they aspire to a gender identity that is conventionally considered to be consistent with their genitalia of birth. Indeed, it is precisely because "passing" *is* conventionally (though regrettably) understood, in Sellberg's words, as "a simple case of pass or fail in relation to one's performance" (see Sellberg, this volume) that a distinction between cisgender and trans is socially created and validated, and that as a result being trans-identified can oftentimes be dangerous.

Now I come to the areas where Sellberg seems to think—mistakenly, I believe—that we disagree. I *agree* with Sellberg that "a gender performance is neither right nor wrong" (see Sellberg, this volume), and in fact, my argument was intended to make precisely that point. I was arguing *against* those who make moral judgments about gender performances. My argument was that, contrary to many social and legal conventions, it is not morally wrong to adopt a gender presentation that is not conventionally consistent with one's genitalia of birth.

Sellberg seems to assume that I am making all kinds of claims about true and false gender representations, but that is precisely what I am arguing against. I never use Sellberg's awkward term "falsity," although she puts it in quotation marks as if she were quoting me (see Sellberg, this volume).[32] I also never use the terms "true" or "false" with respect to gender aspirations or performances. Contrary to what she imputes to me, I do not say that "passing as a gender is in many ways 'as real' as being of that gender" (see Sellberg, this volume). I do not use the word "real" in any non-ironic sense with respect to genders; instead, I am *critical* of any deeply metaphysical use of the concept of "reality" with respect to genders. And I do not make a contrast between "passing as a gender" and "being of that gender"; part of the point of my argument was precisely to *deny* that one can legitimately make such a contrast.

Instead I argue that the reason that "gender 'passing' is not deceitful or fraudulent is that genuine deceit and fraud must be based on misrepresentation. Yet the trans person is not engaged in misrepresentation: Far from being deceitful, her/his gender aspirations are in fact quite public; s/he is manifesting the gender with which s/he identifies" (see Sellberg, this volume). Fraudulence or deception is not possible when truth is not applicable. It is precisely because there is not a "true" gender for any of us that an individual cannot be "guilty" of "passing," and that it is both unjustified and unjust to accuse such a person of being "deceptive" or "fraudulent."

A Response to Overall

Karin Sellberg

In response to Christine Overall's question "what is a good role model?" I would like to emphasize that the term "role model" has several different connotations and in my argument, I use it in a way that specifically emphasizes its aesthetic qualities—as a fictional character that gives rise to imitation. Overall is unable to see how Myra Breckinridge can be a suitable *moral* or *political* role model, and I think that both Kate Bornstein and Gore Vidal would back me up wholeheartedly when I agree with Overall that she most certainly *is not*. Overall admits that Myra could be "a role model in some sense so metaphorical that I can't figure it out." This is the problem here. Overall's response does not register the most crucial point of Bornstein's and my conception of passing: its metaphorical subsistence and its playfulness.

As I explain in my response to Overall's chapter, I do not believe that gender should be considered in terms of morals. It is an ontological rather than a moral issue. Considered from a moral perspective, Myra Breckinridge is an abominable character. All her projects are entirely self-serving and she uses and abuses all the people around her. Vidal's depiction of Myra is not a serious one, however. She is a caricature. Vidal is making fun of the binary division between masculinity and

---

32   I use the term "false" only in evaluating the truth-value of certain philosophical claims.

femininity. Myra/Myron represents the gender war of late twentieth century Western society. When it comes down to it, *Myra Breckinridge* and *Myron* break down the absolutism of the gender divide. Vidal attempts to show that there is no such thing as a full man or a full woman. These are concepts or ideas (in the Platonic sense) that we all dance around and engage with, but they can never truly become fully embodied (at least not in the non-fictional "real" world).

Instead of responding to Overall's moral objection that a "megalomaniac sadist" who rapes and maims young men should not be an example to follow, or her metaphysical complaint that Vidal's descriptions of Myra and Myron's "selves" are both essentialist and unconvincing—both of which I believe most of us (including Vidal himself) would unquestionably agree with—I will thus attempt to shed some further light on the philosophical framework behind the playful formation of self that I am tracing in my work. I am interested in Vidal's Myra/Myron because of his/her development or becoming. The two characters do not merely oscillate between one to the other—they continually develop into something slightly different.

This is what I want to emphasize in my argument: gender is a process of becoming rather than a state of being. It is an *internal* fluidity rather than a superficial flux. Overall dismisses my reading of Bornstein's ritualistic gender "dance" as a "typical postmodern view of selfhood." It is unclear exactly which of the numerous postmodern formulations of the self that Overall believes that my analysis falls into, but I can certainly concede that I share certain basic notions with Judith Butler's work on performative selfhood.[33] However, I do not advocate what is arguably its most postmodern aspect; the anti-essentialism often attached to Butler's work.[34] I prefer a Deleuzean ontology, in which essences constantly transform, to the conception that there was never an essence in the first place.[35]

Rosi Braidotti argues that subjectivity should be considered in terms of transpositioning. Corporeality (which encompasses both body and mind) is a marker of subjectivity-in-becoming. It continually moves through essentialized and corporealized subjective "locations." These are not to be considered separate

---

33   It should be noted that Overall's own analysis also adopts this most 'typical' facet of Judith Butler's ontology.

34   If Butler's most canonical works, *Gender Trouble* and *Bodies that Matter*, are read separately they certainly do form an anti-essentialist idea of self. Butler indicates that there is no such thing as a subjective basis underneath our numerous self-formulating performances: "[t]here is no volitional subject behind the mime who decides, as it were, which gender it will be today ... gender is not a performance that a prior subject elects to do, but gender is *performative* in the sense that it constitutes as an effect the very subject it appears to express" (Butler 1991: 24). Butler's later works, such as *Undoing Gender* and *Giving an Account of Oneself*, reformulate this idea and constructs a more subtle approach to subjective formation, however.

35   This is not an unusual approach to gender performativity in gender and queer studies at the moment, advocated most explicitly by writers such as Elizabeth Grosz, Elspeth Probyn, Claire Colebrook, and Rosi Braidotti.

from each other, but rather as planes intermeshed by chains of memory (Braidotti 2002, 2006). Braidotti describes it in terms of speed perception: "Just like travellers can capture the 'essential lines' of landscape or of a place in the speed of crossing it, this is not superficiality, but a way of framing the longitudinal and latitudinal forces that structure a certain spatio-temporal 'moment'" (Braidotti 2006: 172). This momentary subject-positioning is continually transposed. It is a recurrent conditioning of connective events that lead to new becomings.

According to this conception of the self, gender (and transgender) identity encompasses a number of subject positions. We attempt to pass as masculine and feminine in various ways as we travel along the landscape of being. The essential line itself is not gendered, however. It is this journey that we call our "self." In my reading of Vidal's *Myra Breckinridge* and *Myron* neither Myra nor Myron is an actual "self." They are subject positions; binary opposites within the gender spectrum. They are not characters in and of themselves, but the development of *one* character; *one* process of gender characterization or gendered becoming. This is why I emphasize Myra's femininity and transgenderism (in their most abstract and fluid sense) rather than her feminism. Myra does not truly have a political or ethical consciousness as we know it, because she is not actually a full character.

I would argue that the concept of the "role model" usually functions in this way. It is an image we attempt to emulate— a platonic idea we strive towards. When Kate Bornstein says that she would "like to call Myra her sister" she briefly inhabits Myra's feminine and transgender space. She attempts to *pass as* and *pass through* this location. Bornstein does not want to act like Myra (I do not believe that any mentally stable transgender activist would). She wants to harness Myra's feminine and transgender power. Passing in this sense can be seen as the engagement with various abstract transformative subject positions. It is the means by which we develop our selves.

References

Bartky, S. 1990. *Femininity and Domination: Studies in the Phenomenology of Oppression.* New York: Routledge.

Bettcher, T.M. 2007. Evil deceivers and make-believers: On transphobic violence and the politics of illusion. *Hypatia*, 22(3), 43-65.

Bettcher, T.M. 2009. Trans identities and first-person authority, in *You've Changed: Sex Reassignment and Personal Identity*, edited by L.J. Shrage. New York: Oxford University Press, 98-120.

Bornstein, K. 1995. *Gender Outlaw.* New York: Vintage Books.

Bornstein, K. 1998. *My Gender Workbook.* New York: Routledge.

Bornstein, K. 2004. An interview with Kate Bornstein, in *On our Backs Guide to Lesbian Sex*, edited by D. Cage. Los Angeles, CA: Alyson Publications, 220-4.

Braidotti, R. 2002. *Metamorphoses: Towards a Materialist Theory of Becoming.* Cambridge: Polity Press.

Braidotti, R. 2006. *Transpositions: On Nomadic Ethics.* Cambridge: Polity Press.

Butler, J. 1990. *Gender Trouble.* New York: Routledge .

Butler, J. 2004. *Undoing Gender.* New York: Routledge.

Butler, J. 2005. *Giving an Account of Oneself.* New York: Fordham University Press.

Califia, P. 2004. Femmes: A love letter, in *On Our Backs Guide to Lesbian Sex*, edited by D. Cage. Los Angeles, CA: Alyson Publications, 199-203.

Currah, P. and Moore, L.J. 2009. We won't know who you are: Contesting sex designations in New York City birth certificates. *Hypatia*, 24(3), 113-35.

Frye, M. 1983. *The Politics of Reality: Essays in Feminist Theory.* Freedom: Crossing Press.

Garber, M. 1992. *Vested Interests.* London: Routledge.

Green, J. 2006 [2000]. Look! No don't! The visibility dilemma for transsexual men, in *The Transgender Studies Reader*, edited by S. Stryker and S. Whittle. New York: Routledge, 499-508.

Halberstam, J. 1998. *Female Masculinity.* Durham, NC: Duke University Press.

Lane, R. 2009. Trans as bodily becoming: Rethinking the biological as diversity, not dichotomy. *Hypatia*, 24(3), 136-57.

Overall, C. 2000. Return to gender, address unknown: Reflections on the past, present and future of the concept of gender in feminist theory and practice, in *Marginal Groups and Mainstream American Cultures*, edited by Y. Estes et al. Lawrence, KS: University Press of Kansas, 24-50.

Oxford English Dictionary. 1989. 2nd Edition. Oxford: Clarendon Press.

Salamon, G. 2009. Justification and queer method, or leaving Philosophy. *Hypatia*, 24(1), 225-30.

Shotwell, A. and Sangrey, T. 2009. Resisting definition: Gendering through interaction and relational selfhood. *Hypatia*, 24(3), 56-76.

Stone, S. 2006 [1991]. The empire strikes back: A Posttranssexual manifesto, in *Transgender Studies Reader*, edited by S. Stryker and S. Whittle. New York: Routledge, 221-35.

Vidal, G. 1989. *Myra Breckinridge and Myron*, edited by G. Vidal. London: Grafton Books.

Vidal, G. 1999a. The gay sunshine interview by Steven Abbott and Tom Willenbecher, in *Sexually Speaking: Collected Sex Writings*, edited by D. Weise. San Francisco, CA: Cleis, 219-51.

Vidal, G. 1999b. Sex is politics, in *Sexually Speaking: Collected Sex Writings*, edited by D. Weise. San Francisco, CA: Cleis, 97-114.

Index